Towar

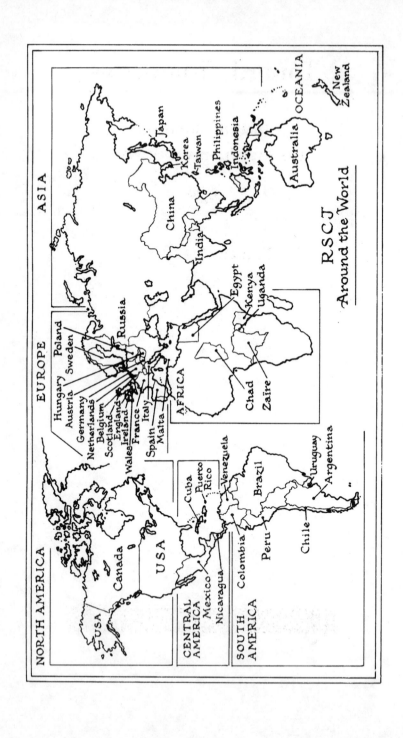

RSCJ
Around the World

Towards Tomorrow

THE SOCIETY OF
THE SACRED HEART OF JESUS

Frances Makower

DARTON·LONGMAN+TODD

First published in 2000 by
Darton, Longman and Todd Ltd
1 Spencer Court
140–142 Wandsworth High Street
London SW18 4JJ

ISBN 0–232–52373–8

A catalogue record for this book is available from the British Library

Designed by Sandie Boccacci
Phototypeset in 10/13½pt New Baskerville by Intype London Ltd
Printed and bound in Great Britain by
Page Bros, Norwich, Norfolk

To friends, colleagues
and fellow sisters,
past and present

CONTENTS

ACKNOWLEDGEMENTS

I would like to express my gratitude to the community at Duchesne House, and to my sisters at Blythe Road, my present community; they sustained me by their interest, patience and prayer. I also want to thank Patricia García de Quevedo rscJ, the Superior General of the Society, for her generous foreword.

I owe a special debt to Joan Faber rscJ, without whom the project could have been neither started, nor completed. In addition to constant support and availability, her extensive knowledge of the Society was essential in ensuring a global perspective. I would also like to thank Anne Leonard rscJ, our General Archivist, who helped me to research and suggested solutions to problems; she also spent hours checking the MS (but any inaccuracies are mine, not hers).

My panel of critics, Doreen Boland rscJ, Teresa de Bertodano, Helen McLaughlin rscJ, Joan Faber rscJ, Andrée Meylan rscJ, Jean Taylor and Prue Wilson rscJ played a key role in the project. Their positive criticism and imaginative suggestions were invaluable, as were the translations of Mary Barrow rscJ, Clara Betzler rscJ, Joyce Blackwell rscJ, Lorna Brockett rscJ, Marion Charlie rscJ, Josephine Heywood rscJ, Ursula Hoare and Andrée Meylan rscJ.

I am indebted to Martin de Bertodano who once again helped me with political notes. On the practical side Dorothy Cooper gave me invaluable back up while my editors Morag Reeve and Brendan Walsh provided affectionate and professional expertise; indeed all the staff at Darton, Longman and Todd were unfailingly helpful.

Many were involved in the production of this book, but were

I to thank each individual these acknowledgements would be without end. Please be assured that every contribution, suggestion and comment was sincerely appreciated. I thank you all in prayer, confident that God will honour my debts.

FRANCES MAKOWER rscJ

AUTHOR'S NOTE

The aim of this book is to provide a survey of the Society of the Sacred Heart in the period leading up to its bicentenary, in the year 2000. It is a survey furnished by the membership themselves; rscJ have sent scores of letters, faxes and e-mails, criss-crossing the globe, describing the means through which they were making known the love of God. Theirs are the accounts that have created this book.

Since the past may provide a key to the future, the first chapter outlines Madeleine Sophie's story and briefly notes the key events and the progress made from 1865 to 1964 under the government of her successors. A summary of the renewal that followed from 1964 to 1994 has been contributed by Rosemary Bearss rscJ, and is to be found in Appendix I. Mrs Josephine Barcelon, an Australian alumna and editor of the AMASC website (Association Mondiale des Anciennes et Anciens du Sacré-Coeur) kindly agreed to contribute Chapter 11. Thus Chapters 2–10 and 12 illustrate the way in which religious of the Society, assisted by colleagues and friends, were attempting to communicate their love of Jesus Christ – a love which for them was no less a passion than it had been for Madeleine Sophie.

Many of those contributing have written of their love of the Lord and of their desire to share this joy; others have been more reticent, leaving their commitment to give tacit witness to their devotion to the Sacred Heart of Jesus. Inevitably there have been ministries that have not borne the hoped-for fruit; these of course must be addressed, but they are hardly the matter for a bi-centenary volume. The purpose of this book is to testify that at the end of the twentieth century rscJ continued to make known the love of God through teaching, or administration, or in accompanying pilgrims on their journey to God. There were also 'prophets' and 'pioneers', pursuing unique and often hazardous ministries: what each one did was secondary – what mattered was the attempt 'to contemplate and experience reality with the Heart of Jesus' (cf, 1982 Constitutions # #21, 22). Comparisons between the various ministries undertaken would be both invidious and misjudged, for 'whatever the service entrusted . . . we stand together, united in our common mission' (1982 Constitutions #30).

Finally, in attempting to illustrate the response to the call to follow Jesus in the Society, this survey has endeavoured to be even-handed in the portrayal of each province. For very good reasons this has not always been possible, but the generous response of all who were approached has been such that I received too many, rather than too few contributions. I deeply regret that lack of space has prohibited the use of all the material I received.

FRANCES MAKOWER rscJ
Hammersmith, January 2000

GLOSSARY

Affiliée A lay woman who has committed herself to follow the spirituality of the Society for life.

AGSC Archives Générales du Sacré Coeur.

AMASC Association Mondiale des Anciennes and Anciens du Sacré Coeur (Past Pupils Worldwide Association).

Associate A lay woman who has committed herself to a closer following of Christ by undertaking to live according to the spirituality of the Society. This commitment is renewed annually.

Coadjutrix sisters rscJ who were principally concerned with the children's material welfare, and domestic duties, as distinct from the choir nuns, who were generally teachers or administrators, and were required to recite Office (the Hours of the Blessed Virgin Mary). In 1964 the two categories of choir nuns and coadjutrix sisters were fused.

CEB Basic Ecclesial Communities.

CEDC Center for Education Design and Communication.

Cloister/to keep cloister synonymous to keeping enclosure.

CRIS Congregation for Religious and Secular Institutes.

District An administrative entity. See Province.

Exercise Instruction for the novices.

JRS Jesuit Refugee Service.

Mater (Admirabilis) A fresco painted by a young postulant on a wall of Trinita dei Monte in Rome 1844. Mater Admirabilis has become the patroness of all Sacred Heart schools.

Post-Christian Generally used of a person who has been reared in a Christian milieu, but has discarded his or her beliefs in adulthood.

Postulant   A woman seeking entrance to the noviceship; also known as a candidate.

Probanist   An rscJ who is part of an international group preparing for final profession.

Probation   A five-month period of international preparation for final profession.

Province   An administrative entity of which there are various different types, provinces and districts being most common. Cf. Supplement to 1982 Constitutions, #168e.

RSCJ (rscJ)   Religeuse du Sacré Coeur de Jésus.

SJ   Society of Jesus (Jesuits)

SMSF   St Madeleine Sophie Fund.

Solidarity Fund   Money available for the support of lay initiatives.

Vicariate   Administrative entity which was replaced by province.

YP   Young Professed: rscJ who have made temporary vows.

In Ireland:

IRA   Irish Republican Army, opposed to the division of Ireland.

UVF   Ulster Volunteer Force, a Protestant group in Northern Ireland opposed to union with the South.

FOREWORD

Portraiture is a difficult art for it must capture a person in all his or her vitality, diversity, history, activity, emotions and experience in one sole moment. Even more difficult is a family portrait in which, added to the individual traits and differences of the unique individuals, is the indefinable family likeness, that element which unites the members. Well nigh impossible, then, to portray a family of 3,500-plus members of diverse nationalities (more than fifty), culture and backgrounds and at the same time communicate their essential oneness. Frances Makower has set about doing just that in this book; she describes her undertaking as 'snapshots' of the Society of the Sacred Heart at the moment of its 200th anniversary. She has brought to the task her considerable skills as a writer, as well as her love and appreciation of the Society of which she is a member.

Our Society, whose story she sketches in the beginning, has had a rich and varied history throughout the world during the past two centuries. Like almost every religious order and congregation in the Catholic Church and like the Catholic Church itself, the Society has undergone radical transformation during the years since the close of Vatican II. It has literally been re-founded. As women who are situated in the world, allowing ourselves to be confronted by it, we have undertaken a process which, during the last thirty years, has profoundly changed our apostolate, our style of life, of government and of formation, and has given us a different outlook on our spirituality, mission and community life. In the appendix Rosemary Bearss, who lived through this process, describes it fully.

Before Vatican II we had a certainty about our identity and

our place in the Church and the world, and we did not speak of re-founding. Like every religious congregation, we passed through a crisis, and this crisis led us to experience not only the struggle for survival, but also the beginning of a serious and deep journey that would be not merely a renewal. We have understood that religious life is not the only 'way of perfection', but rather a way of living out our Christianity in the following of Jesus, in an apostolic congregation, by means of the vows and in the context of community.

We have taken seriously the reflection on our experience; and the last General Chapters have given us direction and helped us to define with greater clarity what we want to live. The Society of the Sacred Heart from its origins has been characterised by a contemplation of the situation of the world – the contemporary reality. Conscious of the situation of women, and with a vision of their role in the family and society, Madeleine Sophie Barat saw the education of women as a response to the urgent needs of society. The educational ministries described in Chapter 2 point to the new frontiers of our educational mission today. While some are working in traditional settings, others are reaching out to the world's poorest people. The ministries described in Chapter 3 illustrate the underlying conviction of all the Society's work: that every human being has a need and a right to be educated.

The manner in which we situate ourselves in the world and contemplate reality, going from the pierced Heart of Jesus to the pierced heart of humanity, was one of the factors that moved us and led us to search for a new way to address the challenges presented to us by the world and by the Church. Vatican Council II led us to see the world with new eyes and to situate ourselves in it in solidarity with the sufferings and hopes of humanity. This shift in focus meant changing, for apostolic reasons, from a conventual to a more open community life. It was no longer a question of waiting for people to come to us, but rather of going out in search of them. The religious who tell their stories in Chapters 4 and 5 describe situations of war, violence or injustice in society with their consequences in human suffering. They exemplify in their life and work the new possibility of being in situations of greatest need and of acting with others to accompany, to alleviate misery and to be advocates for the voiceless. Their apostolic choices spring from contemplation of our world and from the need to make a response.

The bridge-building endeavours recounted in Chapter 6 are rooted in our self-understanding as women of communion called to strive for peace and reconciliation, whether among different races, nations and cultures or among religions and social classes. Those religious who speak in Chapter 7 confirm in their insertion among the poor the call we have heard since Vatican II, along with the rest of the Church, to exercise 'a preferential option for the poor'. All those who are engaged in spiritual accompaniment and pastoral work witness to the paramount value of prayer, of the contemplative dimension of the Christian life. Finally, those who serve in the government of the Society see their work as contributing to the strength and health of the whole body of the Society in whose name each religious of the Sacred Heart exercises her particular ministry.

In presenting these 'snapshots', illustrating how several individual rscJ are responding creatively to need, Frances Makower has portrayed the Society of the Sacred Heart in the present, and has sketched in new developments that continue to communicate the love of the Heart of Christ for all humanity – for each individual human person.

PATRICIA GARCÍA DE QUEVEDO rscJ
Superior General
Rome, Casa Generalizia
1 January 2000

CHAPTER 1

The Society: A Brief Overview

On a spring day in 1796, Madeleine Sophie Barat waited apprehensively to board the coach for Paris. She was sixteen years old, and had grown up with her family in the small town of Joigny that lay a few miles north of the border of Burgundy, in the Province of Champagne. Sophie was reluctant to leave home, but had been persuaded by Louis, her elder brother, godfather, and strict mentor, to pursue her studies with him in Paris. She had cause to be nervous: Paris was a ruined city, where 'The Terror' had only ended the previous year. Memories were still haunted by the sound of the beating drum, announcing the fall of the guillotine, as it echoed through streets controlled by violent mobs.

Louis had had first-hand experience of the Terror. Ministering as a priest, he had been imprisoned and might have been guillotined had not an old school friend contrived to omit his name from the lists. When the Terror ended in 1795, Louis returned to Joigny where he found Sophie absorbed in her books and her concern for her mother. She had been his pupil and had studied a broad syllabus including mathematics, Greek, botany and astronomy, subjects normally reserved for boys. To live a circumscribed life in the family home was not what Louis had planned for his talented sister; her gifts, he had decided, were for God alone. Therefore, ignoring all protest, he insisted that she should accompany him to Paris, to complete her education under his direction. The combined opposition of Sophie and her mother might have deterred him, had not their normally silent father intervened. Sophie was to go to Paris.

In fact Louis' concern for Sophie was groundless: her passion

1

for God was such that she had determined to enter Carmel, although the Revolution had closed all religious houses in France.

When they arrived in Paris, Louis lodged his sister with an elderly spinster in a house on the rue de Touraine. For the next several years she did little but continue her moral and intellectual training under Louis, teach the catechism to a handful of children and sew; gradually several young women came to share in this work. So time passed, until one day in October 1800 her life changed definitively.

Through Louis, Sophie had come to know Joseph Varin, a priest ten years her senior. He had inherited, from Père Léonor François de Tournély,[1] the vision of a new congregation for women. It was to be called 'the Society of the Sacred Heart' and was to be dedicated to passing on to others the knowledge of God's love, by means of the work of education. Neither Princess Louise de Bourbon Condé, nor the Archduchess Marie-Anne of Austria on whom hopes had rested for the founding of the new congregation, had persevered. Once he had met Sophie, however, Father Varin was confident that he had at last found the means of accomplishing his inherited task.

In October 1800, on Sophie's return to Paris from her vacation in Joigny, Father Varin outlined his project. Sophie agreed to think about it. 'When the will of God is known, there is nothing to do but obey,' he insisted. Sophie surrendered; three of her friends agreed to join her, beginning their religious formation immediately, under the direction of Father Varin. Some weeks later, during the Mass of the Presentation of Our Lady, on 21 November 1800, the four young postulants made an act of consecration before the Host. This marked the beginning of their noviceship and the birthday of the Society of the Sacred Heart. 'This was not the way in which Sophie had thought to become a nun, but she was in peace.'[2] Two years later, the group made their vows.

Throughout her religious life Sophie was to experience moments of trial, and quite possibly the first was that of 1802

2

when Father Varin named her superior. Twenty-three and the youngest, 'Sophie' disappeared and re-emerged as Mother Barat. Three years later in January 1806, by the majority of a single vote, she was elected Superior General at the Society's first General Council. By then the Paris house had been vacated and the community was installed in a former boarding school at Amiens, in the rue Martin-Bleu-Dieu. Two additional convents had been opened: Sainte Marie-d'en-Haut, at Grenoble, in 1804, and in neighbouring Bellay in 1805.

Madeleine Sophie was to hold office for another sixty years, transmitting to successive generations her passionate desire to glorify the Heart of Jesus by combining contemplative prayer with the work of education. The rule of the Society was 'essentially based on prayer and the interior life ... [and religious were] consecrated to the sanctification of others'.[3] Speaking of the spirit of the Society, Madeleine Sophie said,

> Our first movement is to linger at the feet of the Master; that is the contemplative life, that is what we must do in prayer. But it is then that Jesus says to us: 'Go tell my brothers ...' Why can we not say to the whole universe: know His Heart?[4]

Thus she described both her ideal of the contemplative in action, and her yearning to tell the world of God's love.

Indeed, Madeleine Sophie's vision was global from the start; from the earliest days she had dreamt of raising up 'a throng of adorers from all nations'.[5] In 1825 she told Pope Leo XII, 'The Society desires to spread Devotion to the Sacred Heart over the whole earth and to set all on fire with divine love.'[6] In Madeleine Sophie's lifetime the Society spread into eight European countries, and crossed the Atlantic with foundations in North and South America, and in Cuba. There were constant requests for new foundations and Madeleine Sophie was grieved when lack of religious forced her to refuse them. While it would be inappropriate to enter into detailed descriptions of the various foundations, it is impossible to omit altogether the heroic journey to America undertaken by St Philippine Duchesne and her companions in 1818. They left Paris on 12 February, embarked on the sailing ship *Rebecca*, and finally reached the mouth of the Missisipi on 29 May, the feast of the Sacred Heart. There they transferred to a steamboat, finally reaching St Charles, in the state of Missouri. This was to be another radial point from which Father de Tournély's vision would eventually spread.[7]

This vision had been inspired by love. De Tournély was a mystic, who had experienced union with Christ, and longed to share his joy by means of education. Madeleine Sophie was at one both with his desire and his belief in education; thus the 1815 Constitutions insist that 'Christian education of youth is the first and most important means which the Society employs for honouring the Sacred Heart of Jesus, to which it is consecrated'. She was certainly a brilliant teacher whom the young found irresistible. Careless of the obligatory curtsy, the youngest children flew into her arms; she could tame the naughtiest and, for her, even altar boys learned their catechism.

As well as boarding schools for the well-to-do, Madeleine Sophie opened free schools and set up orphanages, where vocational courses were given. She also established special schools for handicapped children, and a centre for the formation of catechists. She was wont to say that the Society was devoted not only to education, but also to all that is related to education. She therefore undertook any work of zeal that was in harmony with the Constitutions, whenever sufficient time, place and personnel affirmed the sign of God's will.[8]

Her love of Jesus overflowed into all her relationships. 'How I love you all!' she told her community in 1860. 'You are not my God, but you are the steps that lead me to Him.'[9] Much as she loved her daughters, the children and her many friends, she could be sharply witty, and her anger was formidable. 'From tongues that talk too much, O Lord deliver us!' is an addition she is said to have suggested for the litany; stories of her anger on

4

receiving an ornate carpet and on the purchase of an excessively expensive organ are anecdotes that continue to be told.

As Madeleine Sophie laboured to establish the Society she was plagued by periodic political upheaval, external attack and internal intrigue. Her three immediate successors enjoyed generally quieter times; under Josephine Goetz (1865–1874), Adele Lehon (1875–1894) and Augusta de Sartorius (July 1894–May 1895), the Society was able to expand and consolidate. In 1865 there were 3,539 members of the Society; by 1894 their numbers had increased to 6,649. Each of these Superiors General had known and loved Madeleine Sophie and so each became strongly conservative, eschewing change and clinging to uniformity in their determination to preserve every nuance of her wishes.

After her election Mother Goetz, an Alsatian, said 'I feel drawn to innovate nothing, to start no movements of change in the beautiful uniformity of our laws.'[10] She was responsible for establishing the Mother House as the venue for all probations, for editing the decrees of the General Congregations and for an outline of instructions for all the novices: this came to be known as 'exercise'. Mother Goetz also supervised the completion of the retreat house begun by Madeleine Sophie on the Boulevarde des Invalides in Paris, and managed to deflect Pius IX in his attempt to reopen the debate on the location of the Mother House, which he wanted transferred to Rome.

Mother Lehon interpreted her role as that of guardian of the Society's heritage, and set herself to keep the rule to the last letter. During her generalate foundations were made in New Zealand, Australia, Mexico, Czechoslovakia, Hungary and Scotland. She was succeeded by Mother de Sartorius, an Alsatian, who had battled with ill health for most of her life; she was in office for little more than nine months, but in the time she had, she too fostered tradition. She acquired the Barat home in Joigny, and at the Mother House instituted daily exposition of the Blessed Sacrament, thus fulfilling Madeleine Sophie's long-held ambition that there should be perpetual prayer in at least one house of the Society.

Yet even during these years of comparative calm and determined preservation, changes could not be kept from the
agenda. The tenth General Council of 1874 debated the advis-
ability of vicariates electing one delegate to accompany their
vicars to future general councils. The proposal, although
accepted in principle, was turned down because 'all innovation
was risky'. Another decree recognised the importance of the
human development of young religious, foreshadowing future
changes in the methods of initial formation. Some years later,
the thirteenth General Council of 1894 considered the need for
a revision of the Constitutions; the response was 'not now'! That
'now' persisted for almost a century.[11]

Mabel Digby, the fifth Superior General, was an Anglican who
had become a Roman Catholic; she was English, but had spent
much of her life in France. She was elected in 1895 and was the
last in this office to have had a close relationship with Madeleine
Sophie. Appointed headmistress at Marmoutier, in France,
directly she had made her first vows, she could not be spared
from the school for long enough to make her probation.
Madeleine Sophie therefore instructed the young probanist
herself, during successive summer vacations. Mabel Digby was
finally professed in November 1864, and was among the last
group to receive her cross and ring from the foundress.

Mother Digby's spirituality was wholly centred on the love of
Christ, but nevertheless she could be caustic on occasions: when
a young religious confessed that she had just discovered that she
was a big sinner, Mother Digby is said to have replied with a
smile, 'O no, just a little fool.'

A great deal of this generalate was taken up with finding
alternative communities for approximately 2,500 religious
expelled from France. Anticlerical laws forced all religious
houses to be authorised by the state. Those congregations
refusing to conform could be dissolved; the result was the closure
of the Society's forty-six houses in France and one in Algiers
between 1901 and 1909. The 'refugee' rscJ rose to the challenge.

'Where are you going?' Mother Digby asked one. 'I don't

know, but it's written on my trunk,' was the carefree reply. By 1909 every rscJ had left France, together with most of the chapel furnishings from the confiscated houses. The Mother House itself was transferred to Ixelles in Brussels. These expulsions were not unique, but were on a far larger scale than those that were to follow from other countries in later years.

Worldwide, almost as many new houses were opened as had been closed in France. In hindsight this dispersal came to be seen as a strengthening of internationality; French rscJ were to be found throughout Europe and also in the newer foundations, which were steadily increasing. Between 1903 and 1907 foundations were made in Malta, Egypt, Japan and Uruguay. Inculturation was an idea in the future, but Mother Digby went so far as to recognise that 'diversities . . . add to our religious life a richness, a breadth which we must singularly value . . .'.[12] Mother Digby's generalate was overshadowed by the expulsions, but it was not without consolation.

She prepared the Society for its first centenary in 1900 by insisting that 'the Heart [of Christ] must be an open book where we learn all things, each truth, each feeling, each rule of conduct'.[13] On the eve of the twentieth century, Leo XIII had dedicated the whole human race to the Heart of Christ. This prompted Mother Digby to write in a circular letter: 'The co-incidence of our centenary with the consecration of the world to the Heart of Jesus is not only a powerful motive for confidence, but should penetrate us deeply with the importance of our mission . . .'. The beatification of Madeleine Sophie on 24 May 1908 was a further cause for rejoicing. Many religious were present in St Peter's for the event; Mother Digby, however, was too ill to travel to Rome at that time.

It could be said that Mother Digby's term of office stands as a bridge between the earlier traditionalists who shunned all change, and her successor Janet Stuart who was convinced that 'uniformity in essentials is good, but we cannot become slaves of this idea'. Thus at the General Council of 1910 Mother Digby recognised the need for changes to be made in the Plan of

Studies[13] while reiterating the need to maintain the 'character proper to our education'. Janet Stuart, who was at the Council in her capacity as Vicar of England and Ireland, went further. In a memorial she criticised the system of prescribing reference and text books for all Society schools, and roundly condemned 'text books prepared by the religious... Large quantities accumulate and must be sold, and a worse evil is the stereotyping of teaching for many years when modern discovery and criticism have reached far beyond it.'[14]

Janet Stuart was also an Anglican who had become a Roman Catholic; she had been trained by Mother Digby, whom she succeeded in 1911, governing the Society for three years. In that brief period she made an indelible impression on education, ongoing formation and community life. Her book *Education of Catholic Girls* was published in 1911 and, although it became outdated in parts, has had an enduring influence. Her profound sense of the prayer upon which the spirituality of the Society is based enabled her to give a telling description of 'the mixed life', as the life of contemplative apostolic religious was formerly known. This she insisted was

> blessed with a specially intimate likeness to our Lord's manner of living on earth ... It must consist of an inward spirit of consecration which has two movements, like the vital act of breathing: the outward and inward movements are each incomplete without the other.[15]

In community Mother Stuart encouraged personal initiative; she insisted that each religious had responsibility for her own personal development, to be undertaken through reading, observation, mental discipline and serious thought. The fruits of this continual effort enriched and enlivened the whole community. Everyone was expected to contribute to 'the thought market of recreation' as Mother Stuart called it; she joked about the ordeal of bringing forth 'a poor little thought' which would be minutely examined by the whole community.

On her election Mother Stuart had adopted a six-year plan of constant travel to all the vicariates in order to get to know the whole Society, in preparation for the next meeting of the General Council. The journeys were strenuous; they involved long periods at sea during which she wrote *The Society of the Sacred Heart*,[16] which she described as 'quite a little book of the sea, . . . planned on the Adriatic, begun on the Red Sea, written on the Indian Ocean and finished on the South Pacific'. When she finally returned to the Mother House in 1914 she was exhausted, but with the German invasion of Belgium, this could provide no resting place. It was decided that she must undertake the hazardous journey to England. This was accomplished, but within a few days she had become seriously ill. She died on 21 October 1914.

Four months later, with the Mother House inaccessible, the eighteenth General Council assembled in Rome and elected Maria de Löe, a German, as the seventh Superior General. Afterwards the councillors managed to return to their vicariates, but Mother de Löe had to remain in Rome, where she was cut off from most of her houses. Although her generalate began so ominously there were signs of hope, among them the return of the Society to France.

A Sacred Heart convent was reopened in Lyons in 1915; five years later the number of rscJ who had returned to France was sufficient to warrant the restoration of the French vicariate. Houses continued to be reopened and by 1946 there were twenty Sacred Heart schools in France. This increase was however not without problems, for at this time vocations were beginning to decline. In 1915 there were 6,444 religious; when Mother de Lescure was elected in 1946 there had been only a comparatively slight increase to 6,570. Although considerably fewer young women were presenting themselves, foundations continued to expand. The Society reached China in 1926, and in Congo a school was set up at Kinshasa the following year.

Another formerly intractable problem was solved in 1920 with the purchase of a villa on the Via Nomentana, enabling the Mother House to be transferred to Rome. This move, which was generally approved by the religious, demonstrated the change of climate since Madeleine Sophie's day, when a similar proposal had come near to splitting the Society.

At that time also, Josefa Menendez, a young Spanish coadjutrix postulant at Poitiers, was 'drawn into extraordinary communications with the Lord, who appeared to her almost daily'.[17]

At first the revelations were treated with extreme caution, not being made known until after Josefa's death in 1923. Ten years later the 'Message' received by Josepha was officially accepted by the Society; it inspired many religious, but was never imposed. In 1944 Mother de Lescure, who had been Josefa's superior, and was to become the ninth Superior General, compiled *Un Appel à l'Amour* for general publication. Within six years fifty thousand copies had been sold, and many had been translated: the book has never ceased to be in demand.

Furthermore, it was during Mother de Löe's generalate that the cause of Madeleine Sophie was triumphantly concluded. In St Peter's, on 24 May 1925, in the presence of four members of the Barat family, numerous rscJ, students and friends, Madeleine Sophie was canonised. Seven years later her statue, designed by the sculptor, Quattrini, was erected in the Basilica.

It was therefore in buoyant mood that the twentieth General Council met in October 1928, a mood that was to be shattered less than three weeks later by the unexpected death of Mother de Löe. One evening, feeling indisposed, she had sent an apology for her absence to her counsellors; forty-eight hours later she was dead. She was replaced on 21 November 1928 by Manuela Vicente, a Spaniard, who was to have the onerous task of governing the Society during the turmoil of both the Spanish Civil War (1936–39) and World War II (1939–45).

Mother Vicente drew strength from her passionate faith in the Eucharist, but at the same time she had a profound mistrust of modern ideas which in her view 'develop selfishness, sensuality and easy-going ways'.[18] This attitude was shared by many of the teaching religious, who failed to comprehend what lay behind their students' doubts. A tonic, accompanied by an act of faith, was the antidote suggested to one girl who was questioning a single act of creation![19]

Despite this lack of comprehension, advances were made by a group of prophetic rscJ who understood the need for their students to be equipped for future Christian leadership. Some Society schools began to offer seniors a two-year 'Cours Superieur' for the study of the humanities, as an alternative route to that of university. Tertiary educational institutions were also both increasing in number and strengthening their syllabuses.

A further force for change at this time was the challenge issued by Pius XI in his encyclical *Quadragesimo Anno* in 1931, prompting both school and college students to become personally involved in social needs. At Eden Hall, in Philadelphia, for example, the Barat Association organised retreats for professional women, lecture circles, and various charitable enterprises. Enthusiasm for foreign missions was equally strong. The Society had become established in the Congo in 1927 during the time of Mother de Löe, while in 1940 Sophia College for Women was opened just one year after the Society's arrival in India.

Meantime the situation in Europe was becoming increasingly sinister; the Society schools in Germany (and later in Austria and Hungary) began to be seriously constrained by Nazi rule; in Spain the Civil War between Franco and the Communists forced many religious into exile in 1936. In this bleak situation, the beatification of Philippine Duchesne in May 1940 offered a rare opportunity for celebration. Mother Vicente summoned the vicars to the ceremony in Rome, for although Poland had been overrun by Germany, there had been little further activity in Western Europe. The Vicars of Poland and Austria were unable to travel; the rest assembled, but left immediately after the ceremony, taking their probanists with them. Four days later Italy declared war on Britain and France and all sure communication between Mother Vicente and the rest of the Society ceased, causing isolation for her and consequent stress. In December 1940 she became immobilised as the result of a broken hip and

11

gradually her mental abilities declined. Four months later the Sacred Congregation of Religious appointed Mother Giulia Datti as Vicar General; she was Italian and had previously served many years as mistress of probation. Mother Vicente died in January 1946 and was succeeded in the following September by Marie-Thérèse de Lescure from France.

After her election Mother de Lescure let it be known that her aim was to rule in love and confidence since for the Society 'the Heart of Jesus is the way, the truth and the life'. She faced an awesome task of rebuilding and reorganisation. During the war Malta had endured over three thousand raids, the International School in Japan was destroyed, as were numerous houses in Europe. Mercifully the Sacred Heart Chapel at Roehampton, the resting place of Father Varin, and of Mothers Digby and Stuart, remained intact, but the adjacent main chapel had been destroyed by incendiaries, together with most of the school. The internationality of the Society, and the generosity of areas outside the war zones, lightened the task of restoration; significant aid was also received from the relief fund organised by the alumnae. However, the cessation of hostilities proved to be no guarantee of security for the Society. Communist regimes in Europe and Asia were the cause of further suffering. The Society managed to remain in Poland but only at the cost of persecution and severe hardship; it was expelled from Hungary, Czechoslovakia and China.[20]

This period was also affected by the shortage of personnel. Statistics reflected the inversion of the age pyramid, while for some time the lack of vocations had been a concern. Numbers of students were steadily rising and the variety of courses offered was expanding; it was therefore proving difficult to provide sufficient religious for all the teaching posts. The subsequent solution, of employing secular staff who would bring so much to the schools and colleges, was not generally acceptable at this time.

To add to these practical problems, a general desire for change, in keeping with the needs of the day, was causing a climate of unrest. Many had come to believe that the continuation of cloister[21] was no longer compatible with the current demands of education. Mother de Lescure consulted Pius XII who insisted that cloister formed a rampart protecting the source of religious spirit and the interior life. Consequently Mother de Lescure remained utterly intransigent in regard to both compromise and basic change. However, she was prepared to update and modify to a limited degree. Thus, while the rule of enclosure was strongly affirmed, it was agreed by the twenty-fourth General Council of 1952 to give official sanction to dispensations from cloister for specific needs, notably the care of health, business concerns and apostolic work.

The 1952 General Council also updated various Society documents, including the Decrees of former Councils and the Custom Book, while a series of directives simplified and underlined the principles of formation, temporal administration and education. In line with these changes, both the School Rule and the Plan of Studies were adapted and renamed 'Life at the Sacred Heart' and 'Studies of the Society of the Sacred Heart' respectively. A further important change was the gradual ending of social exclusiveness which had previously restricted entry to the choir nuns' novitiate, to the boarding schools, and to membership of such organisations as the Children of Mary and the Affiliées to the upper echelons of society.

Thus in obedience to the Church, Mother de Lescure loyally upheld the rule of enclosure. Yet ironically her vision of 'a community wide open in welcome [ensuring that] alumnae, visitors of all sorts, workmen, priests, the poor and religous know that we love them and that we love one another',[22] would not be fully implemented until the lifting of cloister. In this matter of 'open' community, Mother de Lescure was ahead of her time. 'Openness, welcome, sharing with others will make the community a sign of communion' is a precept of the New Constitutions of 1982 (#34).

In February 1957, Mother de Lescure, like her predecessor, fell, broke her hip and became confined to a wheelchair; she was also suffering from cancer. In August she named Sabine de Valon as Vicar General, but continued to govern the Society until she died on 31 December 1957. The twenty-fifth Council elected Mother de Valon to succeed her. She struck the key note of her generalate when she said that the Society must come face to face with the reality of today. That reality was also to be faced by the Second Vatican Council summoned by Pope John XXIII[23] in 1962, which Mother de Valon attended as one of the official observers. In a circular letter of 1964 she reflected the mood engendered by renewal which was gathering momentum, both in the Church and in the Society:

> Hope is indeed the virtue of the present moment; we look to God, we look to the future. Something is awakening in the world under the impulsion of grace ... We await a tomorrow prepared by love; tomorrow God will show his marvellous mercy and the eternal youth of his Church ...

Renewal affected the life of the sisters and coincided with growth in the educational, missionary and social apostolates of the Society.

The changes set in train by this renewal have been admirably dealt with by Rosemary Bearss rscJ (see Appendix I); nevertheless, even at the risk of repetition, it is necessary to emphasise one or two key developments. The 1976 General Chapter agreed that 'new educational aspects of our mission have opened new ways of showing forth the love of God revealed in Jesus Christ'. Three years later the Assembly of Provincials held in Mexico committed members of the Society and others to education for justice. This commitment was taken further by the 1992 reflection on Initial Formation, entitled 'The Fate of the Society Is In Our Hands', which stated 'whatever the context of our educational service, the cause of the poor, the dispossessed, the marginalised becomes the compelling motive of our efforts ...'.

This radical development in the understanding of the Society's charism had led to an expansion of ministries. Thus although a large proportion of sisters continued to manifest God's love as

14

they taught in schools and colleges, others were witnessing to the love of God in a wide variety of ways. Some were teaching in refugee camps, others were supporting street children; they were to be found alongside the marginalised, or accompanying pilgrims on the 'Way'.

Paradoxically, this expansion of mission was accompanied by a diminishment of members. The Society, like many congregations, suffered a loss of professed religious in the aftermath of changes unleashed by the reforms of Vatican II. When the second Vatican Council met in 1962, the Society numbered just under seven thousand; by 1999 there were fewer than four thousand members. In several areas, notably North America, Europe and Australasia vocations had diminished or even ceased. A number of Society schools and colleges had been closed, others had been handed over to lay or church ownership; yet in response to the signs of that time new projects and new foundations continued to be undertaken.

The Society strengthened its presence in Central and South America. In 1980 a new community, linked to the Province of Mexico, was established at Jalapa, Nicaragua; there the sisters became involved in the National Campaign for Reading and Writing, and with local educational projects. Eight years later, links were established with the University in Managua, which led to the opening of a second community. In 1988 Margot Bremer rscJ took up the invitation of Victor Hugo Zorzo, the then Jesuit Provincial of Argentina, to go to Asuncion on the western border of Paraguay to assist with Bible classes. A small community was established, linked to the province of Argentine/Uruguay; its members trained local leaders, taught in seminaries and led retreats.

In 1991 a new community was established in Jakarta, Indonesia, in response to an earlier invitation from the Bishop Leo Soekoto SJ. This project was pioneered by Sister Anne O'Neil rscJ (better known as Nance). Sponsored by the Atma Jaya University of Jakarta, Nance, an American, was appointed to the English department, an employment that enabled her to gain the essential work and residency permits. She and the rest of the community also assist poor people, especially street children, for this project began as a commitment to work alongside the poor and to build bridges with what is a predominantly Islamic society. The aim of the Society is to hold the mission in trust until Indonesian rscJ can articulate and develop their own sense of mission in the Society of the Sacred Heart. By 1997 several young women had shown an interest in the Society and by 1999 it had become necessary to open a novitiate.

The region of Chad was founded many years earlier in 1964. Before the secondary school was built at Chagwa, classes were held on the river bank, alongside the fishing nets. In the 1990s the sisters became increasingly involved in pastoral work and three new communities were established: Guelendeng in 1992, a second community in N'Djamena in 1996 and a third at Moulka in 1998 which was half way between Bongor and Guelendeng. The Moulka community was sufficiently close to Guelendeng for the sisters from both communities to meet each week. This enabled them to pray, reflect, shop in the local market and enjoy some leisure together. A notable milestone marked the year 1997, when the first Chadian candidate entered, later going to Kimwenza, Congo, for her novitiate.

The second half of the twentieth century was not without trials for the Society; the religious of Poland, Cuba, Hungary and China all became victims of Communist regimes. While in Poland the religious were allowed to stay in their own country, albeit under stringent circumstances, those in Cuba, Hungary and China were forced to leave. By 1999 rscJ, after considerable risk and drama, had been able to return, in some manner, to all four countries. In 1961 the religious of Cuba had to seek refuge in neighbouring territories.[24] In 1970 Manuela Valle rscJ returned to Cuba from exile in Puerto Rico, and managed to secure a permit of residency. She worked in the parish of Vista Alegre in Santiago de Cuba and served on the Diocesan Catechetic Commission; one year later, in 1972, Raquel Pérez joined her, thus re-establishing the Society in Cuba. Their house was small and delapidated, but in the one sound room a small picture of the Sacred Heart concealed the Blessed Sacrament.

For long periods after this, the two in Cuba were cut off from the rest of the Society. Letters to and from Rome took three months each way and when the rare letter did arrive, little sense could be made of it. They heard nothing of the twenty-ninth General Chapter that was meeting in Rome from 4 to 14 October 1976, until after it had actually opened, while all the rest of the Society had been fully involved in preparing for it. Finally they received a letter from the Superior General, Concepción Camacho. This had been written many months earlier, promising to send all the Chapter documents and asking for an account of life in Cuba. There was no hope of their response arriving before the end of the Chapter, but they wrote all the same, sending the letter via three different routes.

They explained how they were attempting to catechise in a dechristianised milieu in which all religious activities were restricted. 'Much courage is needed', they wrote, 'to dare to place a religious object in full view and yet we can sometimes see pictures of the Sacred Heart and the Virgen de la Caridad (the patron saint of Cuba), through the blinds of the houses.' They also wrote of the harsh conditions: severe food shortages, milk restricted to children and old people, constant queuing and their house little more than a cave. Finally they appealed to their sisters: 'Come and help us, come and share our lives.'

Some time later, in August 1977, they were suddenly told that Agnes Lahey, the then Canadian Provincial (1914–1996), was arriving. She was bringing all the Chapter documents with her and would recount everything that had happpened; as a Canadian it was less difficult for her to obtain an entry permit. Agnes spent a week with them, bringing their isolation to an end; the following year five visiting rscJ renewed their vows with Manuela and Raquel on the feast of the Sacred Heart. In 1978 Florencia de la Serna, an rscJ from Argentina, arrived to stay and in 1980 Concepción Camacho came herself.

From then on the mission in Cuba has continued to flourish

and expand. By 1988 numbers had increased, enabling a second community to be established at La Habana, where the sisters continued to work in the local parishes. A turning point was reached when some young women asked to join the Society and a novitiate was set up; thus by 1999 there were three communities in Cuba, at Santiago de Cuba, La Habana and the novitiate house at Catalina de Guines. At that time two Cuban rscJ were in probation preparing for final profession and there was a growing group of Young Professed, novices and candidates.

The collapse of Communism in Europe had also led to the return of the Society to Hungary. In 1992 a community was re-established in Budapest where the sisters collaborated with the local priest. In time several young women asked to join the Society as the result of contacts made in the parish, and by 1995 there were three houses in Hungary, including a noviceship.

The political changes in both Russia and Poland also made it possible for the Society to establish a community in Moscow in 1991. This project, the response to a request from Polish families living in Moscow, had been the subject of a discernment in which the Polish Provincial Assembly, the bishop and the chaplain to Polish workers in Moscow had all played a part. Once established, members of the community taught students in several different tertiary institutions; it was an exciting time, with many different initiatives in which the Society became involved. In China it was not possible to restore communities, but there were several rscJ carrying out significant ministries, whose contributions will be found in subsequent chapters.

Inevitably this fleeting and somewhat breathless survey of the Society is both incomplete and superficial; nevertheless it is hoped that it will offer a comprehensible context to the main body of the book.

NOTES
1. P. Léonor François de Tournély (1767–1797) was at the seminary with P. Varin; when he died he passed on his vision of a new congregation to P. Varin.
2. Margaret Williams, *St Madeleine Sophie: Her Life and Letters* (Herder & Herder,1965).
3. Abridged Plan of the Institute, 1805.
4. Adele Cahier rscJ, *Vie de la Vénérable Mère Barat* (Paris: De Soyes, 1884).
5. Ibid.
6. 1815 Constitutions Ch. 3, #169.
7. Mgr Louis Baunard, *Histoire de la Vénérable Mère Madeleine Sophie Barat* (Paris: Poussielgue, 1900), Vol. I, p. 307.
8. Margaret Williams, *The Society of the Sacred Heart* (Darton, Longman and Todd, 1978), p. 75, and *St Madeleine Sophie*, p. 489.
9. Margaret Ward rscJ, *Life of Blessed Madeleine Sophie Barat* (Roehampton, 1911), p. 541.
10. Pauline Perdrau rscJ, *Les Loisirs de L'Abbaye* (Rome, 1935), Vol. II, p. 168.
11. *Congrégations Générales de la Société du Sacré Coeur* (1874), p. 74.
12. *Lettres Circulaires de Mabel Digby* (September 1904), p. 184.
13. AGSC Série Conseils Generaux.
14. The first Plan of Studies was drawn up in 1805 and laid down the general principles on which Sacred Heart education was based; it was revised over the years to meet the changing needs of the times.
15. Janet Erskine Stuart, *Society of the Sacred Heart* (Roehampton, 1914), p. 65.
16. Maud Monahan rscJ, *Life and Letters of Janet Erskine Stuart* (Longmans, 1922), p. 201.
17. Margaret Williams, *Society of the Sacred Heart*, p. 191.
18. Vicente Circular Letter, 1933.
19. Margaret Williams, *Society of the Sacred Heart*, p. 220.
20. The Society reached Shanghai in 1926, establishing schools and a university college. When the fighting of World War II spread to the Far East in 1941, the school campus was commandeered to house internees, including non-national rscJ. The property was confiscated in 1952 and all the rscJ managed to leave China with the exception of Margaret Thornton (1898–1977). Having organised the Legion of Mary, whose members courageously defied all attempts to make them abandon their faith, she was imprisoned and did not finally leave Shanghai until July 1952, by which time she had become an international celebrity on account of her defiance of the Communists.
21. Madeleine Sophie wanted her religious to be bound by solemn vows, but these carried the obligation of papal enclosure, a restriction that was incompatible with the Society's apostolate. In 1826 Pope Leo XII agreed to vows of stability, on the proviso that semi-cloister was observed.
22. De Lescure Circular Letter, 1952.
23. Second Vatican Council 1962–65, summoned by Pope John XXIII and continued under Paul VI; the Council aimed to review the life of the Church, update its teaching, discipline and organisation, and strive for the union of Christians.
24. The account of Cuba is based upon Raquel Pérez' *Religiosas del Sagrado Corazon en Cuba*, much of which she kindly translated into English.

CHAPTER 2

❧

The Heart of an Educator

Christian education of youth is the first and most important means which the Society employs for honouring the Sacred Heart of Jesus.
(1815 Constitutions #169 I)

We must educate to a faith that is relevant in a secularized world and to a deep respect for intellectual values. (Chapter 1970)

Our service of education is carried out in a genuine relationship of mutual interaction, where each person both receives and gives so that all may grow together. (1982 Constitutions #14)

In obedience to the call of God, Madeleine Sophie gave up her home, her attraction to Carmel and all possibility of a hidden life. Indeed, much of her time was spent among the many people who sought her advice and support. In addition to her own sisters, she was in constant demand on all sides; church dignitaries, workmen, doctors and lawyers, beggars, children, their parents and her own family all claimed her time. She gave of herself with generosity, but she never lost touch with her deep life of prayer, upon which, she maintained, all apostolic effort was founded. ' . . . our Society is made for the practice of prayer and the salvation of men; [we] must draw [our] strength from contemplation.'[1]

Two hundred years later, those who had responded to the call to follow Christ in the Society of the Sacred Heart were likewise grounded in contemplation. 'This contemplative attitude permeates our whole being, helping us to live ever more united to

Christ in our relationships, our task and our ministry; it becomes a powerful force of conversion and transformation for mission.'[2]

The sine qua non of contemplation for religious of the Society becomes evident in the contributions which make up this chapter. They were written by rscJ from around the world, who were then teaching in Society schools and colleges, and described their attempts to make known the love of God in accordance with the tradition established by Madeleine Sophie.

Teaching in Chad

Françoise de Pous rscJ was not attracted to religious life. Educated in a Sacred Heart school in her native France, she disliked the nuns' black habits, was at times scandalised by them and had no desire to teach. Yet almost in spite of herself, she was drawn to the Society. 'I was struck', she wrote, 'by the witness of these joyful women who radiated the love of the Heart of Jesus. Ignoring the off-putting externals, I began to feel at home in the spirituality of the Sacred Heart.' Françoise entered the Society in 1970, and having completed her religious training and secular studies, she went to N'Djamena, the capital of Chad, one of the poorest countries in Africa. There she taught in the Lycée du Sacré Coeur, becoming increasingly attached to her work and to the country.

These brave people have a hard time, especially the women; they live a traditional life, but have a great longing for change. All our teaching is concerned with the whole person: for me this is making known the love of the Heart of Christ to all the students, including the Muslims. To do this seems a better witness to life, than direct evangelisation.

As religious of the Sacred Heart it seemed natural for us to stay throughout the civil war, the army's seizure of power and all the conflicts which were such an impediment to progress. We stayed as witnesses to Christ's preferential love for the little ones; we stayed to affirm that in spite of suffering and death, the power of the Resurrection is still at work.

In 1992, after many years of teaching and at the request of the local church, Françoise left the Lycée in order to undertake parish work in Guelendeng, a town about two hundred kilometres south-east of N'Djamena.

Around this time a number of lay people were beginning to initiate their own projects, among them was a group of pioneering parents who were attempting to introduce education to an area that had no schools. These women had worked out a method whereby one literate adult could pass on his or her skills to a group of children. Lacking teaching skills, they turned to the Catholic Mission in Bongor for help. Carmen Rosales, a Spanish rscJ, was then working with the Mission, and so she became involved; she sent the following account of her ministry.

From November to the following May, youngsters living in the bush go to school in one of the mud huts which previously had housed goats! The children arrive carrying on their heads the blackboard – the school's sole piece of equipment. Their teacher, a young adult who had abandoned study and returned to the village, uses the international alphabet to teach them to read and write in the mother tongue; later they will learn French. Anyone completing six years 'in class' receives a Certificate of Primary Education. So, once all the proposed schools are functioning, there will be around three thousand children in school.

Two months before the beginning of term, the fifty teachers, who run ten schools between them, come to the Catholic Mission in Bongor for their own instruction. They come by foot, by bike or by hitching a lift. They receive lesson guide-notes with which to practise in groups, and are invited to take part in various activities, including literacy classes. They are also encouraged to reflect on the way the teaching process relates to their own culture.

22

The success of these bush schools, for which the parents themselves took responsibility, is admirable, but the children's future, once their schooling had ended, has been a cause of concern. If the young people left their villages in order to continue their studies, the villages would become derelict and there might well be an increase in rootless, hungry and violent young people, but if they did not continue to study, they would be likely to forget all they had learnt. Setting up a four-year agricultural course in the ten areas where schools had been established seems to offer a practical solution; all the villagers would benefit from any improvement in farming, and therefore it can be hoped that the new agricultural methods will spread. By 1999 pupils from two of the community schools will have completed their studies: by then, therefore, two of these agricultural colleges must be up and running. Madeleine Sophie would surely say to us today: 'It is for Africans to build Africa. Let us help them to do so.'

Teaching Secondary-School Children in Northern Uganda

Josephine Adibo rscJ, a Young Professed from the Uganda/Kenya Province, wrote of the effects on her of teaching in a girls' secondary school in Kangole.

This ministry has been both a blessing and a revelation, which called me to progress from the normal Ugandan academically orientated education, to a more holistic approach.

I was moved by the girls' readiness to share their troubles; they talked of their struggle to get to school on account of the opposition they faced from all their close relatives. They discussed their family problems which mostly concerned poverty; they also spoke of their confusion about themselves: who were they and what did the future hold for them? All this revealed the 'tears of God' on the faces of many who were in need of love and of someone to believe in them.

My daily prayer reminds me that I am to be more than a professional teacher, for I am called to give the love of the Heart of Jesus. How I long to bring each child closer to Christ. How? By giving my time, by listening, by nurturing hope, bringing out the best and concentrating on the positive – in a word, by loving.

It is not easy, but I try to live according to the '94 Chapter:

> The compassionate gaze of Jesus directs our eyes and hearts towards a world where many are like sheep without a shepherd, and brings to birth in us the desire to give our lives, as women of compassion and communion, to nourish life, to help life grow, to defend life.[3]

Teaching in Colombia

Eduvigis Velásquez, a Colombian rscJ, is the Director of the primary school of St Leticia in Huila, a town in the south of Colombia; this is situated in an area dominated by guerillas and popularly known as 'The Red Zone'. Writing of her ministry, she explained that her concern extended beyond her students to their parents; indeed all the staff try to integrate the whole school community: teachers, parents and students.

As rscJ we attempt to give our pupils formation for life, instilling human, ethical and religious values. Consequently we encourage such skills as crop rotation, tree planting and the recycling of waste. We also hold regular workshops to encourage practical activities, leaving the students free to choose which to attend. Those on cookery, dancing and weaving are always the most popular.

In addition to the regular lessons on doctrine, we seek to promote religion by making use of the annual feasts and holy days, with their special novenas, processions and tableaux. When we prepare for the feast of St Madeleine Sophie on 25 May, for example, we use the opportunity to discuss her ideals and achievements and to pass on Society values and traditions. We tell the students about the early days of the Society in France and how from the beginning Madeleine Sophie dreamt of gathering together young girls who would always 'adore' the Heart of Jesus. We also tell them all the well-loved stories of St Philippine Duchesne, and about how she crossed the Atlantic in a sailing ship.

Education in Upper Egypt

The Province of Egypt was established in 1903, at a time when the means of fulfilling the mission of the Society was generally understood to be that of formal teaching in the schools that had been established in Cairo and Heliopolis. Many years later, in 1940, the Jesuit Henry Ahib Ayrout learnt of the desperate needs of the Christian minority in the villages of Upper Egypt. Determined to create a network of small schools, dispensaries and catechetical centres, he set up an Association of 'Responsables', with a training centre in Cairo. Many of those he recruited were alumnae or the older pupils of the two Sacred Heart schools. The religious longed to join their students, but until the lifting of cloister, in the wake of the second Vatican Council (See Appendix I, p. 238) this was not possible. Eventually in 1966 the Egyptian Province established a community in Samalout in Upper Egypt; several others followed: Beni-Ebeid (1971–72;1974), Abou Korkas (1972), Dairout (1974) and Bayadeya (1980).

Maria Teresa Arbeloa rscJ, who had arrived in Cairo from Spain in 1955, was among those who felt called to work in Upper Egypt, but she had to wait until 1977 before being sent to Abou-Korkas; ten years later she went on to Dairout. In all these years she had been unable to master the local language, and was therefore unable to give lessons in religion; instead she taught needlework and knitting. She described her disappointment and explained how she overcame her feelings of failure.

What could I do in this school of the Association at 62 years old? For two months I was lost and discouraged, but during my retreat, I set myself to face my situation. I did have a mission in this school, but what was it? Gradually I realised that I was to be a presence to everyone, especially the poorest. When I left Dairout five years later, I was deeply touched by a young man, one of our teachers, who said to me, 'You have been the presence of Jesus among us.'

The Sophianum College of the Sacred Heart, Lima, Peru

Peru is the oldest Province of South America and has maintained its strong tradition of Sacred Heart education. Most schools and colleges are state institutions, but their administration and leadership are generally in the hands of rscJ. Francisca Quintanilla rscJ, Assistant Director of the Sophianum, a school of 1,230 primary and secondary students, has sent this report of her ministry.

Our aim is to form pupils (and ourselves) to be realistic, integrated people of faith, who proclaim the Gospel, and are committed to building a more just, humane and united society. Thus we attempt to give a solid formation centred on the person of Jesus. We want our pupils to live by Gospel values, and to take Mater as their model.

For the most part, the students work on projects teaching them to be open to scientific and technical progress, while the staff, working as a team, try to foster personal relationships, creating a family atmosphere; they are also concerned for the parents of the students, for whom workshops are sometimes organised.

The pastoral work of the school is also important. The older children organise spiritual work-days for the younger ones. Justice and Peace is one of the class subjects, and all the students undertake some practical social work. An active Student Council has a concern for all the pupils. In sum we aim to educate the students to become apostles of the world, so that through them the reign of the Heart of Jesus may flourish.

Forest Ridge School of the Sacred Heart, Seattle USA

Marcia O'Dea rscJ contributed the following:

For at least thirty years I have found the teaching of literature in Sacred Heart schools in the United States to be a wonderful work. I am always aware that my pupils benefit from the spirituality, education and studies which I have received from the Society. One student commented, 'By your dedication and appreciation of the arts you have inspired us to look more deeply into what is around us.' I thank God for this tribute which reflects the values of the person who made it. Because of my own enthusiasm and passion, I want those whom I teach to read and write for the love of it and to cultivate a growing sense of the breath and depth of the various disciplines and arts.

The tradition of Sacred Heart education prompts me to help young people to cultivate a certain 'inwardness'. This tradition asks the student to attend to the Spirit within, and also introduces her to the 'sages standing in God's holy fire' (Yeats). There, as Mother Stuart, echoing St Paul, has said, they can drink deeply of 'whatever things are true, modest, just, holy and lovely'.

Training Teachers in Peru: A Report from Rosario Valdeavellano rscJ

Since 1995 the Society has been in charge of ISPTA (The Institute of Higher Pedagogy of Tupac Amaru of Tinta). This is a name which is lamentably linked to terrorism: a situation which we were determined to change. This ministry brought us back to our original mission in Peru: that of training teachers.

At ISPTA we were confronted by a series of crises, including the threat to a rural state school of fifty years' standing. Co-operating with the Church, the Society was responsible for some radical changes designed to meet the needs of regional development. The Society was also involved in the pilot plan of teacher training which faced serious climatic and political problems.

The selection of student teachers for the pilot plan is all important; we seek to train free, compassionate, imaginative individuals, capable of fostering democracy at all levels of society, who are themselves ready to receive the love of Jesus. For our part we must improve the humane and academic standard of formation and increase the number of courses on offer. We also have to bear in mind the possibility of unemployment; this is a real threat to our students, although they are generally recognised as leaders.

Risks have been taken to improve the facilities of the twenty-two primary schools of the district. A programme of business formation has been set up, for example, which makes loans to students or settlers. In another school the construction of greenhouses has made it possible to grow organic vegetables for the college students. Andean culture has been enhanced by the People's Theatre Workshop, whose productions tour the region, developing self-esteem among actors and audience alike. Some of these projects have been assisted by the Society's Solidarity Fund. [See Chapter 12, p. 222.] In addition to training students, ISPTA is attempting to encourage new forms of collective work and exchange in the region.

The desire to make the love of Jesus known to all has led to such initiatives as the Workshops of Christian and Citizen Formation for Children and Young People (a form of catechesis), and The Students Assembly of the South, a training scheme for teaching young children.

Rosario concludes her account by saying:

It is moving to witness the joy and receptivity of those who have seldom before been assisted with projects. They constantly thank us, saying, 'Stay with us, you make good things happen.' We know it is the Lord's doing. The good news is always with us.

Sophia University, Mumbai (Formerly Bombay)

The pursuit of excellence has always been one of the goals of the Society, as has the development of a social conscience. In Madeleine Sophie's day the boarders asked for coal or gravel for the poor school, as birthday presents; in more recent times students have been encouraged to assume some responsibility for the deprived and underprivileged. For example, Livi Rodrigues rscJ, a former principal of Sophia College, introduced an additional course of excellence. This was available to students who undertook some form of social service, additional study, and the maintenance of a continuously high academic standard.

The students who entered on this additional course were expected to take responsibility for designing schemes to assist the less advantaged. For example one group took sickle-cell disease as their concern. During their vacation they persuaded a local hospital to train them in diagnostic skills. On their return to college they gained permission to set up a sterile area where they tested all comers; the results of the tests were passed on to the hospital, whose staff had agreed to undertake any necessary treatment. Other groups organised a street theatre designed to instruct audiences on AIDS; another group taught the canteen staff to convert organic waste into fertiliser; and others helped local science teachers in the municipal schools.

This emphasis on local needs was a deliberate attempt to train students for Christian leadership. By encouraging her students to develop a sound knowledge of Christian values, Livi believed that they would be in a position to exercise true leadership in their professions. 'I wanted their religious leadership to be exercised through their professional leadership,' she insisted.

The Roehampton Institute of London

In 1999, Bernadette Porter rscJ was appointed Rector of the Institute, having aleady served for many years as Vice Rector and Principal of Digby Stuart College.[4] One of her aims was to ensure that all the students fulfilled their potential, which in her experience always extended beyond their expectations, but this she believed would only happen if they were empowered from within.

In her role as Principal, she was also deeply concerned in education for justice, but she knew that the students would never rise to their own innate sense of justice, unless they themselves were treated justly; she made sure that she was always available and if necessary would intervene on their behalf. Over the years the students had established a tradition of active social concern which was furthered by the Social Justice Co-ordinator elected to serve on the Student Union Executive. Bernadette joined the various activities that addressed justice issues, but was careful never to assume a leadership role. She understood that the students' own needs must be met and therefore secured a new accommodation block for Digby Stuart as well as an up-to-date Learning Resource Centre for the Institute.

Bernadette believed that activities unaccompanied by reflection were deficient. 'I would be very worried', she insisted,

if, for example, the students went out on the soup run for the homeless, without considering why a soup run was needed. It is good for them to address the results of injustice, but they must always reflect on the causes. I believe that the Society's gift is to be concerned with integrating our thinking with our heart space. Reflecting on our actions is the form of prayer for which we have a special responsibility; we are committed to examining our consciousness about who we are and what we're doing.

Tertiary Education in Japan

Madeleine Sophie's 'little Society' has expanded across continents and cultures, leading to some difficulties in the transfer of spirituality and traditions. 'It should be noted', wrote Horiguchi Ikiko, a Japanese rscJ teaching at Seishin Joshi Daigaku (the University of the Sacred Heart),

that the spirituality and administration of the Society has been too occidental. It has not sufficiently incorporated the pluriformity of the Asian thrust and thinking, because many European rscJ do not seem to know Asia. I wonder to what extent even the Superior General and her team, after travelling around, have assimilated their experience.

Asia is very pluralistic with many indigenous languages and traditions, but it is frequently regarded as a single whole. The expression 'the making known of God's love' is based on a Christian tradition formed in the West; it needs to be translated into a concept that can be understood by ordinary non-Christian Japanese people.

Having clarified her own position, Ikiko explained how she passed on the charism of the Society to the students at Seishin Joshi Daigaku.

Her teaching was based on her conviction that the love of God deepens as knowledge of God, knowledge of God's world and knowledge of others, grows deeper.

That is to say, when a person learns through study, daily events, encounters with others, and through the experience of joy, sorrow and pain, how God works and how God speaks through the words of the Bible, that person's relationship with God deepens. The mutual relationship becomes one of friendship, adoration and thanksgiving. The Bible is taught as a way of living, a set of values that guide, rather than 'the Sacred Scripture of Christians'. When the values of the Bible are introduced, the long established Japanese values and traditions must also be taken into account.

All the courses offered by the University contribute to the formation of critical thinking and to an understanding that human beings, interconnected and interrelated, are dependent on one another in God. This should lead both to a desire for the peace of the global village and to a concern for ecology. As teachers we ask 'How can we assist the growth of our students? How accompany them in their self development?' We try to leave them to find and tackle the issues that need to be faced and as they do this we share our values with them.

Teaching in Moscow

The account of these early beginnings in Moscow has been based on information provided both by Maria Stecka, a Polish rscJ, and by Mary Totton rscJ from the English/Welsh Province.

In 1990 the Polish Province, in response to a group of parents who were living in Moscow and wanted their children catechised, discerned the possibility of creating a community there. It was to herald the Society's permanent presence in Russia until the time when this became legally possible. By the following year the passage of the decree granting religious freedom had opened the way to Moscow. The Polish Province promptly sent Maria Stecka rscJ to begin organising catechetics in the Polish Embassy School. She arrived on 4 February 1991 and saw the possibility of a wider ministry. RscJ could help the Russian people to reclaim their Christian faith, freely, in the new political/ social/religious climate in which they then found themselves. Consequently two rscJ, Beata Gutkowska from Poland and Mary Totton from England, joined Maria in 1992.

During the next seven years, seven rscJ joined the community, and stayed for periods ranging from two to eight years. The mission to the school remained the community's main financial source of income, since teachers were paid in Western currency. This enabled other members of the community to become more nvolved in teaching in the various tertiary educational in-stitutions in the city, and in work connected with some of the ecumenical, social initiatives such as the special educational pro-grammes for handicapped children, and ecumenical projects to feed the hungry in Moscow.

In the words of Mary Totton,

this was a time when the Society was privileged to be involved in many new beginnings such as the Thomas Aquinas Theological College, founded by Archbishop Tadeusz (Kondrusiewicz) in 1991; its first students were ecumenical, agnostic and atheistic, reflecting the society around them. The College functioned three evenings in the week and all day on Saturdays. By 1993 it had associate colleges in St Petersburg, Kiev, Kalingrad and Zagarov. Different members of the community were working in the University of Moscow, the newly state-established Humanities School, belonging to the Academy of Sciences, and the Catholic Seminary which had been officially opened in 1993. There, there were eleven seminarians hailing from all parts of the Confederation of the States of Russia. This was also the time when the Moscow community was involved in the production of the first official Catholic newspaper since the Revolution and the beginning of Catholic broadcasting in Moscow. Furthermore, their teaching brought rscJ into touch with many religious colleagues, with Dominicans, Jesuits, Salesians and Franciscans and also with Orthodox clerics and scholars.

In addition to teaching, rscJ also ministered to the parish. They helped in its basic organisation and undertook parish visiting. They also worked with Christian families and supported the Anglican initiative which had set up a project to feed the poor of the city. More local contacts were made on First Fridays when the community operated an 'open evening' with the celebration of Mass, followed by prayer, discussion and supper; these First Friday evenings, attended by a wide spectrum from the parish, became an ideal setting for making known the love of God and for spreading the Society's charism. The whole community was also involved in the attempt to create and strengthen links with the children of the parish, and they were also deeply involved in ecumenism, on account of the outreach of its members. Since the arrival of Sister Gabriella Berenyi in 1997, rscJ have also been connected with the highly respected Orthodox Theological College of Father Alexander Men, and with the Biblical Institute.

However, since the New Law on Religion was enacted in 1997, many religious communities have encountered greater difficulties with the State; but by then the Society had made good friends with several Russians and with their fine educational and cultural institutions.

An rscJ in China

From the earliest days, there have been individual religious who have become living legends in their own day. Brigid Keogh has a place among them. An American of Irish stock, Brigid was born in 1909. She entered the Society in 1930 and was finally professed in 1938. Studying history, she developed a fascination for the Far East and was therefore delighted to be sent to Tokyo in 1947.

Her immediate task was to rebuild the International School, destroyed like so much else during the Second World War.[5] This she did, and endeared herself to students, teachers and religious alike. In 1954 she was appointed Vicar/Provincial of the expanding Far East, contributing greatly to the initial foundation in Korea (1954) and the Philippines (1969). She was finally replaced as Provincial in 1971.

After serving briefly as Mistress of Novices, Brigid taught university students in Taipei, boys in a junior seminary and girls in a bush school in Kenya, until she was asked by Concepción Camacho, then Superior General, to investigate the possibility of establishing a ministry in China. Renting a room in Hong Kong in the late 1970s, she made her living by teaching English; meanwhile she contacted every university in China in search of a teaching post. One year later, she was offered a contract to teach English at the University of Beijing.

She was an instant success with her students, who described her methods:

In order to reinforce our memory and understanding . . .
Professor Keogh always accompanied her teaching with vivid
gestures. To explain the word 'plant' she would move as if she
were sowing or hoeing; talking of cats she would imitate cats
mewing . . . When she talks about something exciting, she dances
for joy or snaps her fingers as youngsters do. Both body and
mind are immersed in the circumstances she is describing.

Brigid was a good lecturer; she was also outspoken; this further endeared her to the students, but aroused suspicion among those in charge. It began to be rumoured that she was a Vatican spy; the contract for her third year was not renewed. In 1982, therefore, she returned to Hong Kong, where she spent a fruitless year trying to gain a re-entry permit. After a year teaching in the National University of Nicaragua, she was sent by Superior General Helen McLaughlin to explore the possibility of rscJ teaching in Jakarta at the University of Atma Jaya. She taught there herself from 1984 to 1985 and affirmed that this was a place where there could be a Sacred Heart community. With her mission accomplished, Brigid, then aged seventy-six, was at last prepared to return to Japan and stay put, but this was not to be.

The following year (1986) she received the offer of a contract to teach English at Yan'an University, in the province of Shaanxi, a place so remote that she had never heard of it. She set out immediately, and her arrival made an indelible impression on Shen Pei Chang, the President of the University. 'She came like an extra-terrestial,' he recalled,[6] 'wearing bright red trousers . . . she walked with giant strides, spoke in a strong voice, laughed merrily.'

In the following account, written by Brigid for this book, her passionate concern and belief in her students is self evident.

Yan'an University is the hope of Northern Shaanxi; when they graduate these young people will become teachers in country middle-schools throughout the province. Their task is to lift the educational level of a great dormant whole. These young people hold the key to the future of China (rather than the best and brightest of the big cities). The majority of their parents work in the fields or in small town factories, but by means of a college education their offspring will step into the wider world. The students are looking for something vaguely referred to as 'progress'. We compare the merits of farming and factory work: they are conversant with polution, over-crowding, crime, violence . . . but they want PROGRESS!

'How many years have you been a teacher?' they ask.

'Fifty.'

'Why do you like being a teacher?'

'Because it is better to work with people than with machines.'

'But in China people look down on middle-school teachers.'

'You must change that.'

I am the only foreigner in Yan'an, but far from being unassimilated, I have been swallowed whole. The Chinese avoid confrontations, the Irish temper erupts, they smile and call me a stubborn lao tai tai (old lady). I want immediate action – they tell me kindly that in China I must learn to wait. I give zero to the student who does not write his name on his paper – he praises me for being strict. The leaders are solicitous, friendly,

surprised by my energy. They visit me, they celebrate my
birthday, they bring Christmas gifts.

I write all this because I have a dream which I want to share.
In the whole sprawling region of Shaanxi Province, Yan'an
University is the one institution of higher learning. It is here, in
this valley, that the middle-school teachers are formed. I dream
of the day when Yan'an University will reach its full stature and
will send out well-trained teachers, who in their turn will lift
and stir to life the whole passive countryside.

Brigid's dream is rooted in an unshakeable belief in her
students. Once, at a prestigious reception, an American visitor
was eulogising Ford motor cars; they had made America great,
he said, and they would do the same for China. Brigid, unable
to contain herself, interjected. It was she who was dealing with
the minds of the young people of China, the country's most
valuable resource. China must realise the importance of education, 'then, twenty years on, there will be no need to import
cars – the West will be importing from China.'

So how did this eccentric old lady, with her red trousers and
her Irish temper, win the trust of students and staff alike? Quite
simply she was their teacher and friend. She took them for
holiday picnics and did their homework with them. She discussed, argued and dreamt with them. Every book she owned she
shared. She was equally popular with the teachers who flocked to
her room to discuss literature, talk French, play bridge and drink
beer. The respect in which she was held was mutual. 'They
sometimes frustrate and even enrage me,' Brigid admitted, 'but
they have always helped and uplifted me.'

Brigid did not spare herself and in the winter of 1987 she
developed pneumonia, a disaster which brought to Yan'an Naga-
mine Miki, an rscJ from Japan. Miki explained how this
happened.

When Brigid caught pneumonia, Sr Hayami Yayoi [then
Japanese Provincial] thought that I should go to help her.
Brigid said it was unnecessary. I was very disappointed. Brigid

explained my disappointment to the Yan'an leaders. They were
touched and said that I should come anyway. I came as a teacher
of Japanese, although everyone knew that there would be no
students. I came, I saw, I was conquered by the love of the Yan'an
leaders for our congregation.

What did I do? Well the University is like a village inhabited
by wives, husbands, in-laws, grandparents, children of the faculty
and staff of all ages. Brigid's work was in the University, mine
was in the village. I did teach – English of all subjects – but
this was incidental to my real work of education. I knew every
child on the campus and each new baby. I gossiped with the
old women, visited the grandmothers, played with the children.
I bargained with the vegetable men and produced the beer
and biscuits for Brigid's bridge evenings with the teachers. When
her eyesight deteriorated, I became her eyes. To sum up, I lived
and loved and was, and still am, Brigid's Boswell.

But even her Boswell could not prevent failing sight. In 1990,
at the age of eighty-one, Brigid returned to Tokyo 'to enjoy
doing nothing'; this nothing, however, covered a remarkably full
programme. She ran a scheme to send Yan'an students to study
in the United States, visited Yan'an regularly, where she gave
student classes, and in her spare time she ran a correspondence
course.

On 23 September 1998 Yan'an celebrated its sixtieth anni-
versary. As part of the celebrations a bronze profile of Brigid
Keogh was unveiled in honour of her work for the English
Department and for the University as a whole.[7] In his tribute to
Brigid, Shen Pei Chang said,

Her strong sense of responsibility, unselfish contributions and
hard work have touched and encouraged all our teachers
and students and have become part of the fine tradition of the
University. The language classroom building [for which Brigid
raised $200,000] will remain for ever as a shining monument in
the hearts of the teachers and students. As an outstanding
teacher, Professor Emeritus and excellent foreign expert of

Yan'an University, Miss Brigid Keogh is always praised for her noble spirit of education. Her contributions to the University, together with her name, will remain for ever in the history of Yan'an University.

Inevitably these accounts provide no more than a random sample of the rscJ involved in the ministry of formal education at the end of the twentieth century; in the chapter that follows a broader group of ministries are described. These often developed as a result of the changes following on from the Second Vatican Council, the General Chapter of 1964 and subsequent General Chapters. All the ministries which are described next were concerned with marginalised people such as prisoners, AIDS sufferers, or street children.

NOTES
1. Conference, 1835.
2. 1982 Constitutions #22.
3. 1994 Chapter Document.
4. St Charles' Training College and Roehampton School were bombed during World War II; in the ensuing reconstruction the college was transfered to the Roehampton site and became known as Digby Stuart, while the school moved to Woldingham in Surrey. In 1975 Dorothy Bell rscJ was one of the pioneers of the federation of the Froebel Institute and the colleges of Southlands, (Methodist) and Whitelands (Anglican). This created the ecumenical Roehampton Institute of Higher Education, renamed Roehampton Institute of London (RIL) in 1995. In 1989 Bernadette Porter rscJ replaced Dorothy Bell as Principal of Digby Stuart; in 1999 she was appointed Chief Executive and Rector of RIL; in January 2000 RIL became part of the University of Surrey and is known as The University of Surrey at Roehampton.
5. Gokakko (language School) 1907 was the first institution founded in Japan, which quickly developed into a flourishing primary and secondary school, with all subjects taught in English. It was closed during World War II during which all the buildings but one were destroyed by bombs. In 1948 the University of the Sacred Heart was established on a new property to which the international school, renamed International School of the Sacred Heart (ISSH), was transfered. In 1999 578 students, from Kindergarten through to seniors, of 45 different nationalities, were being educated at the ISSH by a staff of 130 of whom three were rscJ.
6. *The Singing Tree*, ed. Cao Guxi and Hao Yu (Yanan, China, 1995), p. 169. This book, devoted to the doings of a foreigner, represented a quite extraordinary tribute, and caused considerable comment when it was published.
7. Sculpted from a photograph by Wang She Wa.

✦✦

On the Margins

As a body we must learn to see how to glorify the Heart of Jesus Christ suffering in humanity.

> (Concepción Camacho's opening address to the
> General Chapter of 1976)

In prayer we come to Jesus . . . with the sufferings and hopes of humanity.

> (1982 Constitutions #20)

The Society chooses to let the world set its agenda.

> (General Chapter of 1994)

The changes experienced in recent decades have been so rapid and radical that it is tempting to look back on Madeleine Sophie's life as a time of stability. This was far from the case. Madeleine Sophie often spoke of the necessity of keeping up with the times, and when faced by urgent need, she allowed events to guide her response, provided she had the personnel. As a result of cholera epidemics, for example, she founded a small number of orphanages where vocational training was given; she also set up a school for deaf and dumb youngsters. Children from the streets of Turin were clothed, cared for and taught the catechism, and an apprenticeship in glove-making was set up at Grenoble. Although she refused an appeal to sponsor a small community of Arab Sisters of the Sacred Heart in Syria, she did tell the Children of Mary about these Arab nuns, which led to the adoption of one Arab sister by each of sixty-five groups of the Children of Mary. This was an example of the close co-operation of pupils, past and present. From the earliest days they took on projects which the Society had reluctantly refused, generally on account of difficulties of enclosure or the lack of resources.

Madeleine Sophie's flexible approach was in evidence two hundred years later, when the Society extended its service of formal education beyond the classroom and lecture hall; the following descriptions of a variety of different ministries illustrate some of the means by which these religious were communicating the love of Jesus 'in activities for human development and the promotion of justice' (1982 Constitutions #13); for 'within [our] common vocation, each one receives her own unique call' (1982 Constitutions #25).

Supporting Handicapped People in Spain, Kenya, Ireland and Scotland

Spain

Fuensanta Meléndez, a Spanish rscJ, found herself launched into a new ministry in 1977 when Lupe gave birth to Eduardo, who was disabled. Lupe was a secretary in a centre run by the Society in Torrejon de Ardez, a small industrial-cum-farming town, twenty-two kilometres north of Madrid. Eduardo was born with cerebral palsy. Fuensanta described the shock and suffering endured by Eduardo's parents, who were totally unprepared for the birth of a handicapped child. 'In a way,' she commented, 'Eduardo was born to all the sisters . . .'. At that time, there was no provision in Torrejon for the education or support of children with special needs, but after his birth, meeting the needs of this child became a community preoccupation to such good effect that by 1998 excellent facilities existed for handicapped young people.

Thus the birth of Eduardo was the catalyst which prompted

Fuensanta to give herself to the ministry of serving mentally handicapped children; this brought her into touch with national and international organisations. Through ASTOR (The Association of Parents with Mentally Handicapped Children in Torrejon de Ardoz), Fuensanta gained access to professionals through whom a number of projects for handicapped children and adults have been brought to the town. In 1997 Fuensanta had the task of co-ordinating the work of the Association, supervising the graduates, identifying the need for additional facilities and fighting to obtain them. As for Eduardo, he had become a strapping young man and an active member of the centre that provided various facilities for disabled young people.

Kenya

While disability is a universal phenomenon, handicapped children in Africa may well be more vulnerable than those in Europe on account of their endemic poverty. Frances Lynch rscJ, a nurse from the English/Welsh Province, was missioned for Africa in 1981. After many years in Uganda, she was sent to Kenya to care for 'God's poor, God's special children', as she called her handicapped charges. She explained that if you have a large family and not enough money, the disabled child often comes last when it comes to food, clothing, medical attention and possibly, even, affection.

I consider myself blessed in having had so many opportunities in which to express God's love for each one, and I am not talking only of the the children. When we visited their families, or travelled for miles to take a blind boy to a clinic or a mentally defective girl to a hospital, we were often asked by nurses, teachers and even the doctors, 'Why go to so much trouble for one handicapped child?' 'Because God loves her so specially; we need to work together to try to improve her quality of life.'

Another vitally important part of my ministry [Frances concluded] is to pray with and for our children. I say to God,

I will hold your people in my heart, and God says to me, 'I will hold your people in MY Heart.'

Ireland

Veronica Punch, an Irish rscJ, speaks in a similar vein about her work in Priorswood, a deprived area of Dublin. When she retired after years in the classroom, she devoted most of her time to the Travellers.[1] Instructing them in religion, teaching arts and crafts, she visited all their homes and spent most of her time with them. But she reserved one day for the severely mentally and physically handicapped men and women from St Michaels, a neighbouring day-centre. These were people of limited intelligence, who lacked speech and for the most part were unable to walk without aid. Yet Veronica, working with a couple of helpers, enabled each one to craft some object, however crude. Despite their lack of speech, she insisted that communication presented no problem. 'A helping hand or a hug works wonders: the language of the heart is all that is needed.'

Scotland

Christine Triay, a Scottish rscJ, spent many years in Edinburgh, teaching young children with special needs, finding this ministry greatly rewarding. One small boy, in particular, helped her to overcome her fear of disabled children. Aged ten, he was both hyperactive and epileptic, and although heavily drugged had a great sense of fun. 'I was touched by his capacity for joy,' Christine said.

Swimming was popular with the children, but the journey to the baths was an ordeal. Eight handicapped children boarding a bus caused chaos; fellow passengers patronised them, ordered them around and occasionally swore at them. Even when they reached the baths they were liable to abuse from the public. At first Christine was indignant when no distinction was made between herself and her charges, 'but gradually my attitude changed. In hindsight I came to see that I was blessed to have been counted as one with this courageous, resourceful group.'

Supporting Sick Children in Puerto Rico

Ada Duarte rscJ, a Cuban and a member of the Puerto Rican Province, taught in elementary schools until she was sent to the retirement house. In 1998 she was working as a volunteer at the children's hospital. She brought the love of the Heart of Jesus to countless young cancer patients and always insisted that the strength to persevere in this emotionally draining ministry was a grace gained through the supporting prayer of her community.

At the hospital, Ada first visited the Intensive Care Unit; she went from room to room, praying with all the patients. 'I was trying to communicate Jesus' compassion and love for the little ones.' As many of the children were undergoing a course of treatment, Ada saw them at regular intervals and developed strong ties with them all. On one occasion Aramis José, a three-month-old boy, came to the hospital for an emergency operation. Ada arrived in time to discover that the child had not been baptised, so she gave him the Sacrament. 'I had never done this before', she said, 'and it struck me that he was indeed different afterwards – had he not become a child of God?'

Ada also ministered to parents, with a special concern for the mothers, who often stayed at the hospital with their children for days on end. 'It is the things of God', they told her, 'that give us strength and support.' 'I am convinced', Ada concluded, quoting from the 1994 General Chapter Document, 'that our spirituality s a gift to be shared.'

Combating Malnourishment in Brazil and Paraguay

By 1994 the National Conference of Brazilian Bishops had made progress in their campaign to eradicate poverty through the implementation of their 'Pastoral of the Child' (Pastoral del Niño). A key factor in this programme had been the campaign's goal of ending malnutrition in children and pregnant women. This had largely been accomplished as a result of the discovery by Brazilian doctors of 'Alternative Food'. This diet consisted of highly nutritious, efficient and cheap resources such as prepared wheat or rice chaff, leaves from potato plants, ground eggshells mixed with mandioca leaves and other such materials, which would normally have been thrown away or fed to the animals. The Church in Brazil undertook a campaign to educate women in the use of these foods, which were rich in vitamins and nutrients.

During this period, Maria Eugenia de la Arena, an rscJ from southern Spain, was working in Brazil where she had responsibility for five Basic Ecclesial Communities (CEBs).[2] Having worked with doctors and with the CEBs she learnt what alternative foodstuffs could be used and how these should be prepared. The aim of Alternative Food was to cut the mortality rate of infants, but the programme, in addition to improving health, had a marked effect on the mothers. As a woman learnt how to prepare the new diet, she was enabled to assume responsibility for the health of her family; she passed on her knowledge to her neighbours and became a person who would initiate and carry through change in her community; through her the community began to assume responsibility for itself.

Training courses for leaders who had been elected by their communities, also played an important part in the project. Few of those involved were literate, so picture books, videos and posters were used to help spread knowedge and support families who had embarked on the Alternative Food programme. Maria

45

Eugenia was convinced that these changes would incorporate values which would lead to improved human and Christian relationships and to a perception of health that would integrate spirituality, justice and reconciliation.

She spent three years in Brazil and then returned to Spain, only to find that 'I could not live tranquilly in the first world where life is taken for granted. This good news has to be taken to other countries.' In 1994 the Conference of Brazilian Bishops gave Maria Eugenia permission to translate the relevant texts, so that the programme could become available outside Brazil. She chose to work in Paraguay, a country where the mortality rate among mothers was the highest in South America. In 1995 the Pastoral of the Child was launched by the National Conference of Paraguayan Bishops who were determined to take an active part in relieving the suffering of their people.

Many have testified to the effectiveness of Alternative Food, including Monsignor Fernando Lugo of the Diocese of St Peter, Paraguay. 'I have seen so many children recover,' he reported in 1997.

At first they were mere skin and bone, but slowly they put on weight, changed colour and began to smile again. I have seen their families regain happiness. This is a battle of life gained over death. Today we are able to solve the debilitating problem of poverty, although much still needs to be done.

When she had completed her work in Paraguay, Maria Eugenia was hoping to be able to continue her work in Venezuela.

Teaching Nursing Skills in India

Even during the time when most rscJ taught in school, some professional nurses were attracted to the Society, many of whom used their skills in the school or community infirmaries. Some of them, however, felt marginalised because they thought that nursing was considered inferior to teaching. Even in comparatively recent years a debate was held to discuss whether nursing was a 'genuine expression of our [the Society's] charism'; after which nursing was acknowledged as having great potential as an educational ministry. This debate was of particular importance to Prabha Rodrigues rscJ, an experienced teacher of the Indian Province.

'I had decided to be a nurse', she said, 'because I had opted to work among the poorest villagers, and their greatest need is for health education.' Having completed her training, Prabha became Nursing Tutor and finally Nursing Principal of the Holy Spirit Institute of Nursing in Mumbai. 'While teaching students and nurses, doctors, seminarians, sisters of other congregations,' Prabha said, 'I have learnt how to keep close to Jesus. I ask our Lady to be my guide as I travel like a sevika (servant); the calls are numerous and my strength is diminishing, but Jesus alone is my strength and joy.'

In addition to teaching, Prabha was always involved in 'hands-on' nursing. She described how one poor mother, with a two-year-old child who would not stop crying, walked for a whole day searching for her.

At first the stench was too much for me, and I was about to scold the mother, when the words of Jesus in the daily Mass spoke loudly to me: 'This is my Body, do this in memory of Me'. I took the child, gave her a bath and dressed her numerous scabious wounds in which there were maggots. I pulled them off, one by one, counting thirteen in the wounds of the head alone. It took me three hours to rid the child of vermin. While I was working, I spoke to her mother with compassion and love, explaining how to care for the child. As she was very poor, I gave her some milk and a few eggs and vegetables, as I knew that without nourishment there could be no recovery. Finally I asked the woman to bring the little girl back in three days time. When she returned the child was healed. I did the dressing, the Lord did the healing! This is what I love to do, to do the Lord's work and to show his mercy in the shadows of this land.

Nursing in Upper Egypt

Specialist nursing had developed in Upper Egypt, where there was an urgent need for the treatment of burns. The government hospitals lacked the facilities for treatment and sometimes discriminated against patients from the Christian minority. Four rscJ, Reyes Callis, Hedwige (de) Cadolle, Conchita Oliver and Celia (van) Zon, together with some local help, were treating about four thousand patients each year at the clinics in Samalout, Abou-Korkas, Dairut and Bayadeya. These clinics, open to Christians and Muslims alike, every day of the year, never had empty beds.

The majority of accidents occured in the home; most families lived in a single room where a stove burned constantly. Young children would put their hands, or even their faces, into the cooking pots. Sometimes a harassed mother would be careless in adding paraffin to the fire, while it was still alight, causing an explosion; there were also tragic cases of women deliberately setting fire to themselves. One of Hedwige's most dramatic cases was that of a nineteen-year-old; in her determination to escape marriage to her designated husband, she doused herself in petrol and struck a match. She was mortally burned and the hospital to which she was taken sent her home to die. Determined to save her, her family brought her to Hedwige's clinic and three months later she had recovered.

How were such cures achieved? The religious had discovered an effective ointment made from aloes, a local and prolific plant. 'Our concern is to organise preventive measures as part of our apostolate. This gives us the opportunity to demonstrate our love, work with the poorest and provide health education along with our treatment.'

Caring for AIDS Sufferers in Kenya and Uganda

Helen O'Regan, an American rscJ working in Kenya, is an AIDS educator in the Diocese of Eldoret; she uses the Education for Life Programme, started by the Catholic Sisters in Southern Uganda and introduced to Kenya in 1998. Helen sent the following account of her work.

In 1999 the authorities of Kenya acknowleged that there were over 1.5 million individuals infected with AIDS, out of a population of approximately 30 million; there were 250,000 patients who had full-blown AIDS, and among those infected 60 per cent were between the ages of 15 and 35.

Initially the AIDS programme was based on accurate information from a medical point of view; this was my approach until in September 1998 I attended a training course in 'Education for Life', presented in a context of faith and prayer. The course members shared what their lives were like and what they would have liked them to be. Group-counselling played an important part in the programme, which was designed to bring about behavioural change, reflection on life and the acceptance of the reality of AIDS. Participants were called upon to make a commitment, to renew this from time to time and to accept ongoing evaluation. The AIDS programme in the Diocese of Eldoret focused on AIDS Awareness seminars which led into the Education for Life programme.

Helen commented:

I have sometimes given pastoral care to patients in their homes, which has brought me face to face with the ravages of the disease and its disastrous effect on all areas of life. I am always touched by the faith of those who suffer, especially the children who are so often bereaved. Truly this scourge is the leprosy of the twentieth century. Though barely a year into the programme, I feel that God is using all the gifts God gave me, and I am grateful to be of service.

In Uganda

Doreen Boland, an Irish rscJ who spent most of her life in Uganda, sent the following account.

In Uganda, where the AIDS pandemic has been among the most severe, the Government and Church have adopted the slogan 'Live positively with AIDS', and have faced up to the disaster with courage and openness. I serve in the parish team in the Inner City of Old Kampala; we are surrounded by the suffering of thousands of AIDS victims and their orphans; they challenge us with their heroic courage, perseverance and solidarity. Most, having lost their livelihood, eke out an existence in one room. Praying and reflecting together as a team over the years, we have found modest ways of improving life and restoring confidence. Sometimes we can provide small capital grants of not more than $150, which are sufficient for the recipient to start trading on the streets again. We also encourage thrift, by running a savings scheme, which generates a little interest. Word has spread and has brought people with AIDS from neighbouring parishes; we can do so little, but we can give loving concern, making each individual understand that he or she is important to us and beloved of God.

We are deeply concerned for the children; the traditional extended family has in general broken down, so it is not uncommon for a single grandmother to be looking after as many as twenty children. We observed that the anxiety for their children, soon to be orphaned and left without the possibility of schooling, further undermined the health of their mothers. The mothers of those few children whom we were able to help with school bursaries noticeably improved in health. The children themselves were traumatised. Seven-year-old Geoffrey, for instance, lived in a small room with his dying mother, and was her only carer. How can we imagine the effects on a young child who is quite likely to witness the painful death of both his parents? We long to give comfort and counsel to the thousands of children caught up in this tragedy of disease and loss.

I am so often personally challenged by the faith of these people, by Beatrice, for example, who has lived in the shadow of death for years and has just discovered that her eight-year-old daughter is HIV+. At one of our services for the sick, Beatrice told us that she had discovered Jesus in her illness. 'Now all I want to do is sing.' On another occasion, Peter, a friend of mine, came to see me. He had undergone treatment for TB three times, and was living in a rented mud and wattle room with his two children. El Niño (the destructive current) had swept away one wall of his home and in the flash flood that followed he lost most of his possessions. He told me he was tempted to take his life, but 'I went to the Fathers for the Sacrament of Reconciliation and while there picked up a booklet on Hope; it suggested that I thank God for restoring my hope, and then go to share my joy with a friend, and that's why I'm here, Sister,' he said.

There are countless stories of bravery, selflessness and faith in Abba, but nevertheless I sometimes find myself overwhelmed by my helplessness in the face of such anguish. It is then that I experience the reality of 'The pierced Heart of Jesus opens our being to the depths of God and to the anguish of humankind . . .' (1982 Constitutions #8).

Youth Work in Ireland

Parts of Ireland were booming in the 1990s, but there were also areas where unemployment remained high and few young people received tertiary education; only the exceptional escaped poverty and deprivation. Anthony was both gifted and fortunate. As a teenager he had joined a youth group for prayer and discussion initiated by Rory and Kay Keating. Later they invited Eileen Lawless rscJ to join them; she had been working with youth in Chile and had just returned to Ireland.

By then the 'Keatings' group' had named itself the 'Anawim'; they were fostering their own spiritual growth and promoting Christian action in the community. They set up dance and drama groups, organised youth liturgies and ran their own meetings. When the Keatings moved, Eileen stayed with the group but it was Anthony and Pamela, another promising young member, who took over the leadership role. Anthony had begun his studies in theology and psychology, but nevertheless accepted an invitation to join the Parish Leadership team.

Later on the Society set up a youth project in the same area, employing Anthony during vacations as project Co-ordinator and later as part-time Director; he maintained that this responsibility provided invaluable experience, enabling him to develop self-respect. He became a member of the Dublin Corporation, whom he represented on the board of Dublin University, and was one of the youngest candidates to contest a seat, albeit unsuccessfully, in the parliamentary election of 1997. When he finally handed over the leadership of the Anawim, he had become a role model, whom younger members esteemed, just as future members would in turn esteem them.[3]

The Philippines

From its foundation in 1969, the District of the Philippines made the decision to set up no institutions. Instead, a number of rscJ have engaged in youth ministries, supported in many cases by the St Madeleine Sophie Foundation (SMSF) which operated in three parishes.[4] From 1974 to 1982 the SMSF provided funds for the education of poor students, most of whom acquired good white-collar jobs. Gradually it became clear that the fund was benefiting individual families, rather than a whole community. After careful discernment in 1989, it was decided to phase out the scholarships and use the SMSF to target the source of student poverty.

In 1991, as a result of this change, Herminia (Hermie) Noval rscJ was able to run a community-based health programme in co-operation with the NGO, LIKAS. LIKAS trained doctors, nurses and students in hygiene, herbal medicine, and in first aid for common medical crises. The programme was responsible both for a general improvement in health and for highlighting additional needs in the community. Thus when the local health centres became more effective and more accessible to poor people, Hermie made the decision to replace the health programme with schemes for the education of youth and with work for mothers and children. Working with PETA (Philippine Education for Theatrical Arts), the SMSF launched programmes which targeted marginalised and non-school-attending youngsters. They presented socially relevant plays which greatly increased self-confidence. A Youth Formation programme was offered, which attracted twenty-five participants, one of whom joined the SMSF staff part-time, while she worked her way through college.

With the assistance of a group of Vincentian priests, the Grameen Bank Loan and Savings Scheme was set up and run by the SMSF. A small group of women were given a loan of about Pesos 100,000 each, which had to be repaid in weekly instalments; this was conditional on their attendance at weekly sessions in which the simple skills of crafts and bookkeeping were taught. One of the women used this loan to make sweets and peanut butter, enabling her to support her family when her husband lost his job. Having repaid the original loan, she borrowed a further P 1000 in order to upgrade her business. The loan and savings scheme was extended to the children who were encouraged to save for school needs. As an incentive they received practical gifts, brought each year by the Japanese students who came to the Philippines for an Exposure Experience.[5] The novices were also involved in the SMSF schemes, running weekend educational programmes for children. They taught through storytelling, drawing and drama and they cooked with the children. The children thoroughly enjoyed themselves, experienced teamwork and returned home with a greater appreciation of the work involved in running a house.

As for the adults, once the loan scheme was successfully launched it became possible to start up a spirituality programme. By means of a ten-week 'home retreat', prayer sessions were organised in the community. Hermie believed that those who had made the retreat would in turn facilitate small prayer groups and become instrumental in rekindling the spirituality of the parish.

In 1986 the church leaders in the Philippines established a Commission on Youth, appointing Lydia Collado rscJ as co-ordinator and executive secretary. She set up various initiatives to train future leaders in youth ministry, including study days, prayer sessions, and in 1997 a two-year MA degree course in Pastoral Ministry; this combined academic study with practical work. Lydia was assisted by the novices and YPs in the organis-ation of five-day summer youth camps, which were held in beautiful surroundings. The opportunities offered – prayer, study, relaxation and companionship – proved to be extremely popular, attracting many, including several 'unchurched youth'.

Lydia made the following comment on her ministry:

'Christ invites us to enter into the dispositions of his Heart'
(1982 Constitutions #41). We are called forth to be
ambassadors of the Church for the millions of disenfranchised,
unwanted and ambivalent young people who are seeking
direction, who ask for love and a renewal of faith. As we share
in the pilgrimage and mission of the Church through our
ministry of education, we are enjoined to accompany and assist
the formation of our younger brothers and sisters.

Youth Work in Poland, Taiwan and Indonesia

Poland

Hope in the future of Christian faith in Poland rests largely on the post-conciliar renewal movements. For several years Jadwiga Skudro rscJ was one of a group of rscJ who have been prominent in Oasis, one of the principal youth movements. This involved risks under the Communist regime, for although traditional Catholicism was not considered subversive, any movement which encouraged young people to reflect on the Scriptures, especially in terms of their application to daily life, was highly suspect. Whenever inspectors or spies joined the groups, all discussion ceased as everyone said the rosary.

By the 1990s under a third of Polish children were attending catechism classes, so Oasis made a point of attracting to their retreats a wide range of people including school students, families with young children and adults. In the beauty of the countryside, directors animated groups of fifty or so, of similar ages. Conferences, sharing, gospel study, relaxation and common chores contributed, in Jadwiga's words, to 'an atmosphere of joy, which helped to create an understanding of authentic Christian life'. After the retreat, meetings continued with ongoing instruction and preparation for the following year. It was estimated that seventy thousand young people progressed from a traditional to a committed and freely chosen faith as a result of their involvement with the Oasis Movement.[6]

Taiwan

Directed by Chow Ching-ming rscJ, the Centre for Young Friends was established in 1976 in response to an appeal from the Taipei Junior Court for assistance in combating juvenile crime. Ching-ming supervised youngsters under probationary orders, held sessions in the Youth Detention Centre and counselled both children and their parents. She also worked with delinquents referred from the courts, supervised school and professional studies, assisted in the search for employment and helped to develop parenting skills.

Some of her charges did reform. Lily was sixteen when her mother had to leave her to her own devices in order to care for her father in hospital. Lily became involved in drugs and crime and was sent to the Junior Detention Centre; she was there when she heard of her father's death. While completing her sentence, Lily received counselling from Ching-ming to such good effect that she returned to school and finally secured a scholarship, enabling her to train as a hairdresser.

In 1998, Ching-ming was attempting to raise funds to secure official recognition as a Youth Centre. Experience had convinced her that 'problem' children tended to be members of problem families. Difficulties often developed during the school years, but the earlier the intervention, the more likely it was that difficulties would be overcome.

With street children in Indonesia

In Jakarta the rscJ community assisted with the three-day 'Kampores' (camps) run by the Jesuits of the Jakarta Social Institute, an NGO whose main work was the monitoring of human rights. The three-day camps were run for about two hundred and fifty youngsters; some were the children of labourers and scavengers, others were street children from slum areas. These Kampores were no ordinary camps. They provided healthy and entertaining interludes, promoting serious analysis with an educational and social impact.

The young people played games, enjoyed sing-songs and were helped to reflect on their situation through competitions and art projects; they began to take the first steps towards assuming responsibility for their own lives. They composed songs about their environment, and prepared a dramatic presentation of their lives which they performed throughout the following year.

The interlude at the camps helped them to enjoy creativity, to express their feelings and to begin to take pride in their work and in themselves. In 1996 they composed a Declaration of Children's Rights which they read at several public events, including the prestigious Human Rights Award function, when a presentation was made to the head of the Social Institute. In addition to helping the young people to change their lives, these kampores began to affect the society around them.

Working with Prisoners

England

Norah Lester rscJ, of the English/Welsh Province, worked with adult prisoners. She wrote of her educational work with men in Wormwood Scrubbs, a high-security prison in London, where many men were serving the first three or four years of a life sentence. After nine years she commented,

The value of this service is still unfolding for me. For these men, education brings liberation in a variety of small unspectacular ways, like seeds growing in the wasteland that the prison system represents.

Doors are open for those who have gained the ability to master the reading of menus, bus destinations or street names. Being able to add up and to read prices gives greater control over money, with a consequent spectacular growth in self-respect and confidence. Many of the illiterate prisoners had been able to cope with primary school, but had been intimidated by their secondary school and had absconded. For them the street had often become an escape from a variety of dysfunctional family situations. In prison a second chance for education can open doors into worlds that had once seemed out of reach. Qualifications gained represent far more than their face value: they are the passports to joining the achievers, the non-losers.

Norah's main work was to encourage men to gain qualifications: she helped many to enrol for an Open University degree. 'This use of time', she noted,

created a metamorphosis whereby a life sentence could lead to
the fruitful pursuit of knowledge and achievement. Success
often offered families hope: out of tragedy and shame something
worthwhile had emerged. This also applied to the men who
took up craft work. They discovered a variety of skills and had
a chance to develop their feminine side – even the most macho
threaded needles and lived to tell the tale!

Provision is woefully inadequate, but to work with what is
provided is to light a candle rather than to curse the darkness.
As an rscJ, I find it is a privilege to go with others through open
doors and discover that there is LIFE elsewhere towards which
we can walk.

Belgium

All the evenings are sad!
I look at the letters of my companions,
at the post they receive, the post they send,
their family photos. I look at them and I envy them.
I am a solitary prisoner . . .

This is a rough translation of the opening lines of a poem written
by the prisoner, Noel, in gratitude to Micheline Ortegat rscJ,
who visited him in prison.

'This poem', she said,

expresses the needs of prisoners, needs to which I have tried to
respond. There is a real necessity for someone to be there for the
prisoner; to be there regularly, dependably, able to take into her
heart all the anxiety, rejection, poverty and loneliness of being
shut away, which so often leads to illness, or suicide. It seems to
me that the prisoners' families also have needs. I have known
about a dozen young people who have taken their own lives, or

58

have died from an overdose, or from AIDS; the shock to their
families is brutal and overwhelming. The Lord has given me the
gift of his peace, his love and his compassion. I try to share
this with the families who have been plunged into mourning.
Thank you Lord.

Another young man whom I used to visit was suffering from
AIDS. Our conversations were very banal as they were entirely
concerned with fast cars and women. He was a Muslim, but all
of a sudden, without one word to his family, he asked me to
read the Scriptures to him. On one particular day I read him
the story of Jesus sending the disciples out two by two to take
peace to all the villages around. It came to me then, that I had
been sent to beseech the Lord to bring peace to Saladin who
was in such agony of mind, and to all those who visited him.

Some days later I received a telephone call to say that not
only was Saladin now at peace, but so were his family who had
at last accepted that he was dying of AIDS. Saladin and I became
very close, we trusted each other and the Holy Spirit inspired
me with a true tenderness for him; he died shortly after this, a
child of God at peace and ready to meet his maker.

After Micheline had been visiting the prison for about a year,
she received permission to visit the men in the hospital block.
There she found Roger, a Fleming, who understood no French
and spoke to no one.

When I first saw Roger he was lying mute and rigid on his bed,
having become totally disorientated since the death of his wife,
some time before. I will never forget this meeting when Jesus
inspired my every word and gesture; after an initial rejection
of me, the Lord loosed the tongue of this man. Roger opened
his heart to me, told me about himself and the state of his
soul. I was able to talk to him of the Lord's great mercy, of
forgiveness and of the love of his wife and his children. When I
left, I embraced and kissed him. This was a gesture of God's
forgiveness which came not from me, but from God with all
the delicacy of the love of God. The following week, one of the

warders asked what had happened to Roger – he was now a changed man. He was totally relaxed and was talking to everyone. God had set him free – to me it was as clear as the water from the rock. Blessed be God!

Peru

In 1998 there were top security penitentiaries put up all over Peru, to hold the thousands accused of membership of the proscribed 'Shining Path' or of the 'Tupac Amaru' revolutionary movements.[7] Human rights were often ignored in the prisons; many inmates were chained throughout twenty- or thirty-year sentences. Trials were often unjust and the unlimited powers of the police too often became a licence to harass or even torture unconvicted prisoners.

Margarita Recavarren rscJ worked in the penitentiaries of Yanamayo, Puno, and Chorrillos, Lima, where convicted women were housed with their young children. She supported the Christian communities that the women had organised for themselves and helped them to edit the monthly publication that they produced.

Part of her work involved supporting former prisoners after their release; a monthly day of recollection was held, which focused on the difficulties of reintegration into family life. Margarita also worked to change the imbalance that overemphasised retribution at the expense of rehabilitation. Like others she was acutely aware that social influences were compounding factors in the crimes of individuals.

Work with Homeless People in New Zealand

June Kirk-Smith rscJ of Auckland, New Zealand, belonged to the 'Tenants' Protection Association' and worked with homeless and vulnerable people. The Association was a member of the New Zealand Housing Network which had been set up to co-ordinate action and to exert political pressure; those working in it were called upon to solve all manner of housing problems. There was the case of an elderly pensioner whose rent had been raised to the point that she could neither buy food, nor afford to heat her home. The house of a couple from Tonga was flooded with storm water and sewage whenever it rained, and their three children got sick. In another case a property developer destroyed both the shed, where three children slept, and the vegetable patch which was essential for feeding the family.

June and her colleagues were also concerned with international justice, such as upholding human rights, or the alleviation of crippling debt. On one occasion they had all returned from a peaceful rally when the door was burst open by the police who had no search warrrant, but nevertheless attempted to search the premises. June and her colleagues tried to bar the entrance, by sitting with linked arms across the doorway. The police lashed out with their long batons. One young man was struck on the head and went into convulsions, whereupon the police withdrew. At the court hearing that followed, the judge dismissed most of the charges; he pronounced the search unlawful and the force used against the group unnecessary. 'I was petrified,' June said, commenting on the incident, 'but if we respond to the call of the 1994 Chapter for "a deeper commitment to justice", we must surely be grateful to those rscJ who are prepared to risk personal security in their stand for justice.'

This chapter has been mainly concerned with the Society's response to the perceived needs of their time. Chapter 4 is concerned with the rscJ who found themselves, along with countless others, in the midst of war, rebellion and unrest.

NOTES

1. Travellers: also known as Gypsies or Romanies; they are believed to have originated in North-West India from whence they spread to many European countries in the fifteenth century. A nomadic people, they are known for

their horse-rearing skills and fortune-telling; they have been persecuted down the ages, and if they settle often face hostility.

2. CEBs have generally developed in response to the needs of a group of parishes; each is unique, but all share certain traits. Committed to the will of God, members' lives centre round the Eucharist and the Scriptures; they are committed to justice, reconciliation and the defence of human rights.

3. Anthony's story is told in *Best Practice in Youth Ministry*, ed. Martin Kennedy and Brendan Doyle (Columba Press, 1998).

4. SMSF is a non-profit-making organisation, founded in 1971; it is financially assisted by the Sacred Heart schoolchildren of Japan.

5. The Exposure scheme is fully explained in Chapter 6.

6. This piece is based on an article in *Connections* Vol. 3 (1993), p. 45.

7. In the early 1980s a group of landless Indians from the highlands formed Sendero Luminosa ('Shining Path'), which waged war on those it considered class enemies. They were reinforced by members of the Tupac revolutionary movement, another guerrilla force, and government attempts to defeat the guerrilla movements who continued to wage civil war were largely unsuccessful.

CHAPTER 4

Violence and Aftermath

Madeleine Sophie and her first companions were touched and impelled by the reality of the historical moment in which they lived.

(Introduction to 1988 General Chapter)

The pierced Heart of Jesus opens our being to the depths of God and to the anguish of humankind. (1982 Constitutions)

The mystery of the body broken and the blood poured out today, send us to the world to be bread shared, the real presence of the love for others.

(1994 General Chapter)

Madeleine Sophie, a child of the French Revolution, was no stranger to political upheaval. Since her day wars, violence, and civil unrest have continuously affected her little Society, which has attempted to respond as far as it might. In a number of areas rscJ were caught up in violent change and experienced the trauma of warfare. The following accounts are no more than a sample of the ordeals that some rscJ were called upon to face.

In Hungary under the Soviet Regime[1]

Anna Lazár entered the noviciate in Budapest in 1947, but within months the Communists had seized power and taken over the Philippineum, one of the two Society schools in Budapest. The novices were transferred to Italy, but Anna had no passport and therefore went with the rest of the community to the Sophianum, the second school. Communication became problematic; Anna received no letter admitting her to first vows, as she had hoped; instead in 1950 she was told to return home, but at the last moment she received a letter from Mother de Lescure, the Superior General in Rome, giving her permission to make her first vows. Little did Anna know that this longed-for event would be followed by a period of great trial.

Three months later, in the middle of a night in June, the police arrested the whole community. The sisters were deported to Eger where they were held for three months, together with religious from other congregations. Once they were released, all but seven managed to reach Italy; Anna was among those left behind. She found work in Budapest in the household of Dr Meszaros, who had looked after the medical needs of the students of the Sophianum. The father of seven children, Karoly Meszaros was compassionate and generous; he called Anna his eighth child and stood by her when she was imprisoned. Anna, for her part, undertook domestic work in the house. Although the rscJ were scattered, they sometimes met and, despite the risks, kept contact with former pupils.

Anna stayed with the doctor's family for three years, until in 1953 she received a message telling her to join a 'people smuggler' who had agreed to escort the remaining rscJ over the border into Austria. Shortly before they were due to leave, the police arrived and arrested them all. 'We were alone in the cell and didn't know what was happening,' Anna reported, 'but', she continued, 'I always felt the prayer of the whole Society. God never abandoned me.' Anna was sentenced to three years in prison, which were reduced to two, on account of her peasant background.

For the first year no one visited her,

then one day they fetched me to meet Doctor Meszaros and his wife; he had done the rounds asking for me. 'How is my eighth child?' he asked. The doctor told my family where I was, and said that when I was released, I must go back to his family.

There was a Jewish woman in the prison who had become a Communist. 'How can you be so happy?' she wanted to know. 'You have no fresh air, no light, no contacts outside.' 'I believe in God and in God's will. God will not allow one hair of my head to be touched,' I told her.

Some people committed suicide because they had lost hope. I always hoped that I would soon be free. I had my beads in my hand and prayed all the time. I taught this woman to say the rosary and explained how to make the Way of the Cross; she said that I gave her courage. When we were released we wrote to each other, but we never met. I was very conscious of God's presence and was also aware of the prayer of the whole Society. Sr Gutzwiller[2] sent me a parcel with a letter telling me about the prayers for us. I worked so hard that I was released three months early[3] and went at once to the doctor's house. Dr Karoly was greatly concerned for me. Whenever I went out, I always said where I was going, and if I was delayed, I used to telephone to say that I was safe.

In 1956, when the Revolution erupted, my brother-in-law managed to get passports for me and my eldest sister, his wife; he said he would escort us over the border. He drove us to my sister's house and as we left, the first of the Russian tanks were arriving; we only just got away. My home was close to the border, but I could not go there; my parents were living alone with a niece and if I had gone back to them, I would have stayed. Crossing the border was the hardest step I have ever taken, for I believed that I was leaving my homeland forever. My brother took me to his home in Graz. My feet were so swollen, having walked so far, that I could not get into shoes, but at last, to my great joy, I reached our house in Petergrasse, and once there, I was told to come to Vienna as soon as I could.

Six months after her arrival in Vienna, Anna made her probation in Pressbaum; she was finally professed on 22 August 1958. For the next forty years Anna cooked and catered in Society schools. She did not go back to Hungary in 1992, when the

Society was finally able to return, but she went for a brief visit in 1996 and was then asked to stay on. Anna was apprehensive. 'But', she explained, 'when we are asked to do something under obedience, we must obey. When I was needed, I received the grace to stay. I like the atmosphere with the young people [the novices]. I feel happy and free and find I can pray better.'

Poland under the Communists

This account is largely the work of Alina Merdas rscJ, the historian of the Polish Province.

In contrast to Hungary, the Society was not forced out of Poland during the Communist regime. Three of the Society's four schools were shut down, and although the Lycée at Polska Wies was allowed to continue, it was subjected to severe restrictions, enforced by cruel inspection. The teaching of the Catechism was forbidden, as were such subjects as literature and history, the students' parents were penalised and there was no financial assistance from the state. The whole Province was therefore involved in supporting the school. The religious grew fruit, vegetables and hothouse flowers for sale, and they also made vestments; but even this relentless work did not generate sufficient income: Mother House funds made up the deficiency.

Despite all the difficulties during this period, new houses were opened, parish ministries were undertaken and young women continued to be drawn to the Society in Poland. Travel abroad, however, was impossible, preventing the probanists from going to Rome to join their peers, so they prepared for their final profession at home in Poland.

A brief glimpse of Poland under martial law

Maria Gaczol, a Polish rscJ, has a vivid memory of the violence inflicted by the army in the early 1980s during the months when Communist rule was being challenged by the Solidarity

Movement. She had entered the noviceship in Warsaw at the moment when Russian tanks were daily expected on the streets, to crush the growing opposition. In December, two months after her arrival, martial law was imposed. The situation was so ominous that all the candidates were told that they could return to their homes if they wished. Maria stayed and some months later had a brush with the military.

On 3 May 1982 we went with Maria Stecka, our Novice Mistress, to Mass at the cathedral in Warsaw. When the Mass ended we were ordered to return home by a particular route, but sensing danger, we set off in the opposite direction. Our Novice Mistress led us along a road that we found had been closed off by a posse of armed troops. Ignoring the guns that were trained on us, Maria Stecka marched fearlessly up to the commanding officer. 'We are nuns, let us pass,' she insisted. The officer was so astonished that anyone should dare to defy him, that he let us through and we arrived back safely. The rest of the congregation were less fortunate; they were tear-gassed as they left the cathedral and many were badly beaten up. Such incidents were commonplace at this time.

In 1991 Maria responded to a missionary call to Uganda; once arrived she found herself in the unrest that followed the civil war provoked by the misrule of Milton Obote (See below).

Revolution in Chile

The revolution which established General Pinochet's dictatorship in 1973 was based on terror. For some years before the coup, the Society had been viewed with suspicion by many of the powerful families of Santiago, on account of the changes that had been made in the admittance of pupils to the secondary school in Apoquindo. These changes were undertaken in an attempt to open the school to less privileged students in accord with the decisions taken by the Special Chapter of 1967 (see

Appendix I). Parents of the school were informed that scholarships were to be made available to poor pupils and a programme of social awareness was to be implemented. A group of wealthy parents and alumnae, determined to maintain the status quo, made serious accusations against the school.

Thus on the day of the coup, the army stormed the school on the flimsiest of pretexts. The headmistress, Margarita Hurtado rscJ was arrested and taken for interrogation. 'It was then', she later admitted,

that I understood and experienced the truth of the words of the Gospel, 'do not fear what you will have to say: the Spirit will speak for you' [Luke 12:12]. Nothing was proved that could justify an arrest, but we felt vulnerable, as we knew we were under suspicion. The decision was therefore taken to hand over the running of the school to the secular staff.

The abandonment of the school was the prelude to a period of extreme oppression in Chile, which was courageously resisted by numerous protesters among whom were priests and religious, including members of the Society. They took part in protest marches, carrying Bibles, praying the Rosary, reciting psalms, singing and repeating freedom litanies. They helped to organise medical treatment for the victims of government brutality, whom the clinics were forbidden to treat. They also supported families by their presence at wakes and funerals – all too frequent events in the parishes during Pinochet's rule. The three rscJ, Odette Karmy, Maria Angeles Marimón and Sandra Cavieres of La Alianza community were then involved in pastoral and catechetical work in part of the West Zone of Santiago. In the twelve months before the referendum that finally ousted Pinochet in 1988, they undertook political and social formation with the local members of the Christian Ecclesial Communities (CEBs), reflecting in the light of the Gospels on what was happening around them. On the eve of the referendum itself, a first aid group was organised and a communications centre established in the chapel. They were present with many others at the liturgy of 'sending', when the Chilean flag, a ballot box, a broken chain and voting papers were among the eloquent symbols placed on the altar. On the actual referendum day, the rscJ went with their people to the polling station and assisted in the count. This was a powerful experience of solidarity for La Alianza community which they later described as a time when 'together with the CEB we learned to value simple gestures ... and to discern. We learned to be people in the midst of a People ... '[4]

'The Troubles' in Northern Ireland[5]

Any narrative attempting to portray rscJ 'under fire', must necessarily include Northern Ireland during the last decades of the twentieth century. The Irish/Scottish Province included the Republic of Ireland, Northern Ireland (comprising the six counties of Ulster, part of the United Kingdom), and Scotland. Both North and South were subjected to terrorist attack. In 1982 Aideen Kinlen rscJ became head of St Catherine's College, the only Catholic girls' secondary school in Armagh. The County of Armagh bordered the Irish Republic and was always a target for the terrorist violence. Aideen's account of her years as headmistress provides a moving and graphic sketch of the effects of 'the troubles' on the school and the surrounding area.

'How many stories I could tell about "The Troubles",' Aideen wrote.

There was the day we expelled a pupil for assaulting a Protestant member of staff, the day a pupil was killed by a bomb, and the day I turned informer. I could recount my encounter with a converted Protestant terrorist, tell of our visits to the women's prison, or tell you of the gentle IRA man who came to tea. Then there was the killing of a loyalist lorry driver whose daughter said she would never again trust a Catholic, and the murder of one man in reprisal for that of another, while the daughter of one and the sister of the other sat as pupils in the same class in the school. And then there is the story of Emma Donnelly.

Emma was a thirteen-year-old, good fun, good-hearted, a keen games player and popular with students and staff alike. Late one evening she was coming home in a car driven by her grandfather, Barney Lavery. She lived in the village of Benburb, six miles from Armagh, where the sound of the IRA bomb was clearly heard. Just as Barney and Emma were passing the unmanned police station, it exploded, killing them both outright.

I still find it painful to remember the next morning. The whole school was devastated, especially the 160 pupils of Emma's year. We held assemblies, made cups of tea, hugged and talked endlessly. All we could do was to try to contain the trauma and the hysteria. I visited the Donnelly home. Their numbed grief was beyond words. The funeral was probably the most distressing I ever attended. The homily from Bishop Lennon measured up to the occasion in its power, its compassion, its very controlled anger, and its centredness on Christ.

I had been interviewed on television about the bomb and as a result letters poured in from both Protestants and Catholics. One beautiful letter from a Mrs Wilson quoted from St Peter's First Epistle, Ch. 2 vv. 19–24. She told me that she and her husband had prayed together on that text. They were Protestants, from Eniskillen, and they had lost their daughter in a bomb attack; Mr Wilson had spoken within hours of the atrocity, saying that as a Christian he forgave his daughter's killers.

Emma's and her grandfather's death caused a loss of sympathy for the IRA even among the Nationalists, their traditional supporters. Exceptionally people were prepared to give information, and it was then that I turned informer. I was given the name of someone who had been involved in the Benburb bomb and I left a message on the police confidential line. The following day I was asked to go to the police station in Armagh: as I entered the police station I knew fear. I was engaged on such a visible act, 'betraying' a Catholic terrorist to what amounted to a Protestant force, the Royal Ulster Constabulary, known to be anything but even-handed. Many in the Catholic community had been intimidated by the IRA; they were told to keep silent about what they knew 'or else' they would have their kneecaps shot up and be beaten to within an inch of their lives. Now in my own small way I was experiencing the dread that gave the terrorists power.

Against this ominous background, it was wonderful to see the resilience, humour and warmth of Protestant and Catholic alike, not that they mixed with each other; it was also good to see youngsters developing and flowering against all the odds. I tried to sum up what I felt in my prize-giving speech at the end of the year. 'We have much to give us hope . . . but I think this year we have tapped an even deeper, more mysterious and more real source: at the core of the Christian there is a faith, incipient or elusive as it may be, that death is conquered. Life is lived in company with Christ who enables us to face the struggles and tumults of life as we attempt to support each other in love.'

Violence in Uganda under Idi Amin and Milton Obote

For the first twenty years or so of independence, Uganda was at the mercy of ruthless dictators.[6] Neither Amin nor Obote respected the rule of law or human rights and both made use of virtually untrained and ill-disciplined soldiers and police. They had a free rein and they massacred the population at will; the country was rent by civil wars and tribal conflict. Although no rscJ lost her life, the religious suffered along with the people, undergoing pillage, dearth and terror.

Doreen Boland, an Irish rscJ, arrived in Uganda in 1963, and there she remained, apart from six years in Rome on the Central

Council. She was the Provincial at this unsettled time and wrote of her experience.

During those years of insecurity, I found myself looking into the barrel of a gun three times, and on a fourth occasion I had to try to humour a drunken soldier; he was brandishing a hand grenade through the open car window. Meanwhile bystanders were looking on, petrified and helpless. Many people were being robbed at gunpoint: to resist was to court instant death. As Provincial, I therefore ordered compliance, only to resist myself on the first occasion I was accosted!

It happened when I was returning from the city one day, and became aware that I was being followed. I could not shake off the thieves who cornered me, seizing the car and all our belongings . . . On another occasion we were driving through an uninhabited area, when three gunmen leapt out of the bush. We had to stop and ended up lying face downwards on the muddy road. While the thieves stripped the car, we prayed aloud 'Sacred Heart of Jesus, we place our trust in you'. They took everything, but not the car, and so we were able to get away. Such were the daily events of the people during those years; our solidarity with them made it natural for us to undergo similar experiences. The Lord's 'I am with you always' gave me – gave us – strength. I can truly say that I had six happy years as Provincial. The adversity and insecurity which overwhelmed us all at different moments cemented a deep love, union and support among us. A sense of humour was also a help!

Later, in 1986, when the National Resistance Army, led by Yoweri Museveni, captured Kampala and overthrew Obote, Doreen found herself on a battleground. She was then engaged in a pastoral ministry and was living in a flat on the Makere University Campus with Patricia Coyle, an Australian rscJ.

Museveni's army caught up with the goverment's so-called security forces at the University and a hand-to-hand battle ensued on compus. Shells began to fall as we sheltered with a refugee family, a Mennonite woman and a Hindu girl. We tried to drown the gunfire by singing Christmas carols, a prayer to the Prince of Peace. We were Protestant, Mennonite, Catholic and Hindu; we came from Uganda, Australia, India, America and Ireland and we were at one. If only the human race could learn to sing each other's songs and to praise one Loving Lord and Creator!

There were many others caught up in the violence of Uganda, but not all their experiences were negative. Katherine (Kay) Haseler (1943–1998), an Australian rscJ, who spent six years at the secondary school of St Charles Lwanga in Kalungu, related how the school community gained strength and found peace. At the time fear was increasing as the students returned to school with tales of homes raided, cars held up at roadblocks and soldiers looting at gunpoint. 'It was almost Lent,' Kay explained,

and I suggested that at noon each day we would stand together and say the Novena of Confidence for peace in Uganda, while the school bell tolled across the compound. This practice brought us a strength from beyond ourselves. We experienced a power greater than the violence around us: trust replaced our feelings of insecurity. Our circumstances remained unaltered, but we had tapped into our source of strength.

War and Revolution in Nicaragua

In 1985, having completed an eight-year term as Director of Novices in the USA, Mary Catherine (Mickey) McKay arrived in Nicaragua, where the revolution against the Contras (counter-revolutionaries) was in full swing.[7] She found herself operating in a war zone and was seered by the experience which she described vividly and with great honesty.

On my fourth day there, we buried Pedro Palma, while his three-year-old son looked on. In my second week, I listened to Cornelio, an eighteen-year-old campesino (peasant farmer), talk about joining the army to lay down his life for his people, 'because that is what Jesus says we must do'. I think I cried for a week, overwhelmed by the faith and love of this people and by my own backward, barely existent Christianity.

In the years that followed, I was to bury many teenagers who had been tortured to death, or ambushed on the road, or shot by the Contras. I was to spend hours with the parish priests, with our community and with members of the Parish Council as we reflected over the paschal mystery as it was being lived in Jalapa. I could hardly look into Teresa's eyes when she asked 'What shall I do when my son's murderer comes back?' In 1986 a group of us walked the 325 kilometres from Jalapa to Managua on the Way of the Cross for peace and reconciliation. We wanted to make an act of faith in the God of peace and of life. Each day we celebrated a liturgy and prayed one of the stations of the cross as we walked in the burning sun, along the dangerous roads. Each day we listened to the hopes and fears of the people of Nicaragua as we ate and slept in their homes at night. Each day we affirmed our faith and hope that life is stronger than death, and that life will have the last word.

Living in Nicaragua was about living in hope, and I did it badly. Life in a war zone, touching the extremity of people's suffering, opened my awareness of all that is unredeemed, all that is not integrated in me. I experienced times of withdrawal when the suffering was too great and I closed myself off from it. I wanted my own time and space. I was a coward, and although I asked for the grace to give my life if I had to, I really did not want this. We were an international community in Jalapa and we did not do very well at this, either. We were pushed to the extreme and found wanting. I felt useless and powerless and hated it. Only the God who is greater than my heart was able to pull me from the abyss. Only this people of faith and hope and love, by the very wonder of who they are, was able to do what was totally beyond me to do for myself. And yet Jalapa was the most contemplative time of my life and I have often wondered how this could be. I think that there I touched the mystery of life and death, and in the end nothing, I suppose, can be more contemplative than to enter with Jesus into his paschal mystery.

The Society in Congo

In 1999, as this book was being compiled, Congo was undergoing a fearful war involving no fewer than nine countries. In the circumstances it was not possible to ask for individual accounts of ministries. However, Marie-José Nsenga Fwakwingi rscJ, the Congolese Provincial, kindly sent me a description of her province. I much regret that owing to problems of space this had to be abbreviated.

In our province we have a greater number of young religious, some of whom are still in formation; we also have about twelve expatriate sisters. Our priority is our own schools, mainly boarding schools, where we try to witness to the love of the Heart of God for all, according to the desire of Madeleine Sophie. We were sorry that we had to withdraw from Kole, a diocesan school, and from Kasongo-Lunda. Also after a long discernment, we closed the secondary school in Gombe, so that we could maintain the boarding schools, which we see as particularly educative in terms of the Sacred Heart family spirit. However, our sisters are sometimes invited back to Gombe to give spiritual formation to the RE teachers who are working there. In our boarding schools, consonant with our desire for the promotion of African women, the older boarding-school pupils are expected to take some responsibility for the younger ones. There are also retreats and days of recollection which in many instances are animated by rscJ.

In the primary schools the lay staff have taken excellent initiatives; one of these has been the setting up of a pilot scheme collaborating with a Protestant school network. As a result of this, a textbook on citizenship for primary schools has been published. Candidates, pre-candidates and the younger rscJ teach in the primary schools.

This situation is in contrast to the secondary schools where the proportion of rscJ on the staff is very small: at Kipako there is only one rscJ for 100 pupils, at Mbansa-Mboma one for 160 children, and at Kimuenza one for 800. We have three sisters studying in college, and one elderly sister visits the schools twice each year on behalf of the Provincial. The fact that there are few rscJ in the secondary schools is partly because of the high level of studies required, and partly because of the political unrest, but now, in 1999, we have five novices and four candidates which gives us hope for the future. We realise the importance of our lay collaborators and want to share with them our educative mission so that people may become more aware of truth, of love and of freedom.

In 1927 the Society had opened a school for European children in Kinshasa and a mission for the local Congolese was opened in Kapako in 1930. There, in addition to a primary school and a dispensary, courses were given in domestic management and preparation for marriage.

Now, in 1999, we have three secondary schools, three primary schools and one nursery school. Because of the guerillas, two boarding schools are temporarily closed and there are only local pupils at Kipako.

Several of our rscJ nurse in our dispensaries and in the surrounding villages in spite of the poor roads which make travelling hazardous. Our health work is orientated towards human development and the promotion of justice; our overall objective is 'health for all' and education forms an integral part of the nurses' role.

Pastoral work in the villages is the special gift of Josefa Lukadi rscJ, who is one of our oldest Congolese sisters and is held in veneration by the Elders. Some rscJ work in a parish on the outskirts of Kinshasa where there is a CEB which is full of life. Also since 1972 some Spanish rscJ have been engaged in prison ministry, befriending and teaching prisoners, following them up and trying to ensure that they are treated justly. They have also offered days of recollection to the staff of the prisons.

May the coming Chapter of 2000 renew each one in every area of our educative mission.

Work with Refugees and Asylum-Seekers

When historians come to reflect on the twentieth century, they may well name it the century of the refugee. There can be few nations from which men, women, unaccompanied children even, have not had to flee from violence or catastrophe. Therefore in the 1990s many rscJ were to be found working with refugees. As with previous accounts, those that follow are no more than a random and incomplete sample of some of the work that was being undertaken by members of the Society. Often they worked in co-operation with the JRS (Jesuit Refugee Service), or some other NGO (Non-Governmental Organisation).

Maria Dolores (Lolín) Menéndez, a Puerto Rican rscJ, was appointed the JRS Education Resource Person for Africa in 1996; both her background and experience had unknowingly prepared her for the post. Her Spanish parents, exiled from Spain during the Civil War, met in Puerto Rico and settled in the United States. After primary school in Spain, Lolín was at Sacred Heart institutions in Madrid, Boston and Manhattan. When she entered the American novitiate in 1966 she was fluent in French, English and Spanish. Her call to Africa followed her final profession in 1976, and is best described in her own words:

Then the General Chapter of 1976 took place and Concha [Concepción Camacho, Superior General 1970–1982] urged us to contemplate the pierced Heart of Jesus in the pierced heart of humanity. This call, coming so soon after my probation, made its gentle way into my heart. Concretely, it meant that I would go to Africa in 1977. It was just a case of 'come and see'.

77

Now twenty years later, I am still coming, coming back and seeing more.

Working at the government Teacher Training College at Karamoja, Lolín was constantly frustrated by the shortages caused by Amin's misrule.

There were no textbooks, so the students had to spend precious hours copying out lesson notes. I learned much about the meaning of time and about relationships. I also learned about the pierced heart of the people of Uganda who suffered so sorely at the hands of Amin.

In addition to college work, Lolín was involved with the parish and later joined the team where, working alongside catechists, leaders of small Christian communities, mothers, nurses and primary teachers, she was responsible for three parishes.

I went from home to home, learning what the pierced heart of humanity meant in the concrete situation of the homes of my neighbours. My contribution was to enable these people to become their own teachers, leaders, ministers; this was a mutual learning process, for I came to know the riches of several African tribes. I was touched by their values and enriched by their welcome and friendship.

A summons to Rome in 1987 to work in the Communications Team meant working with machines rather than people; Lolín compensated for this by spending her spare time working with refugees. She made contact with Michael Schultheis SJ, the International Director of JRS, who later would invite her to work for refugees full time. 'Again,' Lolín explained,

the signs of the times had made a silent, but constant demand. The number of refugees in the African continent is the largest in the world and is continually growing. This was the pierced heart that I was being invited to contemplate.

On leaving Rome in 1988, Michael Schultheis offered Lolín

work with the JRS project in Malawi, where post-primary education was being set up for refugees from Mozambique.

I worked at the Malawi project for about two years, putting the English curriculum into booklets, so that it could be used as a learning module. I was surrounded by more than a million refugees and I listened to their hopes for a better life, a life in which they could be openly reunited to God, which the Marxist government had rigorously prevented. For me this was a time of growth and learning.

In 1994 Lolín was asked by the JRS to educate Sudanese refugees who had fled to Rhino Camp, in south-west Uganda. There, joined by Florence de la Villéon, a French rscJ, she trained refugee teachers and parents to enable them to take over the running of the schools. By the second year this handover was in sight, when tragically all progress was halted by incursions from Sudan. The Sudanese government attempted to destabilise Uganda by demonstrating that it could not protect refugees within its borders. Roads were mined, vehicles seized, refugees and relief workers were attacked. Joseph Payeur SJ, the JRS Director, made the decision to withdraw his team.

Having left the camp, Lolín was then asked to become the JRS Education Resource Person for Africa, with overall responsibility for planning, staffing, resources and input. Much of her work was concerned with communication with other agencies, with staff in the field and with other organisations working with refugees.

Denise Calder, an rscJ of the English/Welsh Province, had also worked many years in Africa; in 1998 she was at Meheba, in north-west Zambia, which the JRS had set up to take refugees fleeing from the civil wars in Zambia. It was a camp of about twenty-seven thousand, many of whom had been born and brought up in the camp; most had come from Angola, but they had also come in small numbers from the Sudan, Uganda and Namibia. Denise was given a double brief, to teach English and to give training in health education, which for her was the means to achieving something more important. 'Presence', she explained,

is an important part of any JRS ministry, and one that meant much to me. Listening, 'being there', staying and demonstrating that we believed in each individual, was a fundamental part of the brief.

Resettling Refugees

In Australia

From 1990 to 1996, the Australians Kathlyn Ragg rscJ and Marie Rose Droulers rscJ shared the ministry of assisting in the settlement of refugees in Australia; for a couple of years they were joined by Faith McMurtrie, a Young Professed (YP), but she left the Society in 1992, before making her final profession. Under the Australian Government's Community Refugee Resettlement Scheme, refugees were offered asylum provided they could find a sponsor to guarantee accommodation.

Kath and Marie Rose worked for the 'Women at Risk Scheme'[8] and were unusual in that they lived in the same house as the women whom they were sponsoring. Marie Rose has described those days:

Our first refugee was a young woman with a four-week-old baby; after her came two single girls who were followed by a long line of women and children from camps in Thailand, Indonesia and Hong Kong. We have also shared the house with women from Cambodia, Salvador and Iran, but they mostly came from Vietnam.

We were notified by the Immigration Department when our 'guests' were due to arrive and witnessed many emotional scenes of family reunions, when we went to meet them at the airport. But we were total strangers to 'the women at risk' whom we welcomed, and we were also their only contact in Australia. It took time to get to know each other and to comprehend the depth of their feelings of isolation, compounded by culture shock. Language was always a barrier; to my shame, I failed to pick up any Vietnamese – my greatest accomplishment was to learn how to pronounce their names. Fortunately there is no barrier to the language of the heart and they soon began to respond to love and friendship. We did indeed love our people, and did our best to teach them English and to introduce them to the life of their 'new' country. Nor was adjustment all on their side. I never dreamt that I would be learning to cope with screaming babies, nappy-changing and toddlers' tantrums at my time of life! I am in admiration of these women, of their courage and inner strength, their resilience and their uncomplaining acceptance. Living and interacting with them and their children has done much for my own learning and growth. It has broadened my vision and left me humbled.

In Canada

Rita Egan (1917–1998) and Mary Power, both rscJ of the Canadian Province, have done similar work with refugees, taking advantage of the Canadian Goverment's policy of sponsorship. Under this scheme sponsors supported new arrivals for one year. This entailed financing the fare to Canada, paying entry and landing fees, and meeting refugees at the airport; sponsors were also responsible for finding schooling for dependent children and providing an introduction to Canadian life.

For some years, the Canadian Province had set aside a specific sum for the support of refugees, but demands exceeded the budget and some who requested sponsorship had to wait. Equally important to the adjustment to life in a strange culture was accompaniment in the struggle to gain legal rights of residence. Rita, crippled with arthritis, who died in 1998, worked tirelessly and was sometimes successful in getting rejection orders reversed. Describing her work on behalf of one couple, she said,

It took four-and-a-half years, more than seventy-five letters, advice from a friendly lawyer and a well-disposed immigration official, before two fine youngsters from Albania were finally admitted to Canada as refugees. This couple was 'fortunate'; their claims of abuse were corroborated by Amnesty International.

The first refugees to be sponsored by the Canadian Province were Abdul and Adill from Ethiopia in 1986. Anne Roche rscJ, then Secretary General in Rome, appealed to Mary Power, the Canadian Provincial of the time. So a ministry began which has assisted many refugees to become settled Canadian citizens: Abdul became a computer-draughtsman and Adill a nursing assistant. The Ethiopians were followed by four young men and a family from Sudan. In 1998 Maximiliano Meko, from Equatorial Guinea, was waiting in Paris for the outcome of a request for an entry permit for Canada. Mary was alerted to his situation by a phone call from Madrid at 3 a.m. Sadly the current budget was then expended. 'I am very sorry, Mr Meko, we cannot help you now, but it might be possible next year,' she said. On 1 January the following year, Mr Meko reapplied and his case was taken up. The work of the Canadian Province is well known; requests received reflect the internationality of the Society. Asunción (Mariasun) Escauriaza, a Spanish rscJ based in Sweden, asked for sponsorship for a Croatian family from Sarajevo. Mary took up their case, gained acceptance for them, and by 1998 had helped them to settle in Ottawa; a second Croatian family, also recommended by Mariasun, were less fortunate. They were turned down by the Canadian Immigration Department.

Sometimes those who had recently settled would try to help another member of their family; this was the case for Martin who was in Kakuna Refugee Camp on the Sudan/Kenya border. His sister, sponsored by the Canadian Province, was settled in Toronto and appealed to Mary Power on her brother's behalf.

Mary contacted Margaret Conroy, the then Provincial of Uganda/Kenya, who visited Martin in Kakuna; so the process of Martin's immigration to Canada was begun.

One of the happiest outcomes concerned Viviane, from Zaire, who arrived in Toronto, having been separated from her husband and two children at the Kinshasa airport on her departure from Zaire; all she knew was that her family were somewhere in Valencia in Spain. She appealed to Mary in January 1995, who contacted the Society in Valencia; rscJ managed to find the family, who had no documentation and were living in a camp in terrible conditions. The Valencia community invited Viviane's husband and two daughters to stay with them while their papers were obtained. The two girls went to the Sacred Heart school, and with the help of the Spanish Province they were able to rent a small house. Maria Soledad Soler, the rscJ trying to get entry permits to allow them to join their mother in Canada, heard eventually that it would have to be done through the Canadian Embassy in Paris. She turned to the rscJ community there, and eventually in March 1996, having obtained all the necessary papers, the family was reunited in Canada. This happy ending was the result of co-operation between communities in Spain, France and Canada.

In Malta

Malta was also among the more hospitable nations in terms of accepting refugees; they received free medical care, as well as education for their children. It was, however, almost impossible for a refugee to obtain a work permit; consequently those who managed to find a job were often exploited by unscrupulous employers. Catherine (Katy) Mifsud rscJ had a ministry with the Jesuit Refugee Service, teaching English. Her students were from Bosnia, Iraq, Palestine, Algeria, Lebanon and the Sudan; all were desperate to learn English, as their one aim was to reach Australia, Canada or the United States. Malta, they hoped, would be no more than a staging post. Some succeeded, but many remained in Malta. Katy's lessons were a precious lifeline for them; she went to their living quarters to teach them, becoming involved in a great deal more than their linguistic ability.

The rscJ working with immigrants, refugees and asylum-seekers were attempting to alleviate the suffering of victims subjected to injustice; there were also many who were seeking to educate both themselves and others to a deeper commitment to justice. The following chapter is devoted to these rscJ and their ministries.

NOTES

1. The Russians imposed a 'police state' regime when they overran Hungary in 1945. In October 1956, encouraged by the freedom secured by the Poles, the Hungarians held a massive rally in Budapest. Prime Minister Imry Nagy announced a return to multi-party government and the withdrawal from the Warsaw Pact, at which Russian tanks were sent in to Budapest, all opposition was crushed and Nagy was tried and executed.

2. Hildegard Gutzwiller rscJ (1897–1957) was Swiss; she spent most of her life at the Sophianum, which was severely bombed during World War II, and before escaping into Austria she hid many endangered people, including twenty-eight Jews. She was posthumously awarded the title 'Just among the nations' by the Yad Vashem Memorial Foundation.

3. Prisoners sewed garments; for each day they exceeded their quota, a day was remitted from their sentence.

4. The description of La Alianza community is taken from an account in *Connections* Vol. 2, published by the Center for Design and Communication (1992), pp 135–7.

5. By the terms of the 1921 Anglo-Irish Treaty, six of the nine counties of Ulster became Northern Ireland (part of the UK), while the rest of the island became the Irish Free State, later renamed the Republic of Ireland. There was opposition to this partition by Nationalists and discrimination against the Catholic minority in Northern Ireland by Unionists. This led to the civil rights marches by Nationalists in 1969 which later erupted into violence between paramilitaries on both Nationalist and Unionist sides. To restore order the British Government maintained a large military force in Northern Ireland, but violence persisted. Various efforts at reconciliation culminated in the Good Friday Agreement of 1998 which seemed to hold out some promise of a permanent settlement.

6. Uganda gained independence in 1962, but during the two terms of Milton Obote's rule (1963–1971 and 1979–1985) and that of Idi Amin (1971–1979), Uganda was rent by tribal conflict and civil war. Both rulers ignored human rights and ruled by terror. Obote was finally ousted in 1985 by the National Resistance Army led by Yoweri Museveni who became President in 1986.

7. Between 1978 and 1985 Nicaragua underwent civil war between the Sandanista National Front (FSLN) which had staged a revolution and overthrown the

Somoza dictatorship, and the Contras, who supported the Somoza regime and were backed and funded by the USA. Having imposed a trade embargo, the USA mined Nicaragua's ports in 1984. Peace was finally secured in 1987 by joint negotiations undertaken by the Presidents of Costa Rica, Colombia, Mexico, Panama and Venezuela.

8. The 'Women at Risk' scheme gave priority to refugee women registered as being of concern to the UNHCR (United Nations High Commission for Refugees), having been identified as being in danger of victimisation, harassment or serious abuse because of their sex.

CHAPTER 5

Women for Justice

Wherever we are, we commit ourselves to directing our energies, our resources and our choices towards the search for a more just and caring society. (1982 Constitutions #55)

Wherever we are sent, we express a concern for the growth of the whole person, a thirst for working towards justice and peace in the world.
(From the General Chapter Document of 1988)

The General Chapter of 1988 called the Society to recognize more fully the political dimension of our apostolic life and 'to live this political dimension with the attitudes of creative non-violence, in collaboration with others working for justice, human rights, peace and the stewardship of creation'. (From the General Chapter Document of 1988)

Madeleine Sophie was ahead of her time in the field of education; she believed both in the intellectual capabilities of women and in their capacity to influence society. But despite her forward thinking, she remained essentially a woman of her own age. Thus although she fought injustice and prejudice wherever she found it, insisting, for example, on the prompt payment of debts and refusing to tolerate snobbery, there could be no possibility of an involvement in politics. In company with the majority of apostolic congregations, the Society, with its habited members and imposing institutions, remained visible but secluded. When enclosure ended, bringing the full impact of the communication revolution into living rooms and convent

86

parlours alike, politics began to impinge on all areas of the Society's life.

From the 1964 General Chapter onwards, the issue of justice had been of mounting concern. In 1976, in a statement on commitment for mission, the General Chapter pronounced that 'As an international apostolic community, the educational dimension of our mission is inseparable from the call to work for justice.' Twelve years later the 1988 General Chapter acknowledged 'the need to recognise more fully the political dimension of our apostolic life' which demands 'working for justice, human rights, peace and the stewardship of creation'. A further step was taken when the 1994 General Chapter set up an international Justice and Peace Commission, with its own co-ordinating committee to consolidate and co-ordinate the work undertaken in the various provinces.

Non-Violent Peacemaking in the United States

Many rscJ have become involved in justice and peace work in some form and so it must, as usual, be stressed that the following examples are not a complete record of all the ministries undertaken. Among those who were working for peace, Anne Montgomery rscJ made a powerful impact. She was convinced 'that the real disarmament must begin in our hearts' and that 'we must take responsibility for what is done in our name'. She has explained how in 1978, during the first UN session on disarmament, she joined Plowshares[1] and took part in 'disarmament actions' against military sites and factories designed for the use or promotion of nuclear weapons. Fully aware that she was acting illegally, she was prepared and indeed was called upon to pay the penalty of a gaol term.

Later on, in 1990 she again explained how

. . . as it became clear that the US was determined to attack Iraq, I was invited to join the Gulf Team of the Christian

Peacemakers[2] which camped on the border of Iraq and Saudi Arabia, to be in situ as a non-violent presence. We were there when the bombing began and endured it for ten days until we were evacuated first to Baghdad and later to Jordan. This experience convinced me that the time had come to promote non-violent peace teams as an alternative to armed peacekeepers. Since 1990 I have returned every year to Iraq, taking medical supplies with me, and maintaining relationships with a community of Iraqi Dominicans.

Anne has also been engaged in peace initiatives between the Israelis and Arabs. In 1992 she joined a peace walk in Palestine and in the following year she went twice to Bosnia, first with an Italian team to Sarajevo, and then with an American group to Mostar. Finally in 1995 Anne left her part-time work in Harlem in order to be able to make a three-year commitment to the Christian Peacemaker Corps, which was then working with Arabs. In 1995 she moved to Hebron where she shared a flat with fellow Christian activists. The successes of the Corps have been low key, but significant. A group of Palestinian Karate students had been arrested for carrying chains in the street, because chains were classed as offensive weapons by the Israeli police. The Christian peacemakers obtained their release on the grounds that the students had to carry the chains with them, as they were the equipment they used in class. On another occasion Anne refused to leave a roof she had climbed, and thus managed to prevent the Israelis from demolishing an Arab home. She and her colleagues have also fasted for 29 days, i.e. 700 hours, as a protest against the planned Israeli demolition of 700 Arab homes. 'It's what the Gospel is all about – Jesus being a non-violent activist,' Anne insisted.

Work for Justice and Peace in Poland

Brygida Jalowa rscJ, a YP from Poland, working with the boarders
in the Sacred Heart School in Pobiedziska, described how, as a
member of the Polish Justice and Peace Commission, she lived
out her charism in her work for justice.

When I meet Jesus in prayer, I know that he is LOVE, that he
loves everybody, desires our happiness, wants us to know his
love and to love ourselves and one another. Above all the world
needs love!

When I look at the world I see love and I see suffering; the
world is divided and unjust. I see Jesus living in the slums and
I recognise his maltreated body in the form of a raped woman.
Jesus comes as a child begging for bread because his parents
are unemployed and penniless. Jesus is in these people; he invites me to stay with him. He invites me to be with poor people
in real situations, to feel as they feel and to create greater justice.

After 1989 when elections took place and Poland became free
of Russian domination, our political, social and economic
system changed radically: along with new opportunities, old
problems re-surfaced with greater intensity. The rich grew
richer and the poor, poorer. Criminality and violence suddenly
erupted, as did unemployment. The opening of our borders
brought migrants to our country and traffic in women became
a problem. Caritas,[3] to which I belong, has set up a Helpline and
embarked on a programme of education to combat this abuse.
Every injustice is a wound on the body of Jesus and this is the
context from which I ask, what does Jesus want of us, want of
me, an rscJ, now, in 1998? How can I reveal his love?

For me, as a member of the Justice and Peace Commission,
the first real challenge was the civil war in Zaire/Congo. We
expressed our solidarity by praying and writing letters to our
sisters; we also petitioned government institutions.

Another concern nearer home is the situation of

neighbouring families in Pobiedziska. They had been
agricultural workers on the state farms and had lost their jobs
when the farms were privatised. Unemployment has continued
over the years, with the ensuing problems of drugs, alcohol,
violence and sexual abuse. Furthermore, there are many
neglected children among these families who do not receive
adequate care. Some of the students from our school have
made contact with these children; they help them with their
homework, play with them and show them how to express and
receive love. This interaction is mutually beneficial. Another
small step is that the province is freeing a community room
for a young people's club, which is to be run by an rscJ in
collaboration with the local authority.

In 1998 I spent two weeks in Brazil, attending a workshop on
the prevention of violence against women and young people.
This experience changed my image of the world. Now when I
hear that two-thirds of the world suffer from malnutrition, I see
real places and faces. Brazil helped me to reflect on the
structures of injustice and how they might be changed. I also
realised how much poor people can teach us – they give far
more than they receive. I am learning to accept their attitudes,
and as I experience my own weakness, I become aware how little
I can change, so I trust in God, our only support. I gain peace
and strength from the conviction that our world and its future
are held in God's hands. Caught up as I am in the desires of
Jesus' Heart, I yearn for people to grow as human beings, as
children of God.

Justice and Peace Commission in Northern Spain

Contributions for this book have generally been received from
individuals, but some collective accounts were sent, including
the following from Northern Spain. It was clear that the Province

as a whole had a heightened feeling of responsibility in regard to justice, fostered by attendance at regular courses and workshops.

The Justice and Peace Commission had involved all the members of the Province and had increased its effectiveness by deliberately collaborating with other organisations. The main focus had been in the areas of immigration and social marginalisation; Spanish rscJ had joined national and international campaigns to denounce unjust laws and had collaborated with other groups working for change in political structures. They were also involved in promoting the rights of women and opposing discrimination.

By the late 1990s there were more than fifty rscJ in Northern Spain concerned with such issues as immigration, racial discrimination and social marginalisation. Some held salaried posts, others worked as volunteers. Those who worked with immigrants acted as advisors, supporting new arrivals in their struggle to regularise their status; several were running evening literacy classes, and others organised courses for children during the school holidays. Many ministered to prisoners, teaching and befriending them and accompanying them on their release. Four rscJ were working with drug-users on a detoxification programme, others nursed AIDS sufferers in homes for the terminally ill, or worked with alcoholics or prostitutes. In Society schools and centres a policy of non-discrimination welcomed immigrants, Travellers[4] and poor people. Every opportunity was taken to raise the awareness of young people to injustice, wherever it was found.

Korea: Reconciliation through Education[5]

Kim Jeong Hee, a Korean rscJ, worked in a study room for children and young people in one of the poorest areas on the outskirts of Seoul. She sent a description of her attempt to transform the hatred and suspicion traditionally felt by South

Koreans for the people of the North; this account has been put together from her report.

'In schools', Kim said,

there is a continual stress on anti-Communist ideology, with no opportunity for students to gain a true grasp of the reality of a divided Korea. By 1996, however, the general attitude to the North had begun to change: it had become possible to think of reconciliation, even union, between North and South. This was in line with the education that we, as Sacred Heart Sisters, sought to give. We were dedicated to 'nurturing life through education . . . an education which would achieve reconciliation'. This was one of the stated aims of both the 1994 General Chapter, and the Korean Provincial Assembly of 1996. It had become possible to think of reconciliation because of the change in attitudes. Indeed union between North and South Korea had become the aim of a citizens' movement which had been taken up by the Hankyoreh newspaper. The paper had launched a 'North–South Mutual Help Movement' and was running various activities to foster reconciliation.

We decided that the Study Room community should join this movement. All the pupils' savings were sent to the newspaper; letters were written to North Korean children and we drew pictures of ourselves and sent them those. On 27 April 1997, we were having a special Mass to celebrate the fifth anniversary of the Study Room; we decided to build this celebration around sharing all that we had received. As a theme for this Mass we therefore chose 'a thankful heart and an opportunity to share what we have with North Korea'.

While these activities were undertaken enthusiastically by the younger students, we discovered that for the seniors there was a serious clash between the anti-Communist education in the schools and the reunification education of the study centre. We therefore made two decisions: further education was required on the division between North and South Korea, and the summer expedition should be related to the work of the previous term. We planned a 'Reunification History Trip' which was to last two days for the juniors, and three for the seniors. We would visit several places close to the border on the 38th parallel. Before this took place the students did further research on their own; they studied the topography of the North, discovered the games played by the North Korean children, and enjoyed playing them themselves.

When we returned from the History Trip we drew up a programme of resolutions for reunification. The students decided to become members of the Reunification Association, to take an ongoing interest in North Korean news and to raise funds by holding a 'Bring and Buy' sale in November, for which they themselves would take responsibility. The sale was a great success, raising $250 (252,300 won) to send to the North Korea Medical Supply Fund. The sale also provided an opportunity for spreading information, through the video *Recent News of North Korea*, which had been obtained from the newspaper office.

Ecology Ministry in the Philippines

'Justice has its roots in the land and the natural order. Natural justice consists of a balance and harmony in which the welfare of the whole is protected.' This view, amplified in an article by Joyce Blackwell rscJ (1912–1999),[6] was being lived out by several rscJ. Luz Dolalas, an rscJ from the Philippines, combined her ministry as Secretary of the Philippine District with that of environmental protection. She explained this ministry.

I have been involved in ecology since 1995; my work as a volunteer covers the task of secretary-cum-liaison officer of an environmental NGO, Sagip Kalikasan ng Montalban, Inc (SKMI). We have been trying to protect the mountains and rivers of the Montalban Marikina area. Thirty mountains had already been dynamited, blasted and quarried, exposing the region to flash floods; these are inevitable when what naturally protects rivers from silting is removed. About a third of the mountains were already levelled and were being worked as open pits. The rock obtained was crushed and transported to the many construction projects; it is thought that about 63 per cent of the aggregates required for the infrastructure of Metro-Manila will be extracted from this region. Montalban's mountains are being used for the progress of Metro-Manila, at the expense of the local population who face catastrophe as a result of flash floods.

We are networking with other NGOs, submitting complaints, securing hearings with bureaucrats and organising petitions which have been signed by thousands of people. Critical as the situation is, SKMI has made some progress. A moratorium has been declared on new quarrying permits and on the renewal of existing ones. Many scientific investigations on the quarrying and crushing sites have been carried out. We keep on working in the hope that the danger caused by this destruction will be recognised and brought to an end. We have also set up an Ecosystem Awareness and Response Campaign in a public high school in Montalban, and have recruited two core groups of students who help us to organise ecological awareness seminars. We peservere in the struggle, drawing courage from the young David who successfully overthrew Goliath!

Support for the East Timorese from Australia

Mary D'Arcy, rscJ of the Australian/New Zealand province, whose main ministry was with migrant women, was for many years involved with an ecumenical group supporting the people of East Timor in their struggle for self-determination. 'Christians in Solidarity with East Timor' (CISET) was formed under the auspices of the Jesuits with the aim of 'informing and educating Australians on the injustice and genocide of our neighbour'. In 1985, for example, CISET organised a silent, prayerful demonstration in the centre of Melbourne to coincide with the tenth anniversary of the invasion of East Timor. Mary, backed by her Province, also disseminated a leaflet on East Timor to all justice and peace groups in the Catholic Church worldwide, and to governments in the West. Demonstrations supporting the self-determination of East Timor were regularly held in all major Australian cities and by 1998 had gained the support of the Catholic Church.

Reconciliation in Sydney, Australia

In 1988 Dorothy and Patricia Ormesher rscJ came to live in Redfern, a Sidney suburb where many Aboriginals had their homes. There they became involved with the effort of reconciliation between Australia's indigenous peoples and the wider Australian community. Indeed the Redfern Residents for Reconciliation (RRR), held their meetings at 'The Gathering Place', where Dorothy and Patricia were living. It was natural for the two of them to be involved in the planning of the 'National Sorry Day', held on 30 May 1998; this is their account of the event.

On the day, Aboriginal and non-Aboriginal people came to a local hall in Aboriginal territory to share a meal amidst much laughter and chat, while music played in the background . . . Came the silence. An awesome sound from the didgeridoo (Aboriginal horn) introduced a smoking ceremony performed by Elder Max Eulo. It was then that all non-Aboriginals present, wherever they stood, proclaimed together a full-throated, heartfelt apology to our black brothers and sisters:

> With deep respect and in a spirit of healing and bridge-building, we apologise to all Koori, Murri, Anunga and Islander people on and around the 'Block', for the injustices suffered by you all, as a result of Europeans coming here and taking your land. In particular I offer my

95

personal apology for the hurt and harm caused by the
forced removal of children from their families, and for
the effect of government policy on the human dignity and
spirit of Indigenous Australians.

The apology was received with humility and deep emotion. It
was a highly significant moment for us all. Elder Joyce Ingram
announced with wonder in her voice, 'It has never happened
here before.' In the months since that first reconciliation event
there seems to have been a growing awareness of a new dawn.
There is a consciousness that black and white can walk and
work together.

Working with Women

The capitulants of the 1988 General Chapter stated that rscJ are
called 'to ensure that, true to our charism, all our educative
work enables women to take their rightful place'. This was the
first General Chapter to articulate a specific concern for the
position and rights of women.

In Ireland

Anne O'Keeffe, rscJ of the Irish/Scottish Province, writes of her
involvement with the Shanty Educational Project in West Tal-
laght, on the outskirts of Dublin, an area of severe economic
and social disadvantage. Anne explains the nature of this project,
founded in 1986.

It is a centre of second-chance, affordable education, enabling
women to achieve their full potential through personal
development. It was founded on the belief that empowerment
through education is the basis for enabling women to counter
the effects of poverty; ultimately it will bring about fundamental
changes. During the last twelve years, more than 1,300 women

96

have become proficient in a wide range of skills such as computing, literacy and crafts.

Anne had a three-part involvement in the project. She was responsible for hospitality, taking care of the practicalities which ensured a warm welcome. She tutored women who were examining the link between the image of God as taught in school and the psychological, social and political effects of that image; she also belonged to the group which came together for a monthly celebration. 'Participation in this Shanty project has given me an opportunity to indulge in many of my passions,' she said,

my passion for spirituality, for feminism, for justice and for being with forgotten communities. Participation for me and for many of the women I have come to know, has been a healing, exciting, empowering, world-changing experience.'

In Peru

In Bambamarca, to the North of Peru, several rscJ were working with the local people, and visiting them regularly. They wanted to evangelise and also to develop the cultural and religious values of the people. When she began her visits Elisa Castillo rscJ found the women to be ill at ease and fearful; gradually they gained in self-confidence, learning to express themselves so that instead of leaving everything to the men, they began to take a more active part in their communities. By 1994 they had set up their own Women's Centre, organised a Parish Pastoral Group and a Health Service Group and in so doing had developed the confidence to reach out to others beyond their own areas. The first National Women's Congress, which took place in 1994, witnessed to their growth in self-assurance.

In 1997 Elisa and her team organised training courses in faith reflection and in the practical skills of literacy, craft-making and cultivation. The women developed a genuine desire to share their experiences, discuss their rights and their role in society and realised, therefore, the importance of communication and organisation. Yet many difficulties remained. Daughters were still not sent to school, there was no market for the goods they produced and the prices paid for them were too low to provide for basic necessities. Furthermore the different sects in the region were opposed to the union achieved among the women and did what they could to undermine it. Elisa remained confident:

I watched the wives and mothers become defenders of life and promoters of justice and peace, and I had developed a real respect for these women. They were tenacious, inspired by hope and possessed of a talent for celebration.

In the Philippines

In 1986, at the invitation of the Bishop of North Samar in the Philippines, a new rscJ community was established in Catarman, one of the poorest dioceses of the country. This account, centring largely around the issue of empowering women, has been compiled from information contributed by Caroline Joy Luz, an rscJ from the Philippines.

The Bishop's invitation to the Society was originally intended to secure help in forming and organising Basic Ecclesial Communities (CEBs). Joy Luz became involved with the CEB of Catarman in 1995 in response to the need for adult catechesis. Within three years the original CEB had grown and divided into three groups each with between fifteen and thirty members, the majority of whom were women. Many were the wives of fishermen, all were poor and had little understanding of the structural roots of their poverty. In general they had little conception of their dignity as women and remained passive when confronted by authority, especially that of the Church. Joy gave an account of their activities.

I ran weekly sessions with the CEB members, basing them on
the Scriptures and addressing such issues as the root cause of
their poverty, their empowerment as women, and their dignity
and equality, especially in matters of sexuality, for rural women
often experienced gender-related oppression and violence.
Convinced of the importance of a holistic approach, I focused
on child-bearing and upbringing, family life and community-
building, attempting to involve all the family members, if at all
possible. I did not want to target the women on their own, but
hoped to influence the men and children also. My hope was
that eventually the whole community would work together.

In Upper Egypt

Adela Blanes rscJ came to Egypt from Spain and spent many
years in Upper Egypt in charge of a centre for young girls. She
worked on the principle that there was more to education than
the imparting of knowledge and was guided by one of Madeleine
Sophie's favourite maxims: 'To teach a boy is to teach an individual – to teach a girl is to teach a family.' So Adela understood
her task to be that of accompanying the youngsters, compre-
hending and listening to what they said and to what they left
unsaid.

My principal concern is to form Christian women of solid faith,
who can incarnate the Gospel in life and life in the Gospel. I
want to awaken a respect for the basic values, respect for willing
service, for freedom and truth, for pardon and reconciliation
and above all for love. They needed to learn to grow and develop
throughout their lives and so to develop to their full potential.

Adela had fifteen assistants, five of whom had passed through
her hands at the centre; they took over some of the teaching,
but Adela never delegated religious instruction.

We start very simply with their everyday lives, and gradually they
begin to express themselves, make up their own minds and

reflect on their traditions. They become aware of the serious consequences of premature marriage and of the harmful effects of female circumcision, which so seriously undermines their dignity as women. When they first arrive they are awkward and inept, but after the six-year programme each one grows in stature as a child of God.

Work for Justice in the United States

Joan Kirby rscJ described her work for justice in New York.

We are good friends. We have coffee together once a week. Tamara seems to trust me. She writes amazing short stories; her attention to detail makes for powerful writing. All my teaching instincts want to ensure she gets a good education, but Tamara is homeless; she lives in the Queens Interfaith Family Inn. Her mother is hopelessly addicted to drugs, so when she disappears to the streets, so does Tamara. We search for her, we ask at the Inn and one day Tamara calls me at home to say 'Thanks for what you have done for me. I have to make it on my own now.' I have never seen her again.

In 1980 we came to live and work in the midst of people deprived of housing, decent education or job security, and this has changed us. We were four rscJ in a small apartment in an old-law tenement in midtown Manhattan, near the docks but also near Times Square and the theatre district. Our goal was not just to live poorly, but to learn what it means to be condemned to poverty in New York City. Mr McNaulty lives alone, in 1998 he suffered a heart attack. Rosa is a mother on welfare in an apartment no bigger than ours; she stayed at home to raise seven children, who have all become self-sufficient and have good jobs. Jimmy at the gas station, Paul in the lumber yard and Dave in the auto repair shop, are among the many whose homes are threatened, because New York City is offering developers an Urban Renewal Area for luxury housing on

Tenth Avenue. Poor people have no resources and for them subsistence is not a given. When housing, job or income are threatened, we have to find others in a similar situation and organise ourselves in order to gain strength in numbers. In times of need, we learn something else: 'What I have is yours.'

We four rscJ have learned something precious in the eighteen years we have lived here together. Patience, when the building is overrun with mice and the landlord stalls, promising an exterminator who never shows up. Forbearance, when for days there is neither heat nor hot water because the landlord has not paid the oil bill; tolerance of each other in our cramped quarters. With shared values comes a deeper understanding and love for each other. We are humbled by our good fortune: we have the security the poor do not have.

At first we came to do no more than share the life of our neighbours. Very soon the unjust political and economic structures made us realise that to struggle for justice was our mission. We organised, petitioned, demonstrated, and we attended meetings with our neighbours. In the late nineties, we see that the cutbacks in social subsidies and education funding, the repression of labour unions, the migrations of the poor looking for work and the environmental degradation have global implications and are universal causes of the suffering of the poor. We are challenged to develop new forms of mission. Solidarity with the poor now requires a new vision of 'who is my neighbour?' How are we to become global citizens in solidarity for the poor of the world? This will be our challenge in the decades to come.

In Defence of Human Rights in Colombia

The long Colombian armed conflict has been characterised by the violation of human rights. Year by year thousands of non-combatants die, disappear, or are taken hostage for ransoms of vast sums, destined to finance the warring factions. All sections of society have been severely affected, especially the rural population, against whom attacks were intensified in 1998. Forced to abandon their homes to seek refuge in nearby towns, the country people were housed in refugee hostels in dire conditions. It was thought that there were two million displaced persons, a situation which led to escalating injustice and division, creating a great open wound in the heart of Colombia.

The most seriously affected zones were in the North-West where problems of crime, often exacerbated by drug production, were acute. Furthermore the livelihood of thousands of defenceless campesinos was threatened by the proposed canal, intended to connect the Pacific to the Caribbean Sea, and by the determination to extract oil at any cost, to further so-called development. In 1994 the Conference of Religious of Colombia, aware of the current and impending catastrophe, committed themselves to provide a team to accompany both those who were at risk and those who had already been displaced.

Many Colombian rscJ have found themselves in high-risk areas and take what part they can in alleviating distress; three members of the Province, Maria del Carmen Guerrero, Maria Teresa Caicedo and Alette Latorre all had ministries with displaced people. Maria del Carmen Guerrero, a member of the Justice and Peace Commission of the Colombian Province, has been an active member of the inter-congregational team since it was first set up. In this capacity, she and her colleagues have denounced abuses against civilians and have had some success in deterring attacks. The team members accompany civilians who have been terrorised and offer assistance in their attempts to organise resistance.

At the turn of the millennium the abuse of human rights appears to be endemic in an increasing number of regions. It could well be said, therefore, that the efforts of a small, relatively unknown group of women could have no more than a minimal influence. Might they not be more effective in an area where there was a

more realistic hope of effecting change? But the religious concerned are committed to the following of Christ, they have been
missioned to make known the revelation of God's love. Inspired
by that love their 1982 Constitutions proclaimed 'the pierced
Heart of Jesus opens our being to the depths of God and to the
anguish of humankind' (1982 Constitutions #8). Few conditions
have created more anguish than those of war and injustice; every
member of the Society therefore, is committed to work either
directly or indirectly for justice and peace. A natural progression
from this commitment is the attempt to create reconciliation,
building bridges between nations and cultures divided by hostility, intolerance, or misconception – this is the subject of the
following chapter.

NOTES
1. An active peace organisation at work in the United States organising 'disarmament actions' against military targets and focusing on ships, missiles and
   planes designed to launch nuclear weapons.
2. A non-violent peacemaking corps, established in 1984.
3. An international confederation of Catholic organisations founded in 1950 for
   charitable and social action.
4. Cf. Ch. 3, note 1.
5. In 1945 Korea was occupied by US troops south of the 38th parallel of latitude
   and by Soviet troops in the north. When the occupying forces withdrew in
   1948 border clashes frequently occurred, culminating in an invasion from the
   North leading to the fall of Seoul in 1950. The UN sanctioned military action
   against the North Koreans, who were finally repelled in 1951; after prolonged
   negotiations a peace treaty was signed in 1953, and an uneasy peace was
   restored between the Communist North and the democratic South.
6. Published in the *RSCJ Newsletter* Vol, 20, No. 5 (October 1998).

CHAPTER 6

Building Bridges

*Through the Eucharist we are drawn into the gift of Jesus to His Father
for the life of the world, and in His Body we are gathered into one.*

(1982 Constitutions #5)

We wish to be women who create communion.

(1982 Constitutions #6)

*We are called to be women of communion, women of compassion, women
of reconciliation, nurturing life by education to reconciliation.*

(General Chapter 1994)

Madeleine Sophie's passionate love of the Sacred Heart of
Jesus, and her desire to spread this love throughout the
world was evident in all her actions. By the time she died in 1865
rscJ had not only crossed the Atlantic, but had also spread widely
in Europe. For unity to be preserved within the Society in the
context of the continuing international rivalry and enmity among
nations, it was essential for the members to be unremitting in
the pursuit of reconciliation. Madeleine Sophie herself was
frequently confronted by misunderstanding, intrigue and be-
trayal; both publicly and personally she cultivated the spirit of
reconciliation in her determination to preserve amity and unity.
Devotion to the love of the Heart of Jesus demanded more:
compassion and communion have always been at the heart of
the Society's charism.

International Links

Japan and the Philippines

As a young professed in the 1970s, Nagano Koko rscJ left her own province to study theology in the Philippines; she returned again in 1978 for probation and final profession. Moved by her own exposure, Koko longed to provide her students with a similar experience. The chance came in 1986 when, as the headmistress of the Obayashi school, she had to find a new summer project to visit instead of the Institute for the Handicapped in Hiroshima, which had unexpectedly closed. Koko believed that 'through the appreciation of a different culture, the students would emerge from a mentality centralised within their own country... enabling them to live in a truly global society'.[1] The Philippines had much to offer: a Catholic country, where English, learnt in school by the Japanese students, was the language of the Society and where the apostolic works included formal education, parish and environmental support and accompaniment of the poorest. Moreover since the hostility between the two nations had been so bitter, for Filipino rscJ to offer hospitality to a group of young Japanese gave this exchange a deep significance.

The enthusiasm of Minda Caoile rscJ, then Director of the Filipino novices (1993–95), matched that of Nagano Koko. Minda realised that the exchange provided an opportunity for the novices to get to know the mission of the Society in Japan and to undergo an intense experience of internationality. When she became Provincial in 1995, Angelita Walker rscJ followed her as Director of Novices and became no less committed to the exchange. The communities of Metro Manila were pleased to be involved in entertaining the Japanese students at the District Centre.

A new link was forged in 1989, when Arita Yuka rscJ, an alumna of Japan, chose to enter the Society in the Philippines, where her vocation had been confirmed. Her first experience of the country had been when she was an undergraduate in Japan and

105

had taken part in the immersion programme; fluent in Filipino, Yuka has been one of the many who have helped to ensure the success of the project.

Towards the end of each tour the Japanese group stayed overnight at the novitiate at Montalban, a visit where they could relax, pray and reflect. There they met the students and youngsters who had benefited from the money sent to the St Madeleine Sophie Foundation, which was subsidised almost entirely by the Japanese Sacred Heart students. The SMSF was then assisting three very depressed areas in the process of forming a CEB; the students, for their part, enjoyed visiting simple homes and meeting Filipino children and young people.

When completed, each visit was followed up with an analytic report in which the benefits were so clear and the change in individual students so marked, that in the nineties the project was opened up to all Sacred Heart students. Indeed several Catholic schools in Japan independently embarked on their own exchange programmes.

Japan and Taiwan

A Society bridgehead between two nations has often been forged by one individual, as was the case when Miyama Atsuko, a Japanese rscJ, was missioned for Taiwan in 1980. Her official ministry was the teaching of English, but it was hoped that in her person she would be a sign of reconciliation between the two nations. This she achieved, in part, at least, through her ministry of spiritual accompaniment. Her popularity spread by word of mouth, and extended to a large circle that included Catholics, Protestants and both lay and religious men and women.

From 1990 onwards Atsuko also made regular visits to the local leprosarium. Each Sunday a group shared the Eucharist with the twenty-five Catholic lepers, staying on for a meal and a discussion; the group was encouraging the lepers to voice their own aims and feelings, in the belief that with encouragement they could bring about an improvement in their own lives. Commenting on this ministry Atsuko said, 'Lepers give me a balance in my life; they teach me how to appreciate kindliness and give me courage to enjoy life fully, by helping me to see things from a different angle.'

Atsuko's ministry in Taiwan was not without cost.

At the beginning I experienced much frustration: I had no language, I was uprooted and confused. In community I sometimes felt that I was treated as a second-class citizen and that I was being exploited. Clinging closely to Jesus, forgiving and constantly being forgiven, I rested in the word of God. 'Love is always patient and kind . . . is always ready to excuse, to trust . . . Love does not come to an end' (1 Corinthians 13). And so I found support and affirmation to live my mission in Taiwan.

In 1998 Atsuko went to Shanghai where she gave an eight-day retreat to a group of religious who were the first to have made final vows since Communist rule was established in 1949.

Haiti and the USA

Virginia McMonagle, an rscJ from the United States, has also forged a transnational link, dividing her time between Haiti and San Diego University, where she was an assistant to the Vice-President.[2]

Virginia's involvement came about in collaboration with Father William Wasson.[3] In 1986 this priest persuaded a reluctant Virginia to accompany him to Haiti, where he was going to explore possibilities. 'I went, I saw and I was hooked,' Virginia reported.

I was offered a year's leave of absence from the University, which enabled Father William and myself to open first an orphanage and then the Père Damien Hospital for 100 babies. The hospital rapidly expanded into an outpatient clinic with its own pharmacy, where free medicine was distributed; by 1998 this had grown to the extent that it was caring for more than thirteen hundred patients a month.

The hospital is staffed by twelve paediatricians, ten of whom are Haitian women; there are also volunteers from fourteen different countries who stay for between one and ten years. They nurse the children, teach them and above all play with them. Teams of doctors regularly arrive from the States to work with the staff; dentists pay annual visits to the orphanage, airlines and hospitals cover the expenses for any youngster needing surgery in the United States.

No words can describe the condition of the hundreds of babies that are brought to us. The parents often go to voodoo doctors first – we are their last resort. Many nursing mothers sleep under their baby's cot, and while the Père Damien is a place of tragic suffering, it is also a place of joy. We are all involved in loving these tiny creatures; we lose hundreds, but we save thousands. At Père Damien we live intimately with the mystery of life and death and eternity. There God walks, giving life, love, hope and, yes, eternal life also, to the little ones God takes to himself.

St Helen's Orphanage in the mountain village of Kenscoff is home to 500 children who live in small groups with a house parent. As so few orphanages will accept disabled children, more space is needed and we have a new handicap home under construction. We hold weekly liturgies in our outdoor chapel where the children's voices echo with the tom-toms through the mountains. The juniors attend our Montessori School before going out to local schools, while at St Helen's we attempt to prepare the young people for adulthood by running practical classes in sewing, typing, bakery, shoemaking, carpentry and dancing.

The celebrations commemorating the tenth anniversary in 1998 emphasised the international links that had been forged. Over a hundred visitors of thirteen different nationalities were welcomed by the children who carried the flags of each country represented. After Mass, celebrated by the Archbishop, two new

kays (cottages) were blessed by our director Father Rick
Frechette CP, and the day ended with a gala picnic.

Virginia concludes her account with both question and plea.
'What can be done,' she asks, 'to save this beautiful race?'
Looking to the great rscJ of the past, she finds her answer in
education:

The United Nations can pour billions into this desolate country,
but without education there will be no hope for these
industrious people, who are eager to work and eager to learn.

Virginia's great longing is for the Society to make a foundation in
Haiti, which is already well known to many; rscJ from Venezuela,
Puerto Rico, Mexico and the United States have all worked there
as volunteers. Mater Admirabilis has a home on the island; the
Sisters of Charity found her in an abandoned building and
promptly installed her in their noviceship. 'Could she be the
means of bringing the Society to Haiti?' Virginia asks wistfully.
In 1999 Patricia García de Quevedo, who was then Superior
General, announced that a community was to be established in
Haiti. Virginia's dream was to be fulfilled at last.

Through Virginia a connection had been made with the
Kenwood infirmary community in Albany, USA. The link was
Elizabeth Shearman rscJ, the Visual Arts Director at Kenwood.
Virginia showed Elizabeth photographs of the orphanage, with
its lines of drying rags, used for the babies' nappies. Shocked,
Elizabeth persuaded the Albany rscJ to raise funds to replace
them; cot sheets and clothes for the children were also sent. In
1998 Elizabeth spent two weeks in Haiti, helping in the pharmacy
of Père Damien Hospital where Virginia was based. Explaining
why she came, Elizabeth said that she wanted to

see how we, in Albany, could best help . . . The small gestures
we are able to make, we will continue. This is no more than a
drop in the bucket, but hopefully it is a drop which will send
out a few small waves for someone.

Ecumenical Bridges

Links with Orthodox Christians in Russia

Gabriella Berényi, a Hungarian rscJ, escaped during the period of Communist rule, entered the Society in Belgium and was professed in 1997. A member of Les Potiers community in Brussels, she taught at Louvain University for six months and spent the rest of the year with the Sacred Heart community in Moscow. There, teaching Scripture at the St Thomas Aquinas Roman Catholic Theological College for the Laity, Gabriella was in contact with Russian students of all ages and backgrounds. She also taught at St Andrew's, the Orthodox College of Biblical Theology. This she found to be stimulating; her students were young, dynamic and something of an intellectual élite, enabling her to respond to her call to build bridges between the Orthodox and Roman Catholic Churches.

Links with Muslims in Egypt

In Egypt the Society's links with Muslims were continually strengthened. The attitude of the Province was summarised in an imaginary open letter written to Madeleine Sophie in 1998 by Céleste Khayat rscJ, a teacher at the Sacred Heart School in Heliopolis.

As you know, the Society has two schools in Cairo: Ghamra, opened in 1903, for between 100 and 200 Christian girls, and Heliopolis, with a small number of Muslim students, opened a few years later. By 1998 both schools had expanded and were each teaching about eleven hundred pupils, half of whom were Muslims.

Relations between the two faiths are good which is very pleasing, because in general there is much fanaticism. Our desire is to be friendly with all our neighbours in this country, where Christians and Muslims have lived side by side for centuries.

We believe that most Egyptians look at the heart of a person, not at her race or religion. Our pupils, from kindergarten upwards, are shown the importance of justice, love and mutual respect. Religious instruction is given in a spirit of tolerance to Christians and Muslims separately, but every morning we pray together at the school assembly. Little by little, good relationships are formed between pupils, which sometimes last through school and into adulthood. There are, of course, some fanatics, but it seems to me that most pupils lose some of their prejudices and begin to open their hearts to the love of God and the love of others. The teaching staff of both faiths have the same ethos: they want to show that we are all children of God. Extra-curricular activities (including shared meals in celebration of the holy seasons of both faiths) contribute to the spirit of unity, reinforcing the belief that we all belong to one large human family. As educators for reconciliation, we relate ecumenically to Catholic, Orthodox and Protestant Christians. We believe in the importance of our mission: our pupils sow the seeds of reconciliation and an appreciation of Christian values in their own milieu. Yes, of course there are difficulties, but ours is such a worthwhile ministry.

Thank you, Madeleine Sophie, for the schools we run in this Muslim country. As our Constitutions say: 'In Jesus, all find their true growth as persons and the way towards reconciliation with one another.' This we believe; this we want to proclaim (1982 Constitutions#10).

Ecumenism and spiritual formation in Sweden

Angela Corsten, a Swedish rscJ and a member of the German/ Swedish Province, sent the following account of the Society's work in Sweden, where Catholics are widely dispersed and make up no more than 2 per cent of the population. Ecumenism is essential in this situation.

We are nine rscJ in a Scandinavian country where for many years secularisation has been a conspicuous phenomenon. However, just because secularisation has been so prevalent for so many years, now, in 1999, deep spiritual needs are beginning to surface. This is giving rise to renewed hope in the possibility that the Catholic faith may be able to start afresh; the Church has an opportunity to address listeners who are as untouched by faith and as curious as were the people of the first century.

In our situation, if the churches are to be credible, ecumenism is a necessity. The Protestant churches are attracted by the universality, the decisiveness and the tradition and faith of the Catholic Church. They need the Church in order to avoid narrowness. On the other hand, because we Catholics are so few, there is little theological debate and some Catholics are tempted to be ultra-conservative as a means of ensuring a secure Catholic identity.

How do we incarnate the love of God in such a situation? Six of us live and work in the Catholic Study and Retreat Centre of Johannesgarden, at Göteborg, on the West coast. The house is open to Christians of all denominations, and in fact the Swedish (Lutheran) Church uses it for retreats for priests and pastoral workers. These are led by an ecumenical team, which includes one of our sisters, and are based on the spirituality of St Ignatius. Groups and schoolchildren who are looking for information on the Catholic Church or religious life also come to Johannesgarden, and some catechetical classes are held there.

Three rscJ undertake parish work in Uddevalla, to the north of Göteborg, in a community that was set up in 1991. There they support Spanish-speaking immigrants who are waiting for entry permits, without which they cannot settle in Sweden.

In addition to my ministry at Johannesgarden I work part-time as the Secretary General of the Scandinavian Bishops' Conference, covering Iceland, Denmark, Norway, Sweden, Finland, Greenland and Svalbard (the Norwegian archipelago in the Arctic Ocean). Although this work is mainly administrative, I enjoy it. It is good to be part of an organisation that is endeavouring to create an effective, but simple, means of

administering the Church. Furthermore, as I am the only
female, I have the privilege of being able to represent a woman's
point of view.

Inculturation in India

Vandana rscJ, who in 1998 was based in a small ashram in the
foothills of the Himalayas, has exercised considerable influence
on the Indianisation of the Christian Church, as well as the
inculturation of the Society in India. Her work has also been
followed by directors of religious formation, who have arranged
a period of time in a Hindu ashram for their novices and seminarians. This has enabled them to experience the prayer life of their
Hindu brothers and sisters. Vandana has also sought to challenge
those responsible for novices and seminarians to reveal the
Indian face of Christ by integrating Indian music, dress and
simplicity into the life of religious congregations in India.

Since the late 1970s, retreats given in Europe, the USA and
Australia have introduced many Christians and 'post-Christians'
to a more contemplative experience of Christ, whereby Christ
has become 'the Antaryamin' or the Indweller in 'the cave of
the heart'.

As a young religious Vandana became aware of the harm
done by the westernisation of Indian Christianity. She was also
concerned to ensure that the contemplative dimension of the
Society's vocation should be seen to be a reality.

I felt, too, that inculturation should be practised by us, so that
the 98 per cent of non-Christian Indians might cease to think
of us as westerners, or westernised Indians.

Her concerns have altered little over the years. 'My hope is', she
wrote in 1999,

that in the twenty-first century, the Church in India will become
a truly Indian Church and that all India will cease merely to
copy the West.

We were inspired by Swami Abhishiktananda [Fr Henri le Saux OSB],[4] and six of us [rscJ] began the Christa Prema Seva Ashram in Pune, in 1978. With my colleague Ishpriya (Patricia Kinsey, an English rscJ, who joined the Indian Province), I spent the next twelve months visiting a number of ashrams; then we received permission to live in the well-known Hindu Sivananda Ashram of Rishikesh. We stayed for six months, and then spent the following six months giving retreats based on Indian Christian spirituality. Requests came from home and abroad, enabling us to support ourselves and our province; this division of the year was to become our pattern for the next six years.

In 1984 Vandana and Ishpriya were offered a property in the small village of Jaiharikhal, lying in the foothills of the Himalayas. There the Jeevan Dhara Ashram was established which became their base and a temporary home for individuals from many countries and denominations. Describing their life Vandana said,

The community is international and is open to both men and women; visitors are always welcome. Our life is based on prayer and silence. As a community we meditate four times a day for the peace of the world.

In 1997 Vandana left Jaiharikhal, 'having heard an inner call to flee from the "crowds" to a quieter, yet active style of life'. She received permission to build a small dwelling on the banks of the Ganges in Rishikesh.

People of any faith, or no faith, any culture or nationality are welcome to spend time with us. On the whole we receive fewer Indian Christians than Western seekers, many of whom are post-Christians. This is a wonderful way of bridge-building and of bringing about peace between warring communities in our country of pluralism, with its present sectarian government.

Vandana's life in Rishikesh may be more peaceful, but she is hardly retired. She continues to give private retreats to in-

114

dividuals and to write books, articles and letters to the press. She is still called upon to address Hindu ashrams and to speak at theological and spiritual meetings; she also remains fully involved in inter-faith dialogue. In 1998 she spoke in Rome on 'The Integration of Indian and Christian Spirituality' at one of the conferences organised by the Missionary Documentation Centre (SEDOS) in Rome.

The riches of diversity in Southall, England

In the English/Welsh Province, Margaret Nourse rscJ works with her community to promote an understanding of 'diversity as riches' rather than threat, by building bridges across the divisions of race, faith and culture. Based in Southall, close to London Airport, in an area attracting large numbers of immigrants, the community is ideally placed for such a ministry. Margaret has herself been to India, staying with Vandana and Ishpriya, and also going to Bangladesh; during her visit she made contact with Hindus, Muslims and Buddhists.

I learnt a great deal and was deeply influenced. The whole experience brought me in touch with people whose spirituality affects everything in their daily lives. They do not differentiate between the sacred and the secular ... art, dance, buildings – everything has a religious significance.

On her return Margaret made contact with Christians Aware, an international, ecumenical organisation, working for justice and peace by building links and developing friendship between peoples. In 1989 she was invited to join Christian Aware's Council of Management; she became reponsible for developing and co-ordinating the Faith Awareness Programme, which formed an integral part of the organisation's work. Supported by her community, and using their house as a base, she ran courses and study days inviting speakers from the major religions: Hindu, Muslim, Buddhist, Christian, Jewish, as well as Sikh, Zoroastrian,

Jain, Rastafarian and others. Speakers gave talks on their faith, their scriptures, their prayer and their traditions.

The community at Southall were all involved in this inter-faith ministry; by welcoming people of all faiths and none, they created a dynamism of unity. Their mission was 'to create a true community by witnessing with our whole life, that union of hearts in diversity of cultures is possible'.[5]

From Buddhist to Christian spirituality

Hayami Yayoi, rscJ of Japan, wrote of her transition from Buddhist to Christian spirituality.

I was baptised when I was a student of the University of the Sacred Heart and I entered the Society in 1957. At first I was very happy and had no doubts about my religious vocation. However, gradually I began to feel that my faith was like a dress borrowed from someone of a different build. I was anxious and was struggling because Christianity did not feel a part of me. This feeling became stronger when I visited Christian countries and met rscJ whose faith was lively and personal. I had always tried to be a good religious, and I thought that in general I succeeded, but I lacked that personal relationship with the living God that I had glimpsed in my sisters.

While I was in this anxious situation, I was given the opportunity to make a thirty-day retreat based on Oriental spirituality. It was the first of its kind to take place in Japan, and was directed by a Carmelite, Father Augustine Ichiro Okumura, a convert, who had previously studied Zen and had been struggling to incarnate Christianity on Japanese soil. Pleased as I was to be given this chance, I was also worried lest the attraction of Oriental spirituality, still deep in my blood, would result in the loss of my vocation. To my great surprise, this did not become a hindrance to my faith in Christ: on the contrary, it helped me to deepen my relationship with the Lord.

The Word of God became much more alive through the

teachings of the Zen masters. The more I understood Oriental
spirituality, the clearer the essence of Christianity became: I am
referring to the incarnation of the Son of God made man. I
had known this intellectually, but now I knew it affectively,
understanding with my heart. Through this experience I began
to feel strongly that the Gospel needed to be shared in a truly
Asian way.

During the Synod for Asia in 1998, a Japanese bishop was
asked why Christianity had not taken root in Japan as Buddhism
had. 'The answer lies', he said, 'in the human heart. In the
West the paternal characteristics are dominant, while in Asia,
especially East Asia, it is the maternal traits that are operative.
The father figure divides and selects; the mother figure
unites and embraces; in the East, therefore, we need to give
greater expression to the feminine aspects of God.' When I
was reading these comments, a passage of the Gospel came to
my mind: 'Jesus bent down and wrote with his finger on the
ground' [John 8:6]. The sight of Jesus bending down was strongly imprinted on my soul. There is a saying in Japan that a
child is brought up by looking at his or her mother's back.
To us Japanese, the back of a person sometimes has a stronger
impact than the front. In the same way, the back of Jesus
meant so much to me. It portrayed his love, tenderness and
compassion, his whole being. Viewing Jesus from the back has
brought him much closer to me. His back proclaims his love
more eloquently than words. This is only one instance in the
Gospel, but enough for me to touch the core of the Heart of
God made man.

Whether we look at Christ from the back or the front, we are
looking at the same Christ. Looking at Christ from the back
made me think that while we respect and appreciate the
Christian heritage of the West, we need to discover and foster
evangelical values, hidden within each culture in the East. Once
a Japanese priest told me that when he was in the noviceship
he could hear the beat of the drums, which stirred his blood,
so that he had to fight against feelings deep within himself. In

117

former days, to be good Christians, we had to set aside our deep inner feelings of our Japanese selves. Thus we were cut off from the spiritual nursery which might have helped the growth of seeds of faith.

To quote again from the Asian Synod, it was said that the enthusiasm for dialogue, apparent immediately after the Second Vatican Council, seemed to have ebbed away. However, I think the Society is very much aware of the importance of dialogue with non-Christian religions and both supports and encourages efforts of inculturation. The General Chapter of 1988 declared:

> The call today is to move beyond the tensions our dialogue may create, to let go our prejudices and become more receptive to others, to accept our differences and the contributions of each culture. In this way we will live our communion in faith, as a vital aspect of our charism.

In Japan there is an old saying that the wider the skirt of the mountain extends, the higher becomes its summit. I think Madeleine Sophie is the one who 'saw' the Summit where all nations will live as co-heirs of God the Father, in spite of the diversity of cultural and spiritual legacies.

The Aghia Sophia-Sainte Sophie Association in Greece

In 1995 Mary Germani, an Associate and an alumna of the Trinita dei Monte, founded this association in order to foster ecumenism, especially in Greece. This was the culmination of a gradual process which began in 1981, when Mary purchased an apartment at Saronis in Attica, which she made available to rscJ and her friends. Staying at Saronis herself, at increasingly regular intervals, Mary made contacts with many Orthodox Christians, including priests, religious and lay people. The project was strengthened in 1985 when Mary was joined by Thémis Sanga, a Greek rscJ and a member of the French Province. Working together and making friends far and near, mutual understanding between the members of the two churches was established.

By 1995 Mary and Thémis were ready to expand their ecumenical venture, which had by then secured the support and encouragement of Patricia García de Queveda rscJ, the Mexican Superior General of the Society. A meeting was convened at Joigny to reflect on the next stage. Attended by rscJ from Germany, France, England and Italy, this resulted in the offical foundation of the Aghia Sophia-Sainte Sophie Association, whose object was the promotion of ecumenism, which was to be fostered through the life of its members and through activities suggested by them. Mary Germani was appointed President, and while the first to join were rscJ, the Association was open to all people expressing good will towards it.

The Association grew steadily; in 1999, the membership of forty-seven included both Catholic and Orthodox Church members, lay men and women and several young people. Mary and Thémis enabled a group of Paris scouts to enjoy a working-cum-cycling holiday in Attica, taking in the holy sites of ancient Greece. Three Greek members who lived in Saronis ensured that groups and individuals could be welcomed at the apartment even when Mary herself was unable to be in Greece. Several people have stayed at the apartment in Saronis, making ecumenical contacts and introducing small groups to the history, culture and religious traditions of Greece. One member worked with young people, helping them to appreciate how cultural difference can be a source of riches rather than a threat, while at school and parish level other members attempt to foster interest and encourage the study of ancient and modern Greece. Membership fees and donations from benefactors have enabled the Association to sponsor a party of young Greeks who were attending a meeting of European Christians at the Paris Forum in 1997. It is hoped also that some Greeks will be at the Youth Forum that is to be organised as part of the Society's bicentenary celebrations. As a result of Mary Germani's mission, the Society has had a presence in Greece since 1995.

The creative ministries described in these pages were generally inspired by the suffering and sadness of division. Similarly the ever-increasing gap between rich and poor, one of the lamentable traits of the last decades of the twentieth century, inspired individuals and communities to make public their commitment to the poor. Following the precepts of the 1994 General Chapter, which directed rscJ to 'be there with the poorest and the marginalised, and be evangelised by them', they worked with vulnerable native peoples, settled in deprived urban areas and worked alongside rag-pickers. Some of these ministries, together with their effects on individuals and communities, form the content of the next chapter.

NOTES
1. Extract from a report on the Philippine Exposure Study, written by Uno Mieko rscJ.
2. Virginia McMonagle rscJ described Haiti as 'a very complex nation with currently practically no government, with rampant crime in many areas, disease and AIDS devouring a country already dying of starvation. Of the population 90 per cent are illiterate, 80 per cent unemployed and 10 per cent hold all the wealth.'
3. Rev. William Wasson founded 'Nos Petits Frères et Soeurs' Organisation in 1953. By 1999 it was running orphanages in Mexico, Honduras, Guatemala, Nicaragua and Haiti.
4. In 1950 Jules Monchanin and Henri le Saux, Benedictine monks from France, founded Saccidananda Ashram in the southern state of Tamil Nadu, where they began to adapt the monastic life to Hindu traditions. When Jules Monchanin died in 1957, Henri le Saux retired to a hermitage in Uttarkashi in the Himalayas, where he wrote several books.
5. Quotation from talk given to the probanists by Helen McLaughlin rscJ in 1994.

CHAPTER 7

Insertion and Solidarity

... It is 'in Christ' that we must build our fraternal communities, within, not apart from the world. (General Chapter 1970)

We are convinced that solidarity with the poor remains our response to injustice in the world. This solidarity asks of us not only interest and presence, but above all commitment and action ... Living this solidarity impels us to encourage insertions among the poor.
(General Chapter 1988)

The on-going work of our inserted communities to discover with their peoples alternative, more human ways of living is as essential as the effort to work for justice at the international level. (General Chapter 1994)

'I would give them my skin!' said Madeleine Sophie indignantly on being told that some garment or article was too good for the poor. She loved the poor with a sincerity that was reflected both in her life and in the Constitutions of 1815.

> If they [the religious] are allowed to have any special pre-ference with regard to the children ... it is evident that this predilection would be just and praiseworthy if it is directed towards the poor children admitted as day-pupils [in the poor schools]; they must therefore consider it a privilege to be employed in classes for the poor, whose state of life had such charms for the Heart of Jesus that He chose to be born, to live, and to die in extreme poverty. (1815 Constitutions #6)

The rules of enclosure, however, enforced one-way traffic: the religious could not go out to the poor, it was they who had to come to the convent. This they did willingly, for there their children received free education. 'If possible there shall be in every house of the Society a place set apart for the instruction of poor children' (1815 Constitutions #203).

As the years passed, however, and state provision of free education became increasingly accessible, the need for free education was generally less acute; consequently an increasing number of boarding schools had no day school for poor children; this meant that many rscJ were cut off from the poor. The Chapter of 1964 responded to the call to renewal by examining the needs of the time, and returning to the roots of the Society. Thus a renewed awareness that preference for the poor was inseparable from the love of the Heart of Jesus coincided with the ending of enclosure, enabling rscJ communities and individuals to be inserted among poor people. What follows are some examples of how this opportunity led to new means of making known the love of God.

Brazil: Insertion with the Myky People

Since 1977 Elizabeth Amarante, a Brazilian rscJ, has followed in the footsteps of Philippine Duchesne by living with a small community of Myky natives of the Iranxe nation, in the Amazonian forest of Mato Grosso.[1]

Elizabeth submitted a contribution for this book in which she both explained the steps that led to her 'call within a call', and reflected on her life with the Myky. What follows was taken from her submission. She wrote of a happy and stable childhood in a family of six children, describing her mother as a woman devoted to her family, caring for prisoners and poor people and consistently working for the rights of natives. Her father, a doctor, had a special concern for the needy: 'He had deep faith and immense tenderness for his children.'

Elizabeth and her four sisters all attended the Sacred Heart Convent in Rio de Janeiro. In 1951 her older sister, Maria Cecilia, entered the novitiate: three years later Elizabeth followed her. Thus Elizabeth's early religious formation took place before the radical changes of the Second Vatican Council, but during her probation in Rome in 1962, she became aware of the revolutionary wind that was sweeping through the Council.

Following the direction of the Second Vatican Council, both the Church in Brazil and the Society undertook projects with marginalised people. In 1969 the first small rscJ community became inserted in the diocese of Itabira, in the North-East of Brazil. Reflecting on this period Elizabeth commented,

We began to discover the political dimension of religious life
and to understand that our place was on the margins with
poor and simple people. We also found that the geographical
and social change of place presupposed a cultural change, which,
in turn, produced a new spirituality. For us it was a return to
the sources of the Society, to drink from the well of Joigny . . . So
in 1973 I left Rio to start a mixed intercongregational
community in which there were two rscJ, the local bishop, a
Carmelite, a Salvatorian and a member of a secular institute.
The five years that I was in that community were years of
powerful experience, enhanced by being in touch with other
inserted communities; we went through a process of reflection
and commitment to the needs of the poor.

During this period a group of missionaries, dissatisfied with the dichotomy between the practice of missionaries and native cultures in Brazil, set up the Indigenous Missionary Council (CIMI). This new organisation, later annexed to the Brazilian Conference of Bishops, began to publish a bulletin explaining incarnation in terms of the protection of the environment and respect for culture. This had a profound effect on Elizabeth:

The first of the CIMI bulletins to reach the Pastoral Centre of
Itabira opened my eyes and my heart. My whole life seemed to

widen out into that call: a hidden contemplative life in a
missionary dimension of incarnation and commitment.

This call was reinforced in 1976 when Hermengarda Martins
rscJ, the Provincial of Brazil, one of her councillors and Elizabeth
visited a community of Charles de Foucauld sisters who were
living in a village among the people of Tapire.

We went to experience at first-hand the reality of incarnation in
an indigenous people according to the new understanding of
the CIMI . . . It was at that meeting that my missionary call took
shape and became viable. So in 1977, after three years of
discernment with the Provincial Council and the whole Province,
I finally left to become inserted. My mission was accepted and
supported by the Province, but as no one else shared this specific
call, I left alone and in darkness, in the simple certainty that
God would arrange all things.

My first stage (novitiate of native life), was with the Iranxe
people, who belong to the same linguistic family as the Myky;
they gave me the opportunity to get to know the Myky. Then in
1979 I moved to Maloca, the 'Village of the Hidden'. The
transition from one world to another was far from simple. It
involved inculturation in a wholly different reality, and being
thus dispossessed was totally demanding. I had to grasp the hoe
and plant the ground, cook over a fire on the floor and adapt
to new food. I was constantly challenged as I learnt to live
sparingly on expeditions, with everything shared, no privacy
and nothing accumulated. This was a hazardous life, imposing
an ongoing, unfamiliar apprenticeship that is never complete.

Elizabeth admitted that in some respects hers was a lonely life,
and especially so at the beginning before she had any grasp of
the language.

Geographically I am far from the rest of the Province, and
without a community of sisters of the congregation. I lived the
first years quite alone here in the village; then in 1983 a lay
missionary joined me. We shared life, reflecting on our work and

the problems caused by the devastation of the forests.
However, the missionary was young, she had her whole life
ahead of her, and she only stayed three years. Then in 1990 an
American sister of St Joseph of Rochester came to the village,
having already spent ten years in Brazil. For six years we shared
our work and our anxieties, facing new problems, and above
all praying together, until in 1997 she gave up her work with the
natives and returned to her own congregation.

Elizabeth might have been alone, but she never felt abandoned.

In all these years, the Myky have really been my community and
my native family; in their midst I am affectionately looked on
as their grandmother. What then does community life mean to
me? I work and reflect with a team of religious and laity of the
CIMI. We do not live together, but I meet them occasionally.
They are companions, living a similar reality of inculturation.
Furthermore I have the support of both my family and my
province who missioned me; I am strengthened by being in
communion with my religious sisters with whom I share my life,
and the problems of the natives. I take part in provincial
assemblies and in our projects of popular education in the
North-East region. Several rscJ have visited me, including Maria
do Rosário Corrêa, my current Provincial and my own sister,
Maria Cecilia rscJ; they had a brief taste of the Myky way of life.
So at the end of each day 'in silence and poverty of heart before
the Lord . . . adoring and abiding in His love' [1982 Constitutions #20] I unite myself to each one of my sisters in the
whole Society.

In 1991 Elizabeth reluctantly accepted an invitation to become
Vice-President of the CIMI. This organisation played a vital role
in the political battle to defend the Indians from illicit land
investors, logging camps, miners and all the so-called projects of
expansion. She held this post for four years but felt

torn between the reality of my village and the more complex
native problems. Furthermore I was constantly travelling, either

to the CIMI base in Brasilia, or to the eleven various regions for which I was responsible. Although as Vice-President I had an influential and enriching contact with native peoples, after four years I became convinced that administration is not for me. I am called to the hidden life of the village where I can be inculturated and can share the life of the people.

Elizabeth kept a diary and the notes she made painted a vivid picture of her life with the Myky.

This night a baby is born to the village. The birth of all Myky infants, their arrival on earth – the sacred earth – becomes a silent discourse on God, on the cosmos and on the human condition. It is in this context that the two poles of the Myky universe can be understood: the house, a symbolic space in which to live is always to 'live with', and 'the way', a word that denotes history. I found a close relationship between the birth in which I had just assisted and the option we had made, as a province, to respond with an open heart to the cry from all peoples, whatever their culture. The blood and water shed in childbirth by a woman: the blood and water shed by his open heart, his consecrated Heart. The new fragile life, alongside the mother's tenderness, has reawakened a fresh awareness of belonging to the Society, together with a desire to be reborn in the strength of the spirituality stemming from the life-giving symbolism of blood and water.

Another diary entry reads:

The children interrupted my prayer. They arrived excitedly bringing fish and manioc meal. I ate, sharing with the little ones, listening to the tall stories of fishing, rejoicing in their joy. In the village every day is a celebration: dividing the catch, sharing food and drink ... Through the years I have discovered the Myky way of living together, of team work and sharing, of being and having. They have an endearing talent for enjoying the details of life and they live in constant praise ...

September is the month that the soil is prepared for

cultivation. The men clear the ground for family and community plots, while the women select the grains, beans and cotton. When the first rains come, it is time to plant! I spent the morning checking the gourds of maize which must produce enough to make the traditional drink for the whole year. We were seated on the earthern floor, talking animatedly, while the children clamoured around us. I can speak, but not fluently, a limitation which is sometimes costly. I have, however, had the help of a linguist; she first established the alphabet and then attempted to produce a system of grammar, enabling us to train a teacher from this community. Then literacy classes could begin . . .

I go into the communal log cabin and find sixteen-year-old Kutyru there. She is sitting, silent and recollected, spinning her cotton thread – [she strikes me as] an image of Mater in a different context, another culture. Today Mary of Nazareth is reflected in many women, for it is the Myky women who play a deeply significant, indeed a theological role, in their society: in the home, the place of procreation and communal life, all that they are and do is directly linked to life. In the community, with the preparation and distribution of food, their work plays an essential part in celebration. And with the dawning of a new day, a day which may prove decisive to their history, it is the women who awaken the village – a symbol of humankind? They have a decisive mission in history; you could even say that they are experiencing, living, witnessing and revealing the Sacred.

Four years ago today, Jurusi died. She was only twenty-five years old. She had borne five children, lost two and her youngest was only three months old. Jurusi was an intelligent woman, a leader and so beautiful! She suffered a swift, mysterious illness attributed to the spirits. I had been given her name, Jurusi (the mythological name for a fish), and being namesakes created a bond between us; she helped me to grow, showing me what it is to be transparent and free, what it is to live in courage and hope. She lived with a serene energy, strove and dreamed, always facing what was yet to be. Yes, she was 'a theology of her people' who are at a crossroads between tradition and an unknown future. Jurusi is certainly with God and today she is invoked as one of the protecting Spirits. Many are the moments when I, too, lovingly invoke my Myky sister.

I am in the 'Village of the Hidden' and the Myky people are carrying out their ritual. They have been singing and dancing since sunset; now it is dawn and the women begin to invoke their ancestors and protecting Spirits. The litany of prayer rises from every hammock, punctuated by the noise of children and the music of sacred flutes, played in the firelight by the men in the village square. It is my turn to pray and I also intone in the Myky tongue which cries to the Myky saints and to the mighty Spirit, a prayer united in faith, praising the one God, whatever his\her name. From the beginning, confronted by an exacting and unifying system of values, I felt that my own spirituality was called to conversion. The Myky live community of goods as an expression of love and they live in communion with the earth. They believe in the immanence of the spiritual in the earth and in history; the earth is sacred. It is utterly impossible for the earth to become an object of commerce. Living here, sharing the feasts and rituals of the Myky people, based on their faith in their ancestors and in both benevolent and evil spirits, I ask myself 'How can I live and witness to Jesus Christ?' In fact this is made possible by the realisation that to enter the native world is to plunge into a specific way of life, understanding that the earth is sacred, because it is the reliquary of the dead. The soil is 'earth-memory,' because in it history and the Way are continued. It is earth-sacrament of new-born life. The existence and resistance of these people depend upon the earth.

People often ask how I live religious life without the eucharistic presence or celebration. Obviously, in these circumstances I live the eucharistic dimension 'in spirit and in truth', otherwise I might fall into emptiness, indifference and ultimately have nothing to celebrate. The absence of the Eucharist, and my longing for it, has enabled me to discover a eucharistic dimension beyond actual celebration. The consecration of the Lord is a continual event, foreshadowing community yet to come. The Myky live communion; every day in the village is a celebration as they divide the catch, and share out their food and drink. And I am learning to unite myself to the eucharist in ways previously unknown; I am communicating with the God who made himself one of us, companion and fellow pilgrim.

From the early days of my arrival, my preoccupation has been to get to know and penetrate the cultural universe of the Myky; to use their language and try to speak it, in order to discover and manifest God present, and Christ acting in Myky history. This demands deep respect for this people's faith, in the belief that they are in communication with the living God. I remember the day when an old man was dying in the family log cabin. From all sides they cried out their prayer in familiarity and trust. I feel profoundly missionary, even if I do not achieve any explicit annunciation according to the catechetical understanding of the expression. What is important is that the Myky go on growing as people, so that 'the glory of God may be the Myky people fully alive, conscious and free'. I mean to go on living like this, listening to events, discerning when, within their history, the time of grace has come for my frail witness to announce God, God of life, of justice and of tenderness.

All that matters is to follow humbly but doggedly in the footsteps of Jesus of Nazareth; through time and place he leaves his footprints along the paths of so many people and cultures. These are the marks of martyrdom that sprinkle the paths of the earth at the crossroads of history; they are the many tears that make the sea saltier, and these footsteps of blood and water are life-giving; they generate hope, the certainty of life.

Solidarity with the Poor in Mexico

I am most grateful to Socorro Martínez rscJ, Provincial of Mexico, for sending me an acount of the way in which the Society implemented their commitment to solidarity with the poor in Latin America. What follows is derived from her contribution.

The years that followed the Second Vatican Council were a stimulating time for us in Latin America; it was a time when we were longing and searching for social transformation. The 1968 Medellin Meeting in Colombia, at which the Latin American bishops met Pope Paul VI, had resulted in the Church dedicating itself to the poor and the oppressed. Any number of documents and movements affected us in those years. Medellin concretised the work of the Vatican Council as it applied to Latin America. Liberation theology, the 'deschooling' of education, CEBs (Ecclesial Base Communities) were all developments which inspired and challenged us. Added to these was our own option for the poor, spelt out and adopted at our General Chapter of 1970.

Many of us went to live in small communities in poor districts in the suburbs and rural areas in an attempt to understand life and the Gospel from the standpoint of poor people. Using the parish as our base we gradually learnt how to analyse and systematise our experience. Collaborating with others we drew up programmes to celebrate the faith in a different way. From all this there developed a network of Popular Education in which many rscJ from the Provinces of Latin America became engaged. [This network will be dealt with in greater detail in the final chapter, which is concerned with recent and future developments.]

Over the years we have noted the results of Popular Education and its effect in virtually every facet of life. People have begun to claim their rights and to take on personal and community responsibilities; leaders have been trained, enabling communities to face problems and set up their own projects and organisations. Poor people have become active co-workers in the Church, women have begun to develop their potential, the general level of health has improved and dignity has been restored. In addition community life has become enriched, young people have begun to be involved and the faith has been celebrated in community.

All this has evolved over thirty years and yet our work for the poor is still regarded with suspicion in many dioceses. Now, in 1999, Latin America is faced by neoliberalism which is another phase of capitalism, resulting from a greater depth of poverty. It is important that we keep up our studies, to enable us to respond as professionals to the needs of the poor in our towns.

We persevere in hope, convinced that those who are disadvantaged deserve the best. Moreover we are aware that this education is a mutual process and that God travels with us all. As followers of Jesus in the Society which has committed itself to solidarity with the poor, we are pledged to the cause of the poor.

Pastoral Work in Chile

This account was contributed by Paz Riesco rscJ, Provincial Treasurer and councillor.

Our province began 'pastoral work' in 1965 at the instigation of the Church in Chile; we were asked to collaborate more closely with pastors by becoming inserted in poor areas, in addition to our educational work. This was a time of many initiatives which were concerned with old and young alike; many groups were springing up for such activities as popular catechesis, biblical reflection and prayer; CEBs were also in the process of formation. While our main concern was to provide education in the faith, many rscJ took part in these initiatives. Several religious served in the diocese helping with administration and with pastoral work. Since we were concerned to educate in the faith, we saw no division between 'popular education' and pastoral work. The defence of human rights was always part of our mission, especially during the time of the Pinochet dictatorship.

Looking back over these last thirty years we are aware of our mistakes and of our sinfulness, but we are also aware of the presence of the Spirit helping us to live in joy and freedom and giving us the grace to manifest the love of the heart of Christ. We have also continued to mature as a fraternal community and to love one another despite our different ages, ideologies and cultures.

Becoming sensitive to the socio-economic reality of Chile, we are constantly urged to respond by making known the love of God. We found ourselves evangelised by the poor; they helped us to celebrate and through them we recalled the Gospel values of solidarity, simplicity, and gratitude.

Now as we stand at the gate of the third millennium and look to the future, we find strength in our roots as we continue to follow the path of Saint Madeleine Sophie, our first shepherdess and companion on the way.

The Mission of the Society in Venezuela

The following account was contributed by Maria Luisa Navarro, the Provincial.

We started in 1968 and are now seven communities. Moving on seems important to us – moving on when things go well, moving on when we make mistakes; looking at the Lord. Our priorities for our mission as rscJ in Venezuela are our solidarity with the poor, remaining committed to life, to human rights and to ecology and our life together. We want to celebrate the little steps forward and to encourage one another with tenderness and sensitivity. Gradually we are learning to be in love with life, the life that is evident in our structures, the life we receive when

132

we respond to calls enabling others to live, and the life that is in the Eucharist in all its dimensions.

We are engaged in the Latin-American education network and we want our work with the marginalised to continue and grow. Conscious of the importance of our role as women and our potential to change history, we want to be an educative and participating presence. Dialoguing with and supporting other congregations and listening sensitively, we need to deepen our inculturation, so that a truly Venezuelan religious life may begin to emerge.

We ponder and question. We think about how best to share our gifts with the people of Venezuela; we reflect on what kind of good news we offer today, and on our links with the international Society. We wonder how to ensure co-responsibility amid the complexities of a horizontal communication network and we consider what we have to give to future generations.

In our process of insertion, we strive for a simple lifestyle, in friendship and solidarity. We want to be creative, reflective, questioning, and leave the initiative to the Spirit. We believe in the future of small Christian communities as a way of being Church today and renewing church structures.

The little Society founded by our holy Mother is very dear to us; she wished it to be flexible, gentle, present wherever the Heart of God is wounded.

Working with Tribals in Torpa, North-East India

The following account is taken from *The Story of Torpa: An Experiment in Alternative Development,* by Jayanti Bannerjee and Jharana Jhaveri, supplemented by a brief discussion with Mary Braganza rscJ. Her ministry with a primitive tribe in Torpa, in the North-East of India, shared many characteristics with that of

133

Elizabeth Amarante. Both Mary and Elizabeth sought to bring the love of the Heart of Jesus to a group of people who had been largely overlooked by the societies surrounding them.

For most of her professional life Mary Braganza had worked in formal education, apart from a brief period when she served on the General Council in Rome. She retired from the post of Principal of Sophia College, Mumbai, in 1988 and was then asked to assist in the updating of Indian Christian higher education. In pursuit of this task, she visited many areas including Torpa, a semi-rural settlement about seventy kilometres south-west of Ranchi in the Chatangpur plateau of Bihar. Torpa was the administrative headquarters of a backward tribal area, in which there were ninety-eight villages, populated for the most part by scheduled caste and tribals. Mary came to Torpa in order to visit the nine university colleges located there, and was appalled by the way that the tribal women were exploited.

Outraged by this situation, Mary persuaded her Provincial, Eileen Gaitonde rscJ, to mission her for Torpa. There she made her base, living in the St Joseph's Diocesan Hostel for girls. This so-called hostel was no more than a dilapidated shed in danger of collapse. The ceiling was propped on poles, every available utensil was catching water from the porous roof and since neither lock nor catch was secure, Mary and the girls were highly vulnerable. Indeed, one night thirty armed men attacked the hostel, miraculously failing to break in before they were put to flight by the priest brandishing a vicious-looking, long-barrelled gun. He had been roused by the cries for help and the bandits, taking to their heels, did not wait to find out that the gun was unloaded. That night was a turning point. Before the bandits came, the local people had been suspicious of the elderly nun in their midst: after the attack, when she had stayed and confronted the assailants, their respect was won. They named her 'Karuna' meaning compassion, a name which she adopted from then on. They listened to her and began to understand how the women and other vulnerable groups were being unjustly exploited. They agreed to work with Karuna and took their first steps in the struggle to acquire equality, dignity and justice.

All Karuna's skill and experience was required to bring about change in the future of these tribal people. Over-exploitation of the forests had ruined their economy, and the consequent need to seek urban employment had eroded their spirit of collaboration, leading to an increase in such problems as gambling and alcoholism. Some assistance was being given by a variety of voluntary agencies, but their activities were so dispersed that their impact was diffused.

From the first Karuna was convinced that with appropriate education it was the women, with their wisdom and positive values, who had the ability to revitalise tribal society. Her unchanging goal was to assist in establishing integrated communities, in which women were empowered to play their part in a development process, based on what they themselves needed and desired. To this end the Centre for Women's Development was set up in Torpa in 1990, a centre to assist in training and the development of skills. Using a system of non-formal, holistic education and working within the indigenous culture, Karuna attempted to provide the students with an education for life.

The provision of training courses for Balwadis (pre-school centres) and kindergartens, lasting six months and nine months respectively, was the main work of the Centre. Karuna's aim was to establish a team of qualified rural women, capable of organising informal pre-school education and of playing an active part in the village community. Trainees, who were aged between fifteen and twenty years, studied a wide syllabus: Mundari and Hindi, English, maths, singing, games, handicrafts and nutrition, with all courses placing much emphasis on literacy. Tribal women who were themselves qualified pre-school teachers undertook the 'hands on' training, under Karuna's supervision, employing the 'Akara' method.[2] They had great success and by 1998 there were fifty Balwadis under the Centre's aegis, teaching 2,000 children, all of whom were being acclimatised to regular school attendance. By 1998 a group of resource persons were undergoing training in a village which had been specially constructed.

In addition to educational training, courses in the production of indigenous medicine, the generation of income from the production of mushrooms, honey, garments etc., and the management of such projects, were being offered at the centre. While Karuna assumed overall responsibility, she left the trainees to manage the hostel. This responsibility enabled them to develop sufficient self-confidence to become active members of the community, when they returned to their villages.

Working with Ecclesial Base Communities (CEBs) in Mexico

This account has been put together from an article written by Margarita Name rscJ, from Mexico.

Margarita spent the first ten years of religious life working in schools, but from the 1970s the call to become inserted in a life among the poor became increasingly insistent. She spent some years studying relevant subjects such as Christology, ecclesiology, social sciences and the methodology of popular education. Finally in 1978 she was sent with three other sisters to La Tarahumara, an extremely poor indigenous area in the North of Mexico. She said of this time,

Little by little I learned to live among simple people; I learned to love them, appraise them and to put my life at their service. I discovered a new vocation within my vocation which filled me with joy.

Three years later, in 1981, Margarita was sent to an inner-city area in Guadalajara where she became a member of an active CEB; since then she has worked continuously with CEBs. Although each community is unique she finds that CEBs have much in common.

Their members are poor and simple; they are called to prayer by the word of God and their lives are centred on the Eucharist, which inspires them to become converted, both as individuals and as a community. They are bound to each other by strong ties, and are deeply committed to justice, reconciliation, and the defence of human rights. Their lives are based on obedience to God's will. CEBs have played an important role in all human development, and it is through them that women have been helped to discover their dignity, their value and their rightful place in the family and society.

My contribution to the CEBs has been concerned with formation and accompaniment. I have always worked in a team with priests, lay people and religious. For me, CEBs are places where I find Jesus alive and incarnated in the poor people, who are a source of great joy. These people represent a call to work for the Kingdom and to collaborate in order to create fraternity, justice, peace, solidarity and love. Working with them I have found a confirmation of my vocation; CEBs have provided a way and a 'space' conducive to the living out of the educational dimension of our charism. It is in these communities that I experience the love of the Heart of Jesus Christ; this is where I can manifest his love.

Accompanying Korean Children

This account is based on a report contributed by Lee Mi Kyung, a Young Professed Korean rscJ who since 1995 has had responsibility for the Huk Bit Study Room in Kohan, a village in the North-East of Kangwon Province, Korea, where coal mining once provided a booming economy. This changed in 1989 when the Korean government made the decision to replace coal with natural gas as the energy source. This led to the closure of the mines, unemployment and a severe reduction in the population. Tourism was proposed as an alternative to mining, but the village

of Kohan lay outside the planned development zone; consequently living conditions deteriorated drastically, and the lack
of funding for education seriously affected the children. In these
circumstances many people left Kohan and those who remained
felt demoralised, and had little faith in a future.

'There were three of us [rscJ], and we wanted to stay,' Lee Mi
Kyung explained,

because we wanted to learn how the suffering Christ was present
in these people, who had suddenly become marginalised, and
were courageously holding on to life in this poor and
deteriorating situation. We wanted to be present, to be in
solidarity and to support and console them. So many of their
trusted teachers and long-time friends had left. In 1995 the
Society set up the 'Huk Bit Study Room' to provide some space
for the middle-school children in after-school hours. The name
means 'to be a light in darkness' and the project was a direct
response to a need expressed by the young people themselves.
By that time there was no library in the village, not a single
cinema and nothing but rows of amusement kiosks, gambling
rooms and empty shacks, all providing endless opportunities for
crime.

We wanted the study room to provide a holistic approach and
to inculcate values which are neglected by the regular schools.
Thirty children come to the Study Room, of whom half are from
one-parent families and the rest see little of their parents since
both father and mother work. We have learnt that the most vital
role of the 'Huk Bit' is that it is a place where the children find
love, warmth and welcome; there they find security and
regularity, enabling them to build up love and trust. When they
first arrive, their hearts are wounded by their broken homes and
they are inhibited by feelings of inferiority, instilled by their
achievement-orientated school education. All the Study Room
activities are directed towards educating the whole person by
means of relationships, dialogue, counselling, reflection,
evaluation. We allow the young people as much freedom as

possible, leaving them to make their own timetables, and to assume responsibility for discipline.

One of those to benefit most dramatically from the Study Room was Myoung Sook, a baffling child, who was stubborn and filled with self-hatred. She was well behaved at home, but had sudden outbursts with us, sobbing, screaming and raging. We learnt that her father was a violent alcoholic and that her mother had walked out and left home for some time. The staff decided to react positively to Myoung Sook's moods, giving her plenty of attention and approaching her with gentleness and understanding. The results were gradual but dramatic; by the end of term, a totally different child had begun to emerge. Most of the children behaved like untamed horses, making huge demands on the staff. We learnt the reality of the incarnation – Jesus so often reversed established practice.

We were encouraged by the children's positive end-of-term evaluation. They said that life in the Study Room was lively and interesting in contrast to school, which they all hated. We wanted to provide something more than class work, to encourage them to search for their identity and find a meaning to life. As a means of achieving this we provided special weekly lectures on different themes, to broaden their experience and inform their choices.

We dream of a future when the people of Kohan will look on a new world in which they are no longer dependent on outside help. A world which they have helped to plan, to which they have contributed and which heralds a new and promising future. So once more we question why we live among the children of those voicelessly suffering, fighting for existence in a life and death crisis of this former mining village. We are answered by the 1994 General Chapter: 'The ongoing work of our inserted communities is to discover with their people, alternative, more human ways of living; this is as essential as the effort to work for justice at the international level.'

Alongside Powerless People in Kenya[3]

'I was sent as a teacher-coordinator to an informal school in the newly established parish of Langas, run by the Divine Word Missionaries.' So begins an account written by Anne Marie (Annet) Nankusu, a Young Professed rscJ from the Uganda/Kenya province.

This was a school for poor children; their parents were failed job-seekers, single mothers or the victims of various tribal disputes: all had fled for their lives. Many of the boys were street children. The parish of Langas is a slum area serving the poor and destitute, who formed the majority of the population. It was like the valley of dry bones (Ezekiel 37): all these people needed flesh and new life, both physically and spiritually. My task lay with the children; I was to educate them, find a place for them to play and instruct them in the faith.

This was a mutual ministry; when I started I barely knew any Swahili: the children taught me as I tried to teach them. However, if I was to bring them life, I had to go to the root cause of their situation, and this could only be done by visiting them at home. I could not hold back my tears as I listened – the pain of being driven from their homes, the loss of all they possessed, the desperation of single mothers unable to find work to enable them to look after their children. But what touched me most deeply were the sad, undernourished, innocent little ones, who were unable to go to school. The poor are touchingly generous; they share the best of whatever they have and we were greeted by smiling faces wherever we went. These visits were enriching, challenging and exhausting. The Lord gave me energy, power and authority, just as he gave power to the apostles. Indeed without the Lord, I could not have carried on.

The love of the Heart of Jesus gives life, and that was the life that I experienced with the children. I taught, I prayed, I played and above all I listened to their problems. Together with

140

the Divine Word Fathers, I shared the love of the Heart of Jesus with my sisters and brothers of Langas. I had great admiration for my colleagues; their salaries were inadequate, but although they were so poor, they served willingly and generously. To extend my ministry of revealing God's love, I worked in the sacristy of the parish and became involved in the children's Sunday School; they flocked there in their hundreds.

One day a colleague told me of a ragged boy who was joining the children at games. He came to me with an unforgettable smile that cracked his face apart. I asked his name, and he asked for a pencil and an exercise book. 'I am Blackie,' he announced, 'king of the street children.' He joined the class as soon as he had been given his pencil and book. He was intelligent and a born leader. 'No more noise,' he said, and there was silence. Sadly he vanished on Christmas Eve, before I could get him into a regular school. I discovered that the uncle who looked after him had lost his sight and had been sacked by his employer. I was sad, but could do nothing for him; there was not a trace of him.

'Who will look after my sheep?' is the call of my ministry. I am ready to go wherever I am sent to discover, reveal and spread the love of Jesus. 'For the sake of one child I would have gone to the ends of the earth,' said Madeleine Sophie. May it always be true of us all.

With the Rag-Pickers in Barcelona

Inmaculada Subirá, an rscJ from Northern Spain, sent the following account of her ministry.

I have had the good fortune to work for ten years with the Engrunes Foundation which runs a refuge and recycling centre in the suburbs of Barcelona, for the accompaniment and rehabilitation of society's casualties.

In addition to commissioning Inmaculada for this work, the Province of Northern Spain gave financial assistance to the Foundation for many years. Its aim was to restore self-confidence and hope, offering education to its clients, as they desired. In 1987, after a process of discernment which included working as a volunteer, Inmaculada resigned her position as a college professor, and became a full-time member of the Engrunes team, with special responsibility for education.

'I worked alongside everyone else, collecting, classifying and selling the bric-a-brac we were given,' she explained.

Surprising friendships evolved between us, as we drove the vans around Barcelona, making house-to-house collections. I was also a member of the co-ordinating group which met every two weeks for reflection and mutual support. As a group we were often bewildered by bizarre situations, but we were determined not to lose hope and to continue to walk with our people who had, for the most part, received such a rough deal from life.

This was an enriching and unforgettable experience. I have begun to understand the Gospel and the world of the marginalised from a very different viewpoint. I have come to appreciate that the traditional criteria of good/bad, truth/lies, just/unjust are deceptive. In certain situations anti-social behaviour has to be seen as a strategy for survival, rather than a destructive quality. It was immediately apparent that to get along with these people, I must avoid categorising them and must put myself in their shoes. I had to acquire greater self-knowledge, recognising my own limitations. In many ways the clients of Engrunes held a mirror to my own behaviour: the differences I observed were minimal!

It has been my good fortune to travel with these socially damaged people, who have been badly served by society; we have worked, laughed and wept together, sharing our hopes and our fears and discovering that it is possible to live, in spite of difficulties.

Neighbours to Indigenous People in Sydney, Australia

In 1987 Pat and Dorothy Ormesher rscJ went to live in a two-bedroomed terrace house, named 'Gathering Place', in Redfern, a suburb of Sydney. Their community was adjacent to 'the Block', a development for Aboriginal peoples which was put up in the early seventies to provide secure housing. Sadly by the time that Pat and Dorothy arrived, it had become run down and vandalised. Many of the people then on the 'Block' had had inadequate schooling and were consequently unemployed; this in turn had led to a high incidence of drug dealing, heroin and alcohol addiction and crime. The Ormeshers embarked on a number of activities aimed at the empowerment of a seriously disadvantaged group, the improvement of race relations and the development of an Aboriginal Catholic ministry.

Our house welcomes people. They come to talk, to use our phone, enjoy a cup of coffee or share a meal. Every Monday evening an unspecified number of guests join us for a meal, followed by communal prayer which we prepare together. Before saying good-bye to our friends we round off the evening with more talk over a cup of coffee. Numbers fluctuate – on some Mondays we manage to squeeze as many as fifteen indigenous and non-indigenous friends into our small community room. Over the years our neighbours' confidence has been built up, although they do not easily trust 'the white fella'. We accept them all, we do not judge and consequently they feel free to discuss problems. Many of the drug-users are anxious to get over their dependency, but waiting times to get into the de-tox centres are lengthy in the Sydney area; often by the time a place comes up, the moment of determination to break the drug habit has passed.

Our vision for our ministry is to empower these disempowered folk by supporting them in as many ways as possible. At this

moment in 1998 we are working with a group of Aboriginal
residents to prevent the demolition of an empty warehouse
adjoining the 'Block'. The Redfern Aboriginal Corporation has
come up with an enlightened plan for its use as a Community
Centre to be available to all residents, both black and white.
Sadly there is a real risk that this Aboriginal initiative,
embodying so much hope, will be blocked, creating yet another
set-back for these long-suffering people.

Working with Junior School Children in Amiens, France

From 1990 to 1993 Elisabeth le Jariel rscJ lived in one of the
poorest districts of North Amiens where she was attempting to
improve the health of six-year-olds. Their families lived in dire
conditions which were much the same as those to be found in
the 'Fourth World', the poorest and least developed countries.

She found that living in an area where she rubbed shoulders
with simple people, who supported life on the bare minimum
or less, 'with nothing left over', helped her in what she was trying
to do for the children. Situated in a fifteen-storey tower block
where violence, aggression and vandalism were commonplace,
the community found this a frightening area. Yet the door was
always open and one or two neighbours did venture across the
threshold to explore 'the mystery of the sisters'. Once or twice
she, too, received an invitation to visit a neighbour, which she
thankfully acknowledged as a small step towards integration.

Our surroundings imposed a style of life, a simplicity expressing
a certain sobriety. We seemed to be called to play our part in
humanising the tower block, and to risk making modest
overtures in order to create relationships. But the most lasting
effect of this experience is the indelible mark that it leaves on
the heart. My outlook has changed . . .

The increasing diversity of ministries inevitably made increasing demands on administration; for many, and most notably for Madeleine Sophie herself, this essential apostolate necessitated a keenly felt sacrifice of a ministry directly involved with the laity. Moreover, authority and obedience could be abused; in the rare cases, when they were not carried out with the love of the Heart of Jesus, this undoubtedly happened. Examples of the exercise of authority together with the methods of initial formation in the years leading to the bicentenary form the subject of the following chapter.

NOTES
1. A small community of twenty-two Myky people were discovered by Jesuit missionaries in 1971; since then their numbers have almost tripled. There are approximately 280,000 surviving Indians in Brazil, speaking in 170 different dialects.
2. The Akara training concept was developed by Bishop Hans, an educationalist. His methods were based on the assumption that life is a celebration in which all are participants. 'Akara' is the dance floor, the centre of cultural life in every village.
3. Cf. 'Growing in sensitivity to the suffering of those who have neither voice nor power' (1994 Chapter Document).

CHAPTER 8

Authority and Administration

For the sake of our corporate mission, we accept freely and in faith, the service of an evangelical authority. Thus obedience is lived as a search for the will of God, in dialogue with others and in the free gift of ourselves which makes us available for the Kingdom. (General Chapter 1976)

Our co-responsibility in government is expressed in a common search for the will of God to fulfil our mission in the world. This discernment will be the hallmark of all our government. (1982 Constitutions #141)

Each one of us, exercising her personal responsibility, puts her liberty at the service of the mission of the Society. (1982 Constitutions #49)

One of the best-known scenes in the annals of the Society is that of Philippine Duchesne flinging herself at the feet of the Mother General and Monseigneur Dubourg, Bishop of Louisiana, on the threshold of the Rue des Postes. The year was 1818 and, accompanied by Madeleine Sophie, the bishop was leaving the Mother House, angered by the further eighteen months that were to elapse before the missionaries for Louisiana were to be allowed to depart. 'Your consent, Mother!' Philippine demanded as she fell to her knees, 'I implore you to give your consent!' And Sophie Barat consented, adding 'I consent, dear Philippine, and now I must find you some companions.' In addition to Philippine's missionary ardour the scene illustrates both the authority invested in the Superior General and the possibility of an appeal against any decision.

Nevertheless, in common with other congregations, authority, in Madeleine Sophie's day, was hierarchical and absolute. 'They [the religious] must receive all orders, even the least sign of the Superior's will, as the expression of God's will' (1815 Constitutions #68). The 1815 Constitutions allowed subjects to 'put their case frankly to their superiors, in all simplicity and humility' (1815 Constitutions #114). However, the practice of co-responsibility and communal discernment, if used as aids in the discovery of God's will, were neither acknowledged nor advocated. The link between Madeleine Sophie's understanding of obedience and the late twentieth-century members of the Society lay in devotion to and knowledge of the dispositions of the Heart of Jesus: ' . . . therefore with regard to obedience, they must consider the love which the Heart of Jesus had for this virtue' (1815 Constitutions #68), which is approximately paralleled by 'Obedience is the bond which unites us all in the heart of Jesus as we seek to fulfil God's plan of love' (1982 Constitutions #53).

The Villa Lante

This book is basically about people rather than places, but if there are some buildings which bridge the life of the foundress with that of rscJ 200 years on, one of these must surely be the Villa Lante. Purchased from the Borghese family in 1837 and built at the foot of the Janiculum Hill, the vast palace was in disrepair, and was being used as a tobacco depot. In addition to its ideal site in the heart of Rome, and its modest price, the estate included spacious gardens. At the top of the climbing paths was a villino (lodge) where Madeleine Sophie lived for some time with the Italian novices. Assuming the function of Novice Mistress, she 'breathed into the Italian novices the authentic spirit of the Society, as she had done at Poitiers for France'.[1]

Madeleine Sophie visited Rome on six different occasions and she most often stayed at the Villa, sometimes for months at a time. The room that she used was converted to an oratory; the church, with a tribune looking into the sanctuary where she

147

prayed, was the first in Rome to be dedicated to the Sacred Heart and was consecrated in 1843. One hundred and fifty years later, it was still in daily use by the community and their guests. The gardens, where at Easter she stood facing St Peter's, with the community around her, and received the Pope's 'Urbi et Orbi' blessing, were redolent of her presence. There, on an outer wall, was a fresco of our Lady of Sorrows. Here, during the crisis over the Constitutions in 1839, Madeleine Sophie dedicated the Society to this mother of sorrows. When the wall was demolished a painting was made for the chapel. On a happier occasion she spoke to the novices 'in words that were like arrows of love ... So often did she speak of Jesus, that Jesus was imprinted on our hearts.'[2]

These tangible traces of Madeleine Sophie are inspiring, but the Villa Lante is more than a memorial. In 1999 it housed the Italian Provincial offices, the archives of the whole Society and a community, whose round-the-year ministry was that of hospitality. There, any number of groups, both religious and lay, were warmly received. In addition to the probanists, researchers and rscJ visitors, there were lay groups, families and individuals. The community also offered hospitality to several young religious, sent by their congregations to study in Rome. In 1999 this group was made up of Koreans, Mexicans and Romanians. The rscJ gave these young students friendship and security, helping them both with practical and academic problems. For their part the young brought life to an elderly community and took a share in the chores of the house. Each one of the community was involved in making their guests welcome and comfortable, and perhaps those particularly evident were the sisters who had charge of the dining rooms. Seldom eating a meal without interruption, they seemed to epitomise the selfless service offered by the whole household.

Aldina Rigamonti rscJ and Giustina Stella rscJ were both invited to say how they showed the love of God to the constant succession of visitors. 'I live in simplicity without thinking about showing God's love,' Aldina replied.

I try to to live in his love and to abandon myself to God. When someone asks me a question, I try to get near to the person who is asking. I am aware that God is within me. I know that this is appreciated. People are open . . . They feel at home here, they thank us sincerely and they want to come back.

Giustina, in reply to the same question, said,

I live trying to meet the desires of others; in general these are quite simple – nothing extraordinary. I always smile because a smile speaks more than words and sometimes I find it difficult to find the right word, and everyone understands a smile. People feel at home; we are like a family. They also like the fresh vegetables that come from the garden.

Carmela Ɗeguara rscJ, of Malta

Carmela has held many posts of authority from school principal to District Superior; in the main she has worked in her native Malta, but she also spent several years in Congo and in England. 'Education remains for me a very tangible means of witnessing to the liberating power of his love,' she insisted.

My awareness of the presence of God in each unique person has helped me to grow in respect and affection for all; similarly my efforts to help each child to discover her own identity, as a child of God within her own culture, have contributed to my own growth. When I was acting as headmistress, I was always aware that ultimate authority rested with me and and yet remained aware and thankful that I was no more than a collaborator in God's work of creation.

Catherine Chapuis rscJ, of France

In 1991, after a lifetime of teaching, Catherine was appointed superior of La Roseraie, an intercongregational retirement community for ninety religious from five different congregations.

This ministry had many facets. I was in daily contact with our numerous seculars: our Director, carers (there were forty or more to care for the sisters), as well as a number of people of various ages and backgrounds who visited La Roseraie. I tried to spread the love of God among all these people. Some who worked for us belonged to other faiths or traditions such as Islam, or the Protestant or Orthodox Churches; this enabled us to embark upon inter-faith dialogue in a modest way. Most of these people were interested in the lives of the sisters, and their questions provided opportunities to speak of the Eucharist or the Sacrament of Reconciliation.

The presence of thirty religious from different congregations also provided a richness that was much appreciated; the exploration of our different charisms led to enlightening and meaningful exchange. Another apostolic field was presented by our aged sisters; they talked of their fear and anguish as well as their love of the Lord. Their one desire was to offer their inactivity, dependence and suffering for the salvation of the world. I was full of admiration for them, for despite their apparent frailty they were in touch with the world and its needs, maintaining their apostolic ardour to the very end.

Some of the elderly sisters remained active and while they wanted to serve their own community, many assisted the local people. They gave language classes to immigrants, coached children through their learning difficulties, visited lonely and sick individuals and undertook voluntary work at the hospital.

Tsai Su-fang, Treasurer of the Taiwan Area

When I was asked to become treasurer in 1985, I panicked. I had received no psychological preparation nor professional training, and for the first time in my life, I felt handicapped. However, after thirteen years of working as an 'inadequate Area Treasurer', I am full of gratitude! During this time I had to open my heart and hold out my hands for help and have experienced God's power at work within me, leading me step by step.

I want to thank my many friends for their trust and accompaniment: for me each one is a special gift from God. 'Friendship is a precious and demanding gift which may be given us along the way of love and faith' (1982 Constitutions #66). This was the greatest joy that I received in my service as Treasurer. Through the help of friends, I learnt not only what could be done, but also how; I learnt to love and believe in people for themselves. In God's loving trust, in union with Jesus, we learned to walk together side by side. 'Our formation is rooted in our everyday experience, and carried on through a network of relationships' (1982 Constitutions #70).

Joan Faber of the English/Welsh Province

For some years Joan combined her work a a psychotherapist with that of the office of local superior of the Duchesne Community, the Provincial infirmary community. During her time at Duchesne she made some keen observations about the needs of elderly and frail religious.

At the end of life we once more need to find someone who can 'hold us in mind' as our mother held us as infants, for it is the mother's awareness of her baby which keeps her infant ever present. The infant needs to be 'held in mind' to avoid the experience of disintegration or that of annihilation.

I feel that those who are close to the very old need to have this sort of reflection in order to hold or contain some of their fears. Such thinking will ensure connectedness, even when the old person is caught in the chaos of senility. Mothers and infants neither have nor need communication, but both have an instinctive knowledge of anxiety, fear and their need for closeness. So at the end of life we should be able to offer safe holding and 'keeping in mind'. We cannot allow ourselves to misconnect, for that will make old people feel that they have lost a part of themselves.

But 'who is there?' As we look at the mentally alert, physically fragile old person, with memories of them in their heyday still vivid, we may be taken aback to find them passive and waiting; they may even be in touch with the child's fear of not being recognised by a mother, after a separation. Once I asked a frail old sister, 'Who are you most looking forward to seeing in heaven?' 'My mother,' she replied, 'but do you think she will recognise me?' Her mother had died leaving a forlorn three-year-old.

Being with the very old, we face reality; nothing is hidden or masked – certainly not death. We are confronted by mystery, the mystery of Christ in his death and resurrection. This has led me to reflect on the mystery of silence. The Lord himself experienced this, both at the beginning and at the end of his life. No words could express his passion, his call to live his exodus and return to his Father. He, like us, had to tread the passage from birth into adult life, and then break through to total abundance in the final stage of transition; the Word which has nurtured during life, can still be received in deepest silence. We see a senile sister, finding her way to the chapel, sitting there in rapt contemplation before, with shining eyes, she receives the host; this she holds in her hands, bending over in silent adoration. Truly, right to the end, there is an inner and consuming fire of love.

Three of our most precious gifts are life, love and time. In this holy and humble period of waiting for the moment of final ectasy, these gifts are still present. We, who silently stand and watch in awe, must contain and keep in mind these gifts; we must validate them, thereby enabling them to be lived without anxiety and in the secret truth of each person's life. We know so little of the final purification and preparation for our true life. At this time there is longing, disappointment, anxiety, depression from the wearisome waiting, and the constant questioning: how is God present? where is God in absence? Again, so much of this has to be intuited, held in mind, for much seems to defy words. Once a person known for her simple, direct prayer appeared to have become depressed; in fact she was anxious. She feared she had displeased the One who was her very life, for he was silent and absent. This fear needed to be put into words and it was the old and favourite quotations about the mercy of the Pierced Heart of Jesus that restored peace.

Each person is different, unique. We who are allowed to be near those in their final life/death experience, need to pray for the gift of reflection, so that everyone, in whatever guise they come to us, may be silently 'held in mind'.[3]

Doreen Boland, General Councillor in Rome 1970–76

In 1963 Doreen left her province of Ireland/Scotland for Uganda[4] where she has served ever since, apart from the six years when she was a General Councillor. She recalled this period as follows.

As Central Team, we were aware that we could not lead the Society forward in new ways of community life, with its emphasis on interpersonal relationships, faith-sharing, community prayer and simplicity, unless we too were striving to become such a community ourselves. We were convinced that

153

this was the way we would become a discerning community, and unless we were, that we could not be a government-in-discernment. I can never sufficiently thank God and my sisters for the deep and loving community we built up, working through our tensions, building up trust, openness, vulnerability, forgiveness and sharing as we travelled together throughout the length and breadth of the Society. During those years I came to know and love the 'face' of the Society – or rather, the heart of so many sisters, generously trying to incarnate Madeleine Sophie's charism in a diversity of situations and cultures. They were willing to share with us, to allow themselves to be challenged, and they challenged us also.

Twenty-five Years in Government: Hannelore (Hanni) Woitsch Reflects

I belonged to that generation of probanists who composed their own profession formula;[5] I spent long hours in prayer in order to express my personal commitment to God in the Society.

Now in 1997 and twenty-five years later on, the expression of this commitment has lost none of its force. I can re-find in the formula the desire to have a part in God's undivided, universal, liberating love; emptying myself and putting all that I am and all that I have at the disposition of others – giving and receiving in gratitude; seeking together to live like Jesus, ever more united to the will of the Father.

In 1972, immediately after probation, I returned to my Province and began to be initiated into government at the service of mission, as a member of the Provincial Council. I confess that I preferred working with young people; previously I had been teaching and had also been the director of a student hostel. Ever since 1976 my apostolate has been that of serving in government: 1976–1982 as Provincial, 1982–1988 as a member of the General Council and then from 1989 to 1997 as Provincial once more. Being named Provincial at the age of thirty-five demanded a clear vision of the nuances between charism, mission and the service of education. I was forced to clarify for myself how to embody my call to live an apostolic/ contemplative life amid all the complexities of provincial government. It was a task that I found stimulating and inspiring and I was sustained by the response and collaboration of the members of the Province. During these post-Vatican II years, we were also much encouraged by the open attitude to change displayed by the Church in Austria.

As a member of the General Council, and influenced by internationality and inculturation, my understanding of charism, spirituality and apostolic service has taken on a new dimension. That the Constitutions of 1982 were a clear expression of our identity was confirmed during our visits to the different provinces. At the same time, the process of approbation of these new Constitutions with CRIS[6] and other experiences of the Church in Rome, put my sense of feeling with the Church (*sentire cum ecclesia*) to the test. This process challenged us to go deep into our roots and their interpretation. Thus the study of the innumerable writings of the Society helped me personally and confirmed me in the gift of vocation.

For me to visit a Province was to discover our charism and mission enfleshed, a discovery that was intensified when the Constitutions, finally approved, began to be studied and discussed. Amidst all the pluriformity which has characterised the Society since 1970, I was able to touch something of the communal effort which forced us to search for an adequate expression of the values, values which we recognised as our spiritual heritage. This has allowed us to embrace such diverse apostolates as dialogue between religions, the implementation of liberation theology, the struggle for justice, formal education or education in its broadest sense, pastoral work and insertion in countries at widely differing stages of development.

Marijke van Eechoud, Superior of an Elderly Community 1991–98[7]

As superior, what was I able to offer to my elderly community? Quite simply I was able to give them love, because I am a member of the Society. We grew up in this special atmosphere of love and caring, firstly for the children entrusted to us and later for our own sisters who had achieved so much and worked so hard until the time came when they became frail and needed to be cared for themselves.

Until the end of 1998, we were sharing our building of Venlo with Marie Réparatrice sisters and a group of Franciscans. Although we each had our own lifestyle, we gave mutual help to each other and formed close relationships, so we were all sad when the time came for us to separate. We moved to Weert in the spring of 1999 where we rented a part of a convent which had been the property of the Franciscans for more than 500 years. We have our meals all together in a lovely refectory; also twice a day we share prayer and we enjoy many informal meetings in the lift or the corridors. We complement each other and have all settled down happily together.

Now we are here, I am again conscious of the spirit of the Society. There is a 92-year-old sister, for example, and although she is a little vague about where she is and has very little energy, she has made relationships with all the brothers, always greets them with a smile and keeps the community informed of their well-being. It seems to me that this old lady is a wonderful example of the living charism of the Society. One day, having met one of the brothers in the garden, she said 'It does people good when you are friendly to them, and it is such a small thing to do.' For her part, she is genuinely amazed and delighted by the obvious affection in which she is held.

The 'Personal Project' of Carmen Comella, Superior of the Area of Cuba

I want to assume those attitudes, convictions and dispositions that Paul adopted towards the Philippians: 'Always rejoice in the Lord, that my thoughts may be those of Jesus Christ; Christ is my life; I give myself to others that they may rejoice in this same faith. I give thanks to God each time I remember each one of you in joy.'

The following regime will help me to live these attitudes, dispositions and convictions. To adopt a serious life of prayer, praying from 6.30 to 7.30 in the morning and for half an hour in the afternoon, paying a visit to Mary, and if possible saying the Rosary; also preparing the following day's prayer in the evening, making an examination of consciousness and taking a day of prayer each month. I will attempt to pursue my personal formation by means of reading serious books and articles.

I want to further community life in the whole region and myself live in joy and with a sense of humour. I want to be of service, but avoid trespassing on others' territory, and to assist and give space to alternative ways of being and living; I want to avoid useless discussion and to nurture a spirit of celebration. I want to work for the Kingdom with passion and to welcome all. I mean to go to bed tired, but not exhausted – I will need the help of others to achieve this.

I want to support the area by helping everyone to feel good, to support the vocation ministry by being creative and to share this project with the community, so that together we may follow Jesus more closely.

Maryvonne Keraly of France, General Councillor (1999), writes of Gospel Authority

Experience tells us that where power is concerned there is little leeway for the Gospel. At all levels we see the dominance of power and the refusal to see weakness as a truly human factor.

In politics and economics and in social relationships, one tramples on another in order to keep up and succeed. Religious life is not immune from this temptation; government structures can become a place of power, where others are dominated and where obedience becomes subservience. It is even more dangerous when attitudes of pride or contempt, fear or resignation are dressed up as spiritual virtues.

Because of the Gospel, it is of paramount importance that power be 'evangelised' and thus give witness to the spirit of Christ. We know of Jesus' constant preoccupation and defence of the little ones and the voiceless. In religious life, government must be based on the Gospel; all structures and actions have to be thought out and expressed in terms of service. This is our way of proclaiming that authority is no longer the rightful use of power, but the transformation of power into service.

Jesus said to the Pharisees, 'Do not call any man on earth father . . . for you are all brothers and sisters' (Matthew 23:8). To govern and to be governed in the spirit of the Gospel is to relate to everyone as sisters and brothers; this includes the relationship of obedience/authority. The will to power and domination must be excluded from all our relationships. In this way, we shall draw closer to the call of our 1982 Constitutions: 'In Jesus, we enter into a new relationship with one another, in faith and love.'

Formation

Religious vocation, or the call to religious life, is always mysterious. Many novices, worldwide, responded to a request for information and although their answers were enlightening in terms of their experience, age and background, the mystery of call remained. In general, novices at the end of the twentieth century tended to be older; many had abandoned rewarding work in order to try their vocations in the Society. Among the candidates of that time there were engineers, computer experts, TV producers, teachers and medical personnel. Many were seasoned church workers by the time they entered the Society. One Cuban novice had a Communist background, and another from the Philippines had spent three years in a Carmelite monastery. In almost every case their introduction to the Society was made through a personal link. Most frequently they had come to know the Society through meeting an individual rscJ, or a community, or in some cases a priest had implemented the introduction.

These women wrote of being attracted by the call to be contemplatives in action, by the internationality of the Society, by the warmth, simplicity and energy that they experienced among rscJ with whom they had worked. Equally some candidates had arrived with a healthy sense of realism; several rscJ communities were open to lay women and some offered a 'live in' period for those seriously considering joining the Society. Thus many would-be candidates had become aware of tensions in community relationships, but those who mentioned problems had not been put off; a few even expressed relief to find themselves joining 'a normal group of people'!

So what of formation at the end of the twentieth century? While much has changed, including (in some places) the title Mistress of Novices, to Director of Novices, the qualities demanded of such a person remained almost unchanged in 1999. According to the 1815 Constitutions 'the Mistress of

159

Novices should be as far as possible a person of eminent virtue, thoroughly acquainted with the spirit and rules of the Institute, gifted with prudence and wisdom, and above all, closely united with the Sacred Heart of our Lord' (1815 Constitutions #85 XXIX). The 1982 Constitutions speak in the same tone:

> The primary task of the Mistress of Novices is to help and encourage the novices to live a true and loving relationship with Jesus Christ, to enable them to appreciate the spirit of the Society and to discover the riches of their calling. To be able to do this, the Mistress of Novices herself will have a deep understanding of the spirit of the Society, a real apostolic sense and the capacity to relate in faith and trust and affection to each novice. (1982 Constitutions #93)

If, however, there has been no real change in the dispositions demanded of those in charge of formation, the training has generally changed. Many entering in the closing years of the twentieth century, especially those from the West, arrived equipped with a professional or technical training, an established habit of personal prayer and an impressive record of apostolic service. Sensitive to the experience of these purposeful women, the 1982 Constitutions direct that the candidate be assisted in 'taking in hand her own formation' (1982 Constitutions #84). Gone are the days of a uniform novitiate with an imposed order of day, assigning a task for every hour. 'When people come,' said Margaret Wilson, the Novice Director of the English/Welsh Province,

> I am aware that I am sitting in front of another adult with a wealth of experience behind her; there is no way that I am going to tell her what to do. I see my role as a reflector, a companion, but above all someone who supports and encourages a person on her journey to God.

Margaret's enlightening insights are based on her considerable experience as Novice Director of the English/Welsh Province, but by her time initial formation was no longer wholly uniform;

it was affected by the many different cultures to be found in the Society.

Despite this deceptively relaxed attitude there is much ground to be covered during the two years of initial formation. 'The novices study the Society's Constitutions, history and the current orientations of the Society in its varied apostolic commitments thoughout the world.' They also study 'the Scriptures, the theology of religious life and the documents of the Church' (1982 Constitutions #86). The latter subjects, together with those that were more general and touched on human development, were often taught in an inter-congregational group of apostolic novices from various congregations.

Learning languages was another serious commitment; few were to become fluent in the three Society languages of French, Spanish and English, but they were expected to be able to communicate in at least two of the three.[8] This somewhat academic diet was balanced by time spent every week in some 'hands on' practical apostolate in the local parish or with some disadvantaged group. In the second year the novices spent three months away from the novitiate, engaged in an apostolic mission.

These various activities provided a framework within which the novices deepened their prayer, ' . . . seeking a personal encounter with Jesus . . . learning to contemplate reality and to experience it with His Heart' (1982 Constitutions #18). They needed to discover who they were and who God is, in order to hear God's call; if this was to happen, unpressured time and sufficient space were essential. Many of the letters received from novices reported that this deliberate 'emptiness' increased their feeling of vulnerability. Speaking of the absence of a 'nine-to-five' job and the reorientation that this demanded, Margaret said:

They arrive and all their supports have gone, along with the way that they had previously identified themselves. They had lost both their job and their financial independence; this was very painful for some, but it led to deeper identification of who they really were as they came face to face with God.

In Margaret's experience, spiritual direction was the cornerstone of the unfolding journey and she also identified the thirty-day retreat[9] as a key moment in initial formation. She found that the experience of the Exercises led to deep prayer together and to the determination to discover how such an experience could be lived out practically, day to day. She spoke of the novices' intimacy, both with themselves and with God.

The more they seemed to understand themselves, the more they allowed God in. I watched people grow and blossom. It was something to do with allowing themselves to be what God wanted them to be. This was the transformation by the Spirit, referred to in the Constitutions. 'The Spirit dwelling within us gradually transforms us, enabling us through His power to remove whatever hinders His action' (1982 Constitutions #21). This was all to do with understanding the contemplative outlook. If the novices managed to get to grips with that, they were able to get to grips with themselves. Then they could be 'at home' in their own skin, at home in themselves and at home in the Society, so that the Society became the place where they could be fully themselves, for God was calling them to be there.

Laurent Mayasari, an Indonesian candidate, shared her reflections on the community in Jakarta, which she experienced as a 'live in'; in November 1999 she was the first to enter the newly established novitiate in Jakarta.

The rscJ community opens its heart to anyone, man, woman, rich, poor, old, young; no distinctions are made on the basis of education, status, way of thinking or way of life. The religious penetrate far and deep into culture, religious plurality, local customs and repression in the country. They use whatever means they see to build up the spirituality of young people.
The rscJ in Indonesia live in the midst of the turmoil of the metropolis, they work hard and they trust so strongly in

the work of the Holy Spirit that they break through the
Indonesian people's doubts about religious life. The life of
the community presents a challenge to young people, prompting
them to search and to take the decision to live as Jesus lived.
The rscJ attract people on account of the way they respond to
human concerns, especially those related to justice. Their spirit
of poverty and their understanding of feminist issues form the
basis of their apostolate and enable them to form healthy
relationships.

I can honestly say that my life and personality have been
gradually formed through living in an rscJ community.
Through prayer that is not rigid, as formal prayer so often is,
and through their way of contemplating life in the midst of
the business of work, I have found it easier to get closer to God,
in freedom. I consider this a grace. I need strength to nurture
it. I am also responsible for sharing it with everyone. When I
first heard about the rscJ, I had a struggle with family concerns
and with my commitment to work for justice. I had many
questions about community life and my own past experiences.
I thought long and hard and reflected seriously and all the time
was supported by friends; finally I decided to join the
community. I trust that God will make up for my limitations.

Before I joined the community I was uncertain about my
spiritual life. I was always struggling. I felt as though I had
involved myself in too many human concerns and began to sense
a lack of humility in my approach. Simple, everyday issues had
lost meaning and importance, I had become cynical and I was
dissatisfied with the way I was developing. I could not
understand what was happening to me in prayer and I was utterly
weary. Now I see that what I needed to do was to face reality.

This chapter has been concerned with the rscJ who were missioned for the administration of the Society; this area underwent
considerable change when limits on the duration of terms of
office were written into the 1982 Constitutions (cf. Government
section ##139–78). And just as those in positions of authority

163

in the Society expected to be replaced after serving their set term, so many rscJ who had undertaken ministries outside the Society found themselves asked to take retirement. But rscJ do not retire! The following chapter witnesses to the creativity demonstrated by some of these so-called 'retired' religious who have continued in their third age to discover alternative means to make known the love of Christ. Also included in this chapter are a number of rscJ who were using an art form as a means of making known the love of God.

NOTES
1. Extract from an informal paper by Jeanne de Charry rscJ.
2. Approximate translation of one of the inscriptions in the garden of the Villa Lante.
3. An extract from *On the Way Home*, edited by Frances Makower and Joan Faber (Darton, Longman & Todd, 1994).
4. The Uganda Province became Uganda/Kenya in 1974.
5. From 1971 to 1978 probanists were free to compose their own personal vow formula.
6. Congregation for Religious and Secular Institutes, concerning itself with all aspects of religious life.
7. In 1998 the Netherlands joined with Belgium to form a single province.
8. In such areas as India, Uganda or the Philippines, novices are required to be fluent in at least one local dialect.
9. The Spiritual Exercises, based on the experience of Ignatius of Loyola and written by him, provide a guide for retreatants. The length of time that a retreat lasts varies, but novices make a retreat lasting for thirty days.

CHAPTER 9

Creative Women

*Our course is nearly run and the end is in sight; reason enough to renew
our fervour, our fidelity in the service of God.*
(Madeleine Sophie, quoted by Adele Cahier rscJ,
Vie de la Vénérable Mère Barat, Vol II)

*When old age makes it impossible to continue in full-time apostolate, we
look for new ways of manifesting the love of God.*
(1982 Constitutions #116)

*. . . it [old age] may be the most contemplative period of our life, keeping
its prophetic power through the truth and depth of our relationships and
the joy with which we bear witness to the fidelity of God's love.*
(1982 Constitutions #116)

Towards the end of her life, Madeleine Sophie asked to retire,
but the 1815 Constitutions ruled that the Superior General
was 'elected for life' (#245) and her councillors would not
consider resignation; she died in office, as did her nine
immediate successors. In 1967, however, Mother Sabine de
Valon's resignation was accepted by the Special Chapter and,
three years later, the 1970 General Chapter limited the mandate
of the Superior General to a maximum of twelve years. This
decision was endorsed by the 1982 Constitutions (#164) which
also set limits on the duration of various positions of authority;
age, however, was never a consideration. Thus at the end of the
twentieth century many rscJ fortunate enough to be blessed with

health, continued to serve in active ministries beyond their three score years and ten.

Since 1967, three Superiors General have been elected and have retired from office. This change was in line with the times, for in several countries rscJ had to comply with a state-imposed retiring age. What follows is a tribute to sisters in their 'third age' who have imaginatively created new ministries for themselves. From the time of Pauline Perdrau, who painted *Mater Admirabilis* at the Trinita in Rome, there have always been rscJ who have made known the love of God through the arts; some of those involved in such ministries have contributed to this chapter.

Ministering in the 'Third Age'
Maria Carmen Nuñez-Lagos, rscJ from Spain

Maria Carmen has been working at the IITD (International Institute of Theology at a Distance) since its foundation by Mgr Augustin García-Gasco in 1973. It was founded on the principle that education, a 'good' to be shared by all, must offer equal opportunities. The aim of IITD was to provide students without access to an educational centre with a theological, pastoral and human formation. The courses were designed to enable students to articulate their faith and to hold responsible positions in ecclesial communities. Using all available means of communication, tutors of IITD entered into a 'faith-culture-life' dialogue with their students. They attempted to foster a commitment to evangelical values which would work towards the transformation of society. For the students, scattered abroad in Africa, America and the Far East, the Institute offered a means of personalised teaching which could be combined with regular employment. Studies are organised to enable the students, rather than the staff, to take the initiative; consequently it is the students who evaluate progress, set their own timetables and organise the pace at which they work.

Obviously in these unusual circumstances the relationship established between tutor and student was of the greatest importance and relied on a specialised system developed over the years. When Maria Carmen first joined the staff in 1973, aged fifty-seven, she assisted in the early development of the Institute. In addition to teaching philosophy, she was also involved with administration, with organising the specialist teaching materials, with the formation of staff and with setting up the structures of the organisation. In 1999 she was still serving the Institute and at that time had been appointed Secretary General of the Executive.

Irène Uyttenhove, rscJ of Belgium

In 1968 when her teaching career ended, Irène studied theology at Lumen Vitae, the Pastoral Centre run by the Jesuits in Brussels. When her course was completed, and she had discerned her future ministry, she began parish work and lived in an inserted community. She became responsible for much of the life of the parish, from preparing the liturgies to giving the homily; she also undertook parish visiting, acted as a guide to the church and visited poor people. In addition she served on the 'Tele Acceuil' (a confidential helpline). Commenting at the age of ninety-three, she said, 'Age has come, so I help ... suggest ... but no longer have any official responsibility ... but I mean to help for as long as the Lord seems to desire it.'

An Older Community in France

The rscJ Bernadette Bovagnet, Odile (de) Rousiers, Marie-Louise Fey and Marie-Thérèse Houdoy were all members of an older community in Montigny-les-Metz, France.

Bernadette Bovagnet rscJ

Having retired, I arrived here in September 1995. I had always
worked in college with middle-class youngsters and now I
wanted to share the gifts that God had given me with
underprivileged people. In 1996 I began work as a Public
Scribe in an office run by a charity. This is located in the midst
of a new urban development area with a population of 25,000,
including Turks, Asians, North Africans and an increasing
number of French families.

At the office we welcome all who present themselves, offering
immediate assistance with filling in claims for tax relief, family
allowances, unemployment benefits etc. I might be asked to
write out a curriculum vitae, or to help with the paying of bills
or rent; sometimes I even write out a cheque or fill in forms
required by the judiciary or the police. Our aim is to assist all our
clients to become independent and to take charge of their own
lives.

In the area in which I work there are large families, but three-
quarters of the adults are out of work; I am in touch with
extreme poverty. However, if people go away happy for the
simple reason that someone has listened to them, my day is made.
It gives me joy to be able to continue this task of education,
spreading his love among these under-privileged people.

Odile (de) Rousiers rscJ

I belonged to the 'ZAI' Association, which was established for
those who find themselves excluded or isolated as a result of
illness; we offer a place where they will be heard, where they
can chat and enjoy themselves and where they will find some
spirituality. To begin with we were almost alone in welcoming
people diagnosed as HIV+, but now these people have less need
of us on account of medical advance and the use of new
treatments. This enabled us to contact the almoner of a local

psychiatric hospital and open our doors to psychiatric outpatients. The mentally ill whom we are welcoming feel increasingly at ease with us and are beginning to make friends among themselves.

These sick people who have been rejected by society, begin to regain their dignity as children of God in a place where they are not judged. Working among them is a new experience for me, but did not Madeleine Sophie instil in us the necessity of openness to new educational situations, and is not the work of 'ZAI' an aspect of our preferential option for the poor?

Marie-Louise Fey rscJ

Since 1966 I have been a volunteer receptionist at the Jean Rodhain Welcome Centre which provides meals for homeless people and is run by Secours Catholique. Between forty and sixty people come to eat breakfast, lunch or an evening meal for which there is a small charge. In addition to the warm welcome and the meals, they can have a free shower, use a low-cost laundry, have a haircut, or consult an expert on money problems and filling in forms. Once a week clinics are held by a doctor, nurse and psychiatrist. Some clients are employed to work in the garden, wash up, stuff envelopes; others undertake simple repair work; those who are employed receive free meals and receive a wage at the end of the week.

My job is to welcome people, register them and issue meal tickets. Our clients are friendly among themselves and generous: those who are in funds insist on giving a contribution on behalf of those who cannot pay. Between meals, I help in the kitchen, prepare the vegetables, make desserts or lay the tables. It gives me great joy to serve these people, and to have a small part in the lives of those who have nothing.

Marie-Thérèse Houdoy rscJ

In 1993 the parish of St Joseph of Montigny embarked on a
project of reaching out to everyone who lives in the area. At
key moments of the liturgical year, leaflets entitled 'A Word of
Friendship' would be distributed to everyone, believers and
unbelievers alike. Passed from hand to hand by messengers,
these leaflets contained local information and concerns; the
aim of the leaflets was to bring people together, rather than to
make converts.

When the scheme had been in place for five years, we noticed
modest signs that pointed to fruit born of the project. At
Christmas time cards and sweets were exchanged around a
Christmas tree; a shared Christmas candle brought joy, as did
the offering of a bowl of rice to a needy person. Furthermore
many of the 'messengers' who had been far from the Church
began to return to the practice of their faith. My small part in
this project is to act as a messenger in my locality.

Edmée Lesne's Ministry at La Roseraie

In 1998, Edmée Lesne rscJ, who was then eighty-eight, was living
at La Roseraie, a community for elderly and frail religious in
Lyons (see p. 150 above). She wrote about the ministry that she
took up when she first came to La Roseraie.

The hour of retirement had struck, but after a lifetime spent
with children and young people, inactivity was unthinkable. It
occurred to me that I might become a guide to Notre Dame de
Fourviere, one of the famous churches of Lyons which is visited
by thousands of pilgrims each year. Moreover, following the
example of medieval churches, Notre Dame de Fourviere presents
a veritable catechism to the visitor, through its works of art.

I undertook all the necessary preparation, attending lectures
on the stained glass, mosaics and carvings. I also brushed up

my knowledge of the Scriptures and history of the Church.
When I give a guided tour, I try to understand the different
individuals in the group: what has brought them to the church
and what does our Lady mean for them? Talking to them and
asking questions, I hope that their answers will come from within
themselves. I never talk directly of the love of the Heart of
Jesus, but I try to reveal the Lord by the warmth and breadth
of my welcome. It seems to me that in bringing the light of the
truth to bear on the Church and its history, I am helping to
break down anti-religious prejudice.

As for me, I find real joy in this ministry. Before I took it on,
I was walking with leaden feet, but once I had begun the
guided tours I flew on wings!

Prayer Links: Lyons and Lima

Many rscJ were assisting in telephone ministries; some, such as
that which 88-year-old Cécile Bigo operated from her room, were
an immediate and compassionate response to requests for prayer.
Each call she received was of value to Cécile, not only for the
opportunity it presented to offer the support of her prayer, but
because in answering the calls she could continue to proclaim
the love of God and thus to glorify the Heart of Jesus. Her
telephone ministry enabled her to enter and share in the
suffering of the world.

Raquel Corrales, rscJ of Peru, ran 'The Friendly Voice', which
was similar, although somewhat more official than the ministry
that was being operated by Cécile in Lyons. Initiated in 1972,
the Friendly Voice was operated from La Acogida (The House
of Welcome) in Lima.

The aim of this ministry was to offer understanding, friendship
and advice to all those who called and who were weighed down
by suffering, anxiety or loneliness. Through the Friendly Voice
many people have returned to their faith, or have discovered the

Lord; lives have been saved by this free service in which
anonymity and professional confidentiality are paramount.
Callers are gently led to find strength from within themselves to
solve their problems and overcome their grief.

Those who make the calls are driven by conflicts of
conscience, anguish and depression; they are beset by such
problems as crises with their children or spouse, drug or alcohol
addiction, debt, illness and unemployment – the list is
unending. All those using the Friendly Voice were full of
suffering and pain, but they found support at the end of the
line. In the hands of Raquel and her community, the
telephone line became a symbol of hope, enabling those who
operated it to perform works of mercy through an unlimited
outreach.

Ministering to the Disadvantaged in Taiwan, China, Argentina and Peru

Lucy Hu, rscJ from Taiwan

'Jesus, I love you, I trust in you . . .' As I croon the child stops
crawling, listens and searches for the source of the sound. He
is a premature infant who became blind and was abandoned by
his parents. I hold him, caress him and talk to him as if I
were his mother. He hugs me tightly and rests his head on my
breast.

There are about ten abandoned, handicapped babies and
toddlers at an orphanage that I began to visit in 1991 and have
carried on doing so for the last eight years. In 1998 I was
seventy-eight and could not do very much, but I embrace the
children, feed them and play with them. I want them to
experience the warmth of my love. This, for me is a most
precious time, for they provide a way in which I can love God
most intensely.

The 'anawim of God' form the compassionate and patient Heart of Jesus within me, and make me realise more and more how I am blessed. I am grateful to these children. I always pray that when they grow up, they will meet kindly, good-hearted people and through them experience the deep love of God; such experience will enable them to break the vicious circle of hatred in our society, within which they could so easily become imprisoned.

Teaching in China

Deirdre O'Brien, rscJ of Scotland/Ireland, had dreamt of being a missionary all her life. As a young child her imagination had been fired by an uncle who was one of the founding fathers of the Maynooth Mission to China; on his rare visits home, he had recounted fascinating tales. After her probation in 1959 Deirdre had offered herself for missionary work, but had spent virtually all her professional life teaching in the Society's schools in Ireland or Scotland. Her final appointment was that of Educational Advisor to Cardinal Grey. This was fortuitous, for she became involved in ecumenical work which led to a link with the 'Scottish Churches in China' group. In 1993, aged sixty-two, Deirdre retired from her work with the Cardinal – what happened next she has described herself.

Aged sixty-two I set out for Beijing with thirty-eight other volunteers, working for the VSO (Voluntary Service Overseas). After three weeks induction I found myself teaching English to doctors, nurses, medical teachers and to the fifteen members of the English Department in Changzhi College of Shanxi Province, one of the poorest areas of China. Normally VSO contracts are for two years only, but I love China and China loves me and the College have asked me to stay on. I hope, if I'm useful, to spend the rest of my life in China. Who knows? I live one day at a time with the Sacramental Presence of the Lord in my little flat on the College Campus. Every day I'm making new discoveries about the survival of the Church in this area, despite almost half a century of oppression. I see the Society's educational work in many different ways, as did Madeleine Sophie. We educate leaders in society, the people who can go into areas of life that are barred to religious. I think this is specially true of family life, where Gospel values are nurtured, hope engendered and above all, the reality of God's love and God's respect for each person experienced. How I long for the time when all may know that they have been redeemed by Jesus and are destined for a life of eternal happiness.

Nelly Ithuralde, rscJ from Argentina/Uruguay

Five afternoons a week, with the help of competent teachers, we [the community of Villa Jardin] run a Centre of Supplementary Classes for about ninety 7–15-year-olds. State schools only function in the mornings, so the Centre keeps the young people safe and off the streets, while their parents are at work. Before the day ends the students receive a nourishing meal of hot chocolate and bread and butter: for some this is the only substantial meal of the evening.

Games – football for the boys and team games for the girls – are popular and boys and girls alike were fascinated by the ten word processors given by a benefactor in 1998. Even more popular were expeditions to places of interest or simply to open country, which offered such a contrast to the overcrowded barrios where they all live. In 1997 we began a new project for eighteen youngsters with special needs. This too is being run by the community, with the help of one volunteer teacher and support given by some of the local institutions.

Maria Velaochaga, rscJ from Peru

We, a community of older sisters, live at the seaside in a large, new, functional house, surrounded by flowers; it is an environment conducive to contemplation.

We begin the day with personal prayer and the Eucharist, after which each one goes to some ministry suited to her capacities. I go to Bethany. This is an attractive room with a large, ample table set in its midst, around which all comers are welcomed: priests, religious, lay men and women, young and old. Some who come are sick or out of work, some suffer from physical or mental problems, others come seeking information – all are Jesus coming to Bethany.

Seated around the table we listen and share in friendship. RscJ and volunteers do all they can 'to be and recall Jesus in everyday life'. In spite of our physical and spiritual limitation, we live our vocation as a free gift to others; in all things we seek to express the faithful love of the Heart of Jesus.

The Ministry of Art

As has been said, there have always been rscJ who were specially gifted with artistic talent. Many of them have used the arts as a means of making known the love of God; often, as will be seen in the concluding pages of this chapter, it is during the 'third age' that these ministries are most fruitful.

Dorothy McMichael, rscJ of the USA, spent her working life teaching biology in Sacred Heart schools. Since her retirement in 1985 she has been working for Neighbourhood Artisans in Detroit, which offers training in screen printing. This organisation helps students from the inner city to learn a craft. It was set up in collaboration with Oonah Ryan rscJ who was appointed Co-Director in 1998. 'My role', Dorothy explained, is to prepare art for the screen-printing process. In addition I paint tiles for kitchens and bathrooms and help out with the workshops for the youngsters who receive very little in the way of art from their schools. I have also been involved in several 'spin off' programmes.

In June 1996, Oonah, Dorothy and Kinue Matsuzaki, an rscJ teaching art in Detroit, spent two weeks in Omaha at Summer ETC (Exploring Things Creatively). Summer ETC is one of the many projects set up by USA Society schools with the aim of sharing their resources with underprivileged youngsters in their area. Directed by Josephine Ellen (JoEllen) Sumpter rscJ, secretary to the Duchesne Academy, Summer ETC held its first session in 1995 and then offered tuition in dance, music, theatre, visual arts and creative writing. The tutors recruited by JoEllen were professional artists or teachers and among them were several rscJ.

Dorothy is committed to the practice of a broad spectrum of the arts. 'As I grow older,' she commented,

I have been drawn more and more to drawing and watercolour as an expression of my admiration and awe of the natural world and as a way of spiritual growth; I have found a great spiritual renewal in exploring Oriental brush painting, as well as Western-style watercolour. I think that creative activity, especially in the visual arts, is an essential part of education and should not be looked upon as 'icing on the cake'. This has so often been the case with educational systems, which tend to cut out the arts when funding becomes difficult.

As for JoEllen, she was delighted to be instrumental in providing high quality arts instruction, participation and exposure for several racially mixed and socially disadvantaged local Omaha schools.

Margret Fühles rscJ taught German literature, Latin and theology to students in Bonn. Since 1983, when she studied psychodrama at the Moreno Institut, at Überlingen in South-East Germany, she has used the method of bibliodrama with students engaged in biblical study.

She described how theologians, priests, and religious, as well as inexperienced students, discovered insights through the medium of drama.

I help my students to play out a biblical scene and encourage them to identify with a specific character. Through this means they come to a new and deeper understanding of the history of salvation and acquire a deeper knowledge of their own reality and truth. It is not possible, however, to plunge straight into dramatic action. Before playing out a scene, the students go through an initial warming-up period in order to become more aware of themselves and their feelings – this also gives them a chance to get to know each other. Next the chosen text is read, roles are allotted and decisions made on the particular viewpoint and emotional slant the piece is to follow. After this preparation, the scene itself is played out. The students might enact Jesus before Pilate, or Moses before Pharaoh, or Martha and Mary. They flesh out the characters, making use of voice, language and gesture, and thereby disclose both biblical and personal reality. Finally the students share and reflect on the feelings evoked during the play, linking the text to everyday life, in order to integrate the experience.

Using this method of psychodrama, some students have been enabled to accept and confront their own challenging or painful circumstances. For example, there was one woman who had recently been uprooted to a strange city and to a different social milieu. She played the role of a leper in the scene that depicts Jesus going outside the city gate in order to approach the outcast. She realised that he had joined her and began to understand that despite the difficulties of her new situation, she was not abandoned. Another student, a pregnant woman, chose the part of Mary visiting Elizabeth; she broke down in tears when she began to speak the words of the Magnificat. 'I did not want this child and now I am expected to praise you for it,' she cried. But as she struggled with the text and listened to what the other 'actors' had to say, she became reconciled to her situation and was finally able to make the words of the Magnificat her own. On another occasion a religious took the role of the man with a withered hand. In her right hand she held her ideals, which she knew well and regarded as a source of strength. The left hand, however was numb, atrophied and almost without feeling. Jesus asked to see it, and she had the courage to show him her useless hand. No longer condemned to hide her deformed limb, she felt good, and gradually recalled 'deforming' memories of childhood.

It is easy to see how intimately religious images are related to the affairs of life; did not Ignatius of Loyola employ similar methods in his Spiritual Exercises? He advocated the construction of a biblical scene and suggested that retreatants should enter into it, interacting with all the characters. Indeed, using every part of myself as I meditate with a group, trying to discern what is the real desire of my life, has become one method that I always find helpful during a ten-day retreat.

As I work with a group of students and we attempt to uncover the vast history of salvation and our own part in it, I am convinced that I am expressing one aspect of the Society's charism.

Phil Kilroy rscJ, an historian, scholar and author, described the experience of writing a new, commissioned biography of Madeleine Sophie Barat; her book was published in 2000.

One September evening in 1993 when I was in Armagh (Northern Ireland), Helen McLaughlin, then Superior General of the Society of the Sacred Heart, asked me to consider writing a scholarly biography of Madeleine Sophie Barat. Its publication would mark the bicentenary of the Society in November 2000. I considered this request for several months and consulted friends within and without the Society before finally accepting this daunting commission. My hesitations were

well founded. I recognised that the task was to examine the vast
collections of original letters, primary manuscripts and texts
on Sophie Barat. Indeed the extent of the archive was a
continual revelation to me, as well as a source of dismay at
times. These sources yielded new aspects of the life of Sophie
Barat. However, before I could read them in the context of
Sophie's life, I had to deconstruct my image of Sophie Barat in
my own mind and memory. Only then could I begin to glimpse
the woman who had evaded close scrutiny for many decades.
Some five years later, in 1998, when I had actually begun writing
the text of the biography, I read a novel by Willa Muir: *Imagined
Corners* (Edinburgh, 1996), pp. 276-7. The following dialogue
spoke to me of Sophie Barat and I chose it as the Preface to the
new biography. The scene is a dialogue between two women;
one is Elizabeth, whose marriage has broken up. The shock has
disturbed her and she has not slept for twenty-four hours. Her
friend Elise has come to tell her that one of the villagers was
found drowned that morning.

Elizabeth: 'I've been sitting here since yesterday, seeing it all,
over all the world. Everything we trust in let us down . . .'

Elise: 'Who are you that you should **not** be let down, as you
call it, by the chances and accidents of life? Who are you that
you should **not** be let down by your feelings and your blood
and your nerves and your reasoning, like any other human
being? The marvel is not that we are fallible and foolish, but
that we have the wit to see it and to go on in spite of it. We
are burdened with error and prejudice, like a rich field
covered with stones, and the marvel is not that we stub our
toes against the stones, but that we have sense enough to clear
them away – even if we only clear the little patch that is
ourselves. And even then, I have realised, we clear it not only
for ourselves, but for the toes of other people who come
after us . . . I don't know whether there is a God or not, but I
do know that there is humanity, that there is a rich field,
and that there are tons of stones to be cleared away . . .'

Researching the terrain of Sophie Barat's life meant delving into fields covered with stones, possible pathways and rocks of potential destruction. I watched Sophie Barat find her path forward, slowly, often painfully, and I saw how in the course of her life she had indeed cleared a way and left a trail. The original terrain of her home ground, Joigny, provided her with both stepping stones and obstacles on her journey. Then new fields of experience in Paris, in many parts of France, in Italy and Switzerland, drew Sophie onwards on her journey. As the Society expanded and the membership increased, so too did Sophie's path become more difficult to tread. Her letters and travels reflect her continual efforts to come to terms with the experience of her terrain, deal with perplexing situations and keep moving forward.

She often faltered on her path and several times was almost defeated by the stones upon the way. Periods of life were shrouded in uncertainty, when she felt her life bore little that was of worth. She often cried out in pain and incomprehension and the years of 1839-51 were a prolonged experience of darkness and personal sorrow. Yet Sophie Barat held on and made pathways where none had existed before. Her life of vulnerability and courage, as well as her integrity and fidelity in seeking a spiritual path, invites both wonder and a response. This has to be rooted in our own time and history, as we search to reveal the love of God in the pierced Heart of Christ. Sophie Barat drew strength from the wounded side of Christ on Calvary. Indeed the image of the rock on Calvary sustained and nourished her; the pathways of her life led finally to this point of resurrection and new life. Today she would invite us to journey along the same ultimate path, finding our way forward in the rich fields of our time . . . where 'there are tons of stones to be cleared away'.

Dolores Aleixandre, rscJ of Southern Spain, is also a writer; she is a Professor of Theology in Madrid and has traced some of the biblical roots of the glory of God.

In the Sinai Desert Moses asked God, 'Let me see your glory.'
Religious of the Sacred Heart could well transform this petition
by saying to God, 'Let me desire your glory.' Such is our life,
for to glorify the Heart of Jesus is the core of Madeleine
Sophie's spirituality. The one occupation upon which the life of
an rscJ is centred, and which unifies what she is and what she
does, is her unique occupation of glorifying the Heart of Jesus.
In this way Madeleine Sophie referred to the permanent bond
that unites rscJ to Jesus' feelings, preferences, choices and to
the constant attempt to adhere to Jesus and his Kingdom. So
the direction of her life is oriented to his as she spends it
contemplating the 'weight' of his love.

I frequently think about glorifying the Heart of Jesus, and
because I am committed to Jesus always and under any
circumstance, what I am doing is irrelevant, whether it be
queuing for a bus, correcting examinations or any other daily
chore.

Whence, I have so often wondered, does this thirst for the
glory of God arise? I have searched the Scriptures to find an
answer. The desire for the glory of God is born of an interior
'drawing' (attraction). To a Hebrew, a person's glory is an inner
'something', it is his density, gravity, strength. When Moses asked
God to let him see his glory, God answered: 'Yahweh, Yahweh,
a God of tenderness and compassion, slow to anger, and
abounding in steadfast love and faithfulness' (Exodus 34:6).
Jesus' life will be overturned, 'emptied' (Isaiah 53:12)
'consecrated' (Jeremiah 1:2) into the glory of the Father; it
will be emptied to obtain for us 'life to the full' (John 10:10).

St Augustine said 'my love is my weight', and we can say that
the love of Jesus was the weight that 'pulled', 'attracted' and
influenced Madeleine Sophie. This was what made her 'come
out of her own love, desire and interest'. She made her own
'Draw me after you' (Song of Songs 1:4), letting herself be drawn
to Jesus, finding in him and his love the axis around which to
gravitate. In a circular letter of 1815, she wrote:

Our Society must be given and consecrated to the glory of

the Heart of Jesus, that all works and tasks undertaken may
be related to this principal end. Interior life is the first need
of our hearts and only the glory of God and the zeal for souls
should cause us to depart from it.

Madeleine Sophie could be thought of as a small stone attracted
to the one unique centre of gravity: the love of Jesus.

The desire for the glory of God is born of a 'com-passionate'
heart. And so the desire for the glory of God seems too big for
us, we have a feeling that it was made not for us, but for truly
filial men and women who recognise everyone as brother or
sister, free people, committed to the Kingdom and its justice. In
fact only Jesus knows how to desire God's glory. When he taught
us, explaining a thousand times in simple everyday words, he
knew how little we understood. The truth is that the problem
lies in our lack of sympathy – we are not attuned to the suffering
of Jesus. Our sickness is that of disenchantment and apathy;
plenty and security have immunised us against desire: we live in
a diminished present to which our digital watches keep time
and we are incapable of passionate desire for the future that has
been promised to us. 'Warm what is cold', the Church makes
us ask the Spirit, as if we were asking the Spirit to bring to birth
in us the very passion from which the desire sprang. For only
the Spirit can put at our disposal the impassioned love of Jesus,
his power to be committed to God's cause and ours, to let
himself be touched by what happens to us, especially the little
ones; to embrace, from the depths of his being, the feelings of
others; to think up and offer to us the radical, utopian alternative
of history according to the mind of God; to believe obstinately
in the possibility of newness for every man and woman . . .

All that is waiting for us, like a great fire that can thaw our
indifference and our insensitivity, like a river in spate, capable
of sweeping away our boredom, apathy and depression. All we
need is to be open to that compassion, to allow our hearts to
beat in time with another heart not made of stone as ours are,
to consent to be invaded by a love greater than our own.

Madeleine Sophie contacted that fire, her whole life was ignited and full of compassion.

The desire for the glory of God is born of a song. The angel's words to the shepherds were for Luke more than a hymn of joy to the Saviour's birth; they were a kind of symphonic overture to Jesus' whole existence. When Paul seeks to express the breathtaking descent of the Son into our history, he uses a surprising verb: 'he lowered himself', he stripped himself of rank, he emptied himself. Theologians of the twentieth century coined the phrase 'the man for others'.

What a strange identity was his, indwelt by a single driving force that Luke expresses as God's glory and our peace. 'I have food to eat that you do not know of' (John 4:32), he was to say to his disciples. We draw our nourishment, we make ourselves strong by making a name for ourselves, whereas he feeds on the Father's word (Matthew 4:4) and seeks only his will (John 6:38). The Father's will is that his scattered children should come home to experience the fullness of blessing and the vitality that the Scriptures call peace. Seeking his Father's will will become such a passion, invading him so utterly that he will live 'de-centred', 'unhinged', because his centre and hinge are his Father and his brothers and sisters.

His relations will even say: 'He is out of his mind' (Mark 3:21), and they were certainly right, for nothing is further from our judicious prudence, our reasonable compromises, our balanced calculations than the life beginning today; already it has gone beyond all sense, all measure. You could say that the hymn of Bethlehem has made him drunk, has thrown him off balance, and from now on he will be unable to live other than alien-ated, beside himself. Squandering prodigality, breaking limits, will be the only possible rhythm of life.

Madeleine Sophie listened to that song in the 'interior dispositions' of the heart of Jesus and walked into his dance. The melody of her life was 'union and conformity with the Heart of Jesus' and she made God's project her own.

Let us risk lying on the bare earth like the shepherds, like

183

Madeleine Sophie, just in case the melody of their song should
reach us: 'Glory to God, peace to his people'. Let us wander
through this place where Someone has begun to-exist-for-
others. Let us come to him without artificial efforts to empty
ourselves of ourselves in order to be like him: it is only when
you have found a treasure that you joyfully sell the rest, as he
will tell us when he grows up. Only when our ears have caught
the music, will our feet be able to dance. We must let ourselves
be carried away by it, hum it, murmur it in the secrecy of our
hearts. And if it is granted to us, let us dance to his rhythm,
mad as it may seem.

Mary Louise (Mamie) Jenkins, rscJ of the USA, is a musician.
She majored in music at Manhattanville College, before entering
the Society. She taught music in school until, aware of her diminishing energy, she made the decision to train as a music therapist,
so that when she was no longer able to work in school, she could
continue her ministry through her music.

I was supposedly retired when I came to Washington in 1989,
but I was appointed Campus Minister for the youngsters at
Stone Ridge Sacred Heart School and am at the school from
eight till noon each morning. I am free in the afternoons and
work as a music therapist at two nursing homes twice a week,
and I also provide therapy to handicapped youngsters.

Most of my adult clientele suffer from Alzheimer's disease and
they are truly *anawim*. The minds of many of them have
diminished, but their spirit and their love of life is unimpaired.
They need to know that they are loved, wanted and esteemed,
and I feel that music is the one gift that can help them. They
need to regain a sense of well-being. I try to say to them, 'Your
memory has gone, but music can help you to relate in a way
that many things cannot.' So I introduce music from the
twenties, thirties and forties, and people who have not spoken
for years begin to communicate. Doctors and nurses are
amazed when patients who have given no sign of life suddenly

begin to relate to me, to their family, friends and to one
another. And what gives life to them, gives life to me.

I feel that God has given me the gift of helping these suffering
people through music; they can still remember significant
things, and to a point can share their memories with others. I
see my ministry demonstrating our charism, because this is
shown forth in the love of the Heart of Jesus. I do this with
children and alumnae, with rich and poor, and with black and
white. I am called to minister through music to people who are
so often overlooked or abandoned. Music enables them to give:
if they cannot sing, they can play an instrument or dance with
me. All are revived by music. Their eyes come alive again and
they are touched by the love of the Heart of Jesus.

Meeda Inglis, from the Irish/Scottish Province, wrote of her art.

Born in 1913 into a family of artists and poets, from my earliest
years I looked on art as a way of life. After twelve years at
Arbroath High School (on the East Coast of Scotland), four
years at Grays School of Art in Aberdeen, I won a scholarship
to the Hospitalfield Post-Graduate School of Painting and moved
back to Arbroath. A few years later, in 1937, I entered the Society.
The novitiate was then at Mount Anville, Dublin, where I was in
for a traumatic experience. At that time, in addition to the
difference between the Irish and Scots, art had no place in
community life, while in schools it was considered to be a non-
essential extra. Part of me survived the noviceship, but I lost
touch with one half of myself.

When I left the noviceship I taught, and continued to feel
half dead. During these years, however, I discovered that prayer
is also a way of life and this helped me to struggle on until my
health broke down, and it was thought that returning to
Scotland would revive me. In Edinburgh I was able to teach art
at Craiglockart College. Until I retired from teaching in 1979,
prayer and art seemed to run in parallel lines and I still had the
feeling that I was not a whole person.

Having retired I was given the opportunity to spend time

painting and very gradually I began to realise that I was whole again. From then on I was aware that prayer was helping my painting and that painting was helping my prayer. Both had merged to become one way of life, the way that leads to God.

For me, art is a means of communication and in my painting I try to communicate something of the peace and tranquillity I experience in the presence of beauty. I want to convey to others my joy and happiness in God's creation and my pleasure in finding beauty in unexpected places; I want to lead people along this path of discovery and fulfilment. Critics have said of my art: 'her watercolours are serene, soft and soothing, full of the peace and tranquillity she finds in beauty . . .'

If we can see how wonderful life really is and recognise beauty in its ups and downs, then we will be well on the way to meeting God. Wonder, it has been said, is the basis of worship and wondering at the beauty of the world around us can lead to God. My appreciation of beauty, and the joy at finding it in my surroundings, does indeed lead along the path to God. And beauty as well as God is found not only in tranquillity and peace, but in the starker aspects of life. I would like to lead people to see the beauty, the power and the wonder of God's creation. To be aware of shape, colour, light and shade in their surroundings and their lives, but especially wonder, which can make life worth living and will surely bring us nearer to God.

Now, in 1999 and in my eighty-sixth year, I thank God for the gift God has given me and for the opportunity to use and develop it in my ministry. In my old age I can truly say with the poet G. K. Chesterton, 'I am glad to be alive for the privilege of looking at a dandelion.' I know that God is reflected in all things and that through them God is drawing us to himself.

The creativity of those rscJ whose ministries have been portrayed above was inspired by their ardent need to make known the love of God, a need which is shared by every member of the Society. Indeed towards the end of the twentieth century an increasing number satisfied the desire to 'glorify the heart of Jesus' by serving in pastoral ministries and in accompanying fellow pilgrims on the 'way'; some of these ministries are described in the following chapter.

CHAPTER 10

Pastoral Work and Spiritual Guidance

The spirit of the Society is essentially based upon prayer and the interior life. (1815 Constitutions #330)

This contemplative attitude permeates our whole being, helping us to live ever more united to Christ in our relationships, our tasks and our ministry. (1982 Constitutions #22)

We are called to be women who know that the source of all energy is to be drawn from prolonged prayer. (1988 Chapter Document)

In a letter to Pauline de Limminghe rscJ, written on 10 November 1829, Madeleine Sophie said, 'An order which unites the contemplative and the active life has a powerful grace which underlines its action. This is what I feel drawn to establish in our Society, before God calls me to Himself.' It is well known that Madeleine Sophie's first attraction had been to Carmel; her desire for uninterrupted solitude and prayer combined with an ardent apostolic zeal was the treasured heritage that she left to the Society. She talked of a 'mixed life': 'Martha blended with Mary'. The Second Vatican Council, however, insisted that congregations make a choice. Either their members were to be contemplatives, living in seclusion, more or less exclusively occupied in prayer, study and manual labour, or they were to be active religious, undertaking specific works. The Society's Special Chapter of 1967, summoned in obedience to the Church, discerned that the Society was 'an apostolic institute in the Church and the world today'.[1] All religious of the Sacred

188

Heart, following Madeleine Sophie's vision, have striven to become contemplatives in action.

By 1999 numerous rscJ were involved in the formation and encouragement of spiritual life. They served in such areas as schools, hospitals and prisons where they were often employed as chaplains; others were working in parishes or retreat centres. For all rscJ, whatever their ministry, the imperative of integrating prayer and apostolic work presented an ongoing challenge.

Retreats and Spiritual Direction: the Philippines and Australia

Eusebia Talastas (Eby), rscJ from the Philippines, has been teaching since the 1990s at the Institute of Formation and Religious Studies and at the East Asian Pastoral Institute. Both are intercongregational, international institutes catering primarily for the formation of 'young' religious. This ministry has brought Eby in touch with many religious and has led to an expansion of her work. In August 1997 she was invited to give a retreat to the Columban Missionaries in Pakistan. As Eby explained in what follows, this turned out to be rather more eventful than had been foreseen.

I was to direct three group retreats for the Columbans and to lead a seminar on 'The Actualization of Human Strengths' for their international mission of priests, seminarians and lay missionaries. Two days after my arrival in Lahore, the community was attacked and I and my hosts were held at gunpoint. Three Pakistani men, posing as religious, had managed to gain entrance. It took them four hours to ransack the house, while we, terrified, beseeched the Lord for deliverance. When finally out of danger, we began to discuss how we had handled the situation. Confronted by a choice between life or possessions, each one of us opted for life; some had been tempted to put up a fight, but had held back for

189

fear of endangering the whole group. Once the ordeal was over, to help us to deal with the after-effects of the trauma, we followed techniques that I had learnt during a renewal session in Montreal.

From Lahore I moved on to Murree, a mountain resort in Northern Punjab, within sight of the Himalayas, where I was to give two retreats, returning to Lahore for the seminar. During this time Peter-Hans Kolvenbach, the Superior General of the Society of Jesus, happened to be in Lahore. While there he invited the local congregations to a conference on the consecrated life, which I was able to attend. It was there that I encountered Sr Philippina, the Novice Mistress of the Sisters of Charity of St Jeanne Antide and an alumna of Tal Virtu Training College in Malta; to my surprise she led me to *Mater Admirabilis* in Pakistan! I had asked a question and Sister Philippina had recognised me as a Sacred Heart sister, and when we met, she told me the following story.

As a student at Tal Virtu she became devoted to *Mater*, and later, working in Pakistan, developed a real longing to see the painting again. To her amazement, while she was browsing in the Lahore Catholic bookstore, run by the Society of St Paul, she found a reproduction which had remained a mystery for over two years. The sister running the store was no less thrilled to have *Mater* identified, than Sr Philippina was to find her; since then there have been several requests for the reproduction and *Mater* is now well established in Pakistan.

Eby ends the account of her ministry by reflecting on her contacts with different congregations.

It has been a humbling experience. Many of those with whom I have worked have either known rscJ personally or have heard about the Society in other countries. They have gained a sense of our charism and I sometimes feel that their trust in me is connected with their trust in the charism of the Society. This has revitalised my own faith in the Holy Spirit's action on the Society as an international body of women, called to show forth

God's love in the world. In a sense it does not matter where
we are, or what we do, because it is the same spirituality that
animates us and that others recognise.

I know that being renewed in my oneness with my Sisters from
all over the world is not enough. I feel an inner demand to
more consistent fidelity and deeper integrity. These days, in my
quieter moments, I have often become aware of the Gospel
imperative to choose the narrow path. When faced with choices
I try to discern which is the broad path that leads to false
fulfilment, and which the narrow, that leads to true life. I see
more clearly now, that the narrow path is inseparable from
intimacy with God.

Mary d'Apice, rscJ from Australia, had completed a medical
degree before she entered the novitiate in Australia in 1946.
After her initial formation, her main ministry was in schools and
colleges where she became increasingly interested in psychology.
In the 1970s she was given the opportunity for further study in
spirituality and psychology. Since then her ministry has integrated the spiritual, psychological and medical aspects of life.
In addition to individual clients (many of whom had been sex-
ually abused), she has received numerous requests for
workshops, seminars and retreats. This has led her to undertake
extensive travel to the United Kingdom, Ireland, the United
States, Korea, Japan and New Zealand. Since publishing her
acclaimed *Noon to Nightfall: A Journey Through Middle Life and
Aging*, she has been increasingly in demand for retreats and
workshops.[2]

Street Retreats

Margaret Mary (Marnie) Kennedy, rscJ of Australia, writes:

In 1984, having worked for ten years in an Ignatian Centre of
Spirituality as a member of a Jesuit retreat team, I was uneasy
and so were my colleagues. Our programmes seemed to be
doing little to effect the social change that we had hoped for.

191

'What experiences', we asked ourselves, 'will help us to move from the desire for justice to action?' Our response to this question was to set up 'Street Retreats', based in the streets of the inner city. Today we need a feet-on-the-ground spirituality which liberates God to be truly 'Word made flesh' and which acknowledges human beings to be the very language of God. Giving retreats in the less sheltered environment of the inner city allows the socio-economic and political realities to sharpen our understanding of the kind of apostolic spirituality needed at the end of the twentieth century. The search begins by placing ourselves at the margins, not at the centre.

Retreatants are billeted in houses to which the powerless and disadvantaged have ready access as friends, for here the 'Word made flesh' is encountered in a thousand guises and is listened to, reflected on, prayed over. To walk the streets with an ever-sharpening awareness of the present moment, of our interconnectedness with the whole planet, slowly unlocks a sense of communion with all living beings. Each evening the group (a dozen at most), gathers for a liturgy where we 'break open' the experiences of the day and share a meal together.

After fourteen years of giving this type of retreat we have found it to be a powerful process for getting in touch with the roots of social sin: with the intolerance, sexism, racism that all of us carry in our hearts. In a Street Retreat there is no sense of 'getting away'. For many of us it can mean a radical shift in our world-view, and it may also change how we hear and respond to the Gospel; this in turn may lead to a change in lifestyle. What it most certainly will mean is that our relationship with God will be deeply affected by the 'cry of the poor' who are themselves so close to the heart of God.

In 1996, in response to the demand for more Street Retreats, Marnie and her colleagues opened a centre in the red light area of Sydney known as King's Cross.

Parish Ministries in Italy, Germany and Japan

> Parish pastoral work is one of the most marvellous means
> of carrying out [our] mission. In contacts with people of all
> ages and with various groups, you have the opportunity to
> talk about the faith and to form individuals in the spiritual
> life . . .[3]

In 1998 Erminia Oliva, rscJ from Italy, joined the National
Missionary Network which runs evangelising missions for parishes throughout Italy.

> We are divided into teams and stay for a couple of weeks in the
> same parish, living with any family that offers hospitality. Our
> aim is to provoke questions about the meaning of life and our
> need of the Saviour. Having delivered the message to every
> house, we prepare a variety of activities and meetings for
> different age groups: liturgies, devotions, Bible study and
> prayer groups. Since it is known that I used to teach, I am usually
> given responsibility for the younger ones or for study groups.
> I approach people with deep respect as I offer them the gift of
> 'living water', and I am always left with the impression that
> ordinary people have a great longing for God, but this can be
> disguised by a number of idols.
>
> This work has been my salvation. Having spent twenty-four
> years in school, I had become disillusioned, for although my
> students were cultivated and well read, they were seldom
> Christians. Eventually poor health culminated in a serious
> illness and a prolonged convalescence; when I tried to return
> to teaching in the state system again, I was turned down on
> account of my age. I was beginning to despair when I discovered
> the Evangelising Network. It is true that there is no possibility
> of establishing an ongoing relationship with those whom I
> initiate into a life of faith, but nevertheless I find my second
> career deeply satisfying and in line with our charism.

Angela Galletto, rscJ from Italy, had trained as a nurse; when she joined the Society, she spent many years in school and community infirmaries, until health problems necessitated a change. In 1986 she gained a teaching diploma and became a class mistress in the primary school in Genoa; two years later she went to Palermo where in addition to teaching she became a member of the pastoral team; in 1999 she was appointed Director of a nursery school.

My parish commitment involves the instruction of both adults and children; I also lead family groups in Bible study. For me this is a joyful experience of seeking together, rather than teaching, enabling me to be in touch with those who are far off, and yet are thirsting for God. I am warmly received as a messenger of the Word and know that in addition to welcoming all who come, it is my task to seek out all those who do not come forward to join the groups.

Today [in 1999], another important element in my life is that I feel at ease with the choices and direction taken both by the Province of Italy and the Society as a whole; I also feel in harmony with the Church, the Holy Father and the bishops. This frees me to welcome in joy and hope all that the future may bring.

Ilsemarie Weiffen, rscJ from Germany, writes:

Since 1980 I have been working as a pastoral adviser in a parish of about eight thousand Catholics in Munich, where there are three primary and two comprehensive schools. My tasks are manifold. I prepare children for First Communion and am responsible for their welfare; I supervise several clubs, visit sick and elderly members of the parish and for several years I acted as a youth leader. I also take an active part in the liturgies, preach regularly and preside over funerals and para-liturgies. Our world is secularised, but nevertheless I find a hunger for God among the people who yearn for a community in which they can feel secure.

In response to the needs of parishioners, I introduced

meditation groups and Bible study circles; for many regular churchgoers this study provided the first real encounter with the Scriptures. It is very rewarding when one of the participants says in astonishment, 'That Bible story is relevant to me!' I have had a similar experience with someone making a Retreat in Everyday Life, which parishioners are encouraged to make during Lent.

The parish has a special devotion to the Sacred Heart; this has been fostered by the Sacred Heart Fraternity, founded in the mid-nineteenth century. Since 1980, First Fridays have been celebrated with a Solemn Mass and a special homily. These begin in September, and culminate in June with the feast of the Sacred Heart; the homilies give an opportunity to explore biblical themes and to set the devotion in its historical context. Thus I find many opportunities to pass on our spirituality in parish life. It seems to me that now, as the twentieth century ends, is the time to make known our heritage. The millennium is being so commercialised and is encouraging such superstition and false prediction, that we who experience the love of God must do all in our power to make that love known.

Yabuki Keiko, rscJ of Japan, was a convert from Buddhism, who entered the novitiate of the coadjutrix sisters in 1952. She described these early days as

like being in a foreign country: the superior spoke to me in English which had to be translated, the refectory was all Western style. Until the fusion with the choir nuns took place in 1964,[4] my only chance of meeting the children was when I was cleaning the class rooms and the cloakrooms, but I listened to the stories about Jesus who was meek and humble of heart, and I was happy enough. After the fusion I was asked to work in the school office. At first I was alarmed, but I thought of Madeleine Sophie talking to the children from her wheelchair and, thinking of her love for them, I prayed that the fire of his love would be enkindled in their hearts while I worked in the office.

Some years later, Keiko was asked to help with cleaning and clerical work in the parish.

Once I had arrived I was asked to prepare children from the parish school for their First Communion. I said no, I was not a teacher and I couldn't do it; but the parish priest said 'This is not a place to teach theology, it is a place to teach how to live through your own way of life.' I had learned a good deal from the Heart of Jesus, and I thought that I should not try to escape this task. I agreed and soon began to realise the importance of prayer. I was sad when I discovered the gap that existed between the families and the Church. On Sundays there were team practices for the different sports which made it difficult for the children to come to church, and when they did come, what they heard had little connection with their everyday life. I thought that for me the most important thing was to make known the love of the Sacred Heart of Jesus and to pray for the children and their parents.

Hospital Chaplaincy in the USA

Elaine Abels, rscJ of Omaha, USA, began working in 1980 as staff chaplain at the Bergan Mercy Hospital; in 1985 she was appointed hospital chaplain.[5]

I worked mostly in oncology, and for me accompanying dying and sick patients has been a true gift. I have experienced this ministry as holy ground. All the years I have been working, I have had a weekly night call, which I have taken as my night adoration. Helping individuals at the time of illness to read or reread the events of their life, 'midwifing' them as they go through some transforming process of suffering, grief or death, has also been both privilege and blessing for me. In this work, the experience of being transformed through love and of being enabled to see with a new vision, has sustained and given meaning to my spiritual life, and has fired me with passion.

In 1997 I published a booklet on the use of a journal as a means of helping patients to get in touch with their inner spirit and healing resources. I was also involved in establishing a TV hospital spiritual channel that patients could tune into throughout the twenty-four hours. All this has been greatly rewarding work.

Prayer Groups in Ireland

Two rscj, Angela Delany and Mary Ethna McLoughlin, ran weekly prayer groups for sixth-formers, parents and friends of the Mount Anville Schools, in Dublin.[6] Most of the groups met at the beginning of the school day, enabling parents to attend after they had delivered their children. Relaxation, reflective prayer, sharing, preparation of Sunday liturgies, together with some specific input from an invited speaker, have made up the regular programmes. Once or twice a year a day of recollection was arranged while at the end of each term all the groups came together for a special eucharistic celebration.

Many members of the groups wrote of this ministry: as will be seen, extracts from some of the letters are full of appreciation. 'Our prayer meeting helps us to relax, meditate and bring the Word of God to our thoughts, to be mulled over, reflected on and much discussed,' wrote Mrs Elizabeth Roe; while Mrs Barbara Bodley declared that her whole prayer life had changed. 'Reading Scripture would have been very alien to me before becoming a member of the group. I now find this is a wonderful way of getting to know Jesus as a person through the Gospels. And for me, the psalms have opened up a whole new way of praying . . .'

Angela summarised the appreciation that she and Mary Ethna have received from the groups.

Serenity, tranquillity, understanding, love, learning, focus, deepening in spirit, friendship, hope, awareness, sharing,

197

communication, are all words that members have used to
describe the benefits they have experienced. Perhaps more
importantly, together we have learnt to live the words 'Be still
and know that I am God'.

Mission to Mainland China by rscJ Tsai Su-fang and Chang Man-ling from Taiwan

In 1987 martial law was lifted in China, enabling a handful of
rscJ to visit the mainland. Among them was Su-fang:

I found a strong spiritual hunger among the people. When I
returned to Taiwan the impoverished lives of my people remained
constantly in my mind and heart. They had no means of
developing as whole persons. They were seen merely as
labouring tools rather than as individuals; in their struggle for
survival they had lost all concept of gratitude or graciousness.
In 1995, after two years of planning and with the support of the
bishop, we managed to establish a foothold in the diocese of
Wuhan (about 600 km to the west of Shanghai), to which rscJ
come and go with sufficient continuity to become a factor in the
lives of the people.
  The ministry continues to grow and develop. In 1997 I spent
almost six months sharing Scripture and psychology with the
young sisters in the Wuhan diocese. There is a desperate need
for spiritual growth. There are some religious and priests in the
area, but they are now elderly, while the new group of young
religious have received little formation. In helping to satisfy
the spiritual hunger of these religious, my own faith has been
strengthened. I have received great joy from seeing the tightly
closed bud open and blossom, as each person receives the shared
faith. My vision for a mission for the Society is to respond more
and more to these people who for so long have been spiritually
deprived and totally lacking in freedom.

Chang Man-ling, also a member of the Taiwan area, compares the people of China to those of the primitive Church.

Catholics have gone through the Cultural Revolution and have been persecuted and deprived of education and worthwhile jobs. Neverthless I am aware, when I make short trips to mainland China, that their faith has remained alive and vibrant. We have a network of people in Taiwan who often link together to minister in China; another group meet regularly to share information about the mainland. In 1996 we began negotiations for a school that would offer general education and skill-training, focusing especially on the needs of women; this was established in China in 1998. I am particularly interested in ministering to Catholic young people who are attracted to religious life or the ministry. Working with a team, I give workshops on self-awareness, personal development and co-operation. We have to keep our work low key, because of the ever-present threat of being denied access, but like the early Christians we persist and make progress.

Contemplative Prayer

It cannot be overemphasised that ' . . . The spirit of this Society is essentially based upon prayer and interior life' (1815 Constitutions #5 V; 1982 Constitutions #17). Madeleine Sophie's understanding of the foundation on which the Society of the Sacred Heart is based is implicit in the life of every candidate, novice and rscJ. Two religious, Rosario Méndez and Tanabe Kin have allowed readers to share something of their life of prayer.

After she made her final profession in 1962, Rosario Méndez, a Spaniard, was missioned for Egypt and became a member of that Province. As she explained, she continued to live there, where despite her difficult circumstances, she was the Director of the

Collège du Sacré Coeur in Heliopolis, a post which she administered most ably and efficiently from her wheelchair.

On 24 April 1975, coming back by night from Wazlet Ghattas, a
small village on the edge of the desert, I did not see a badly
parked lorry and crashed into it. My three companions were
killed. I was severely injured and was taken to Barcelona. I
spent a year of rehabilitation there, learning to live within the
limits imposed by paraplegia. I can never thank my rscJ sisters
enough for what they were then for me and for what they
continue to be. I am sure that I owe to their prayer and love a
very special grace from God: the realisation that the accident
was only another way of 'losing one's life', one that I had never
previously thought much about. Before the accident I had served
God with great activity. Now I would move about less, but in one
way or another, I continue in union and conformity with Jesus.
I myself am amazed at my peace and inner serenity. Even the
memory of the three rscJ who died, sad though it is, does not
overwhelm me with anguish as it might have done. It seems to
me that my three sisters who were killed look on me with
forgiveness, and intercede for Egypt and its people.

I must also thank the people responsible for our province at
that time for allowing me to come back to Heliopolis. I adapted
myself very well, and the whole community assist me in
overcoming my limitations. The teachers and all the staff are
very helpful and thanks to the collaboration of everyone, the
school functions well.

I have experienced the living strength of the community in
their prayers for me, in the love and practical help I constantly
receive. I believe that community is essential as the place where
we live the experience of God together; in community we help
one another to respond to God's demands; it is a centre for
discernment, for the 'sending' and supporting of mission. Each
one must share her life of faith deeply and sincerely: the
community grows as its members share. I am convinced
therefore, that we must be attentive to all the activities we share

together – meetings, prayer, meals and times of relaxation, so that our interaction can create an atmosphere conducive to deep spiritual communication.

For me personally, the contemplative outlook is fundamental. By that I mean prolonged prayer, attending to new insights of the ongoing call, allowing the Spirit to bring about transformation in the depths of myself, and living all this in the joy of his presence in the simple details of life.

From 1987 to 1992, Tanabe Kin, rscJ of Japan, was a member of the international formation team, then went to assist with initial formation in the Philippines, until recalled to Japan to replace Nabeshimo Noriko rscJ who had unexpectedly died at the end of her first year as Novice Director. In 1999 Kin was living in a small community in a rundown area of Tokyo.

One day I was walking in a slum area and suddenly I realised that I was feeling happy that I did not belong to the people living there. It hit me as a shock, but I had to acknowledge the fact. Then I knew that Christ was with the people on the other side. I had to accept my own helplessness at being on the discriminating and exploiting side, making use of that same evil power that causes inhuman and unjust situations for so many people. I could not change myself immediately. What I could do was to become aware of the reality of social evil within and without and desire and ask to be changed, while trying to change my own way of life. I think that there and then my perspective began to shift; that means that I was no longer standing where I used to be. I knew, however, that in order to keep being transformed, so as to work for justice and peace in the world, I needed to live in touch with this reality of poverty and injustice – where and how I live became very important.

Since the mid-1990s my main ministry has been giving retreats, workshops and individual spiritual accompaniment. I have been struck by the reality of wounded humanity. God has given us the Good News through Jesus; when individuals are wounded and weak, and become aware of their weakness, they are ready to enter a right relationship with God, and God reigns in their hearts. God puts no conditions, no limit to love.

On several occasions I have been graced with a penetrating and transforming encounter with Christ, but as I grow older, God is inviting me to the prayer of silence and emptiness. No longer does word, idea or feeling help me to enter God's presence. I am passive: God does all. Although I feel nothing, I have a deep sense that I live in the moment of Christ's death-resurrection. In the depths of my being, God keeps me alive and impels me to go out and be with people, that they may become aware of God's gratuitous, unconditional, life-giving love. At the same time, I hear a new call, to live the mission as an rscJ in the world of the twenty-first century, a world which apparently has so much violence and chaos, where many people are forced to live deprived of human dignity. What does it really mean at this time to follow Christ, to witness to the love of the Heart of Christ in the educative mission? Each day this question grows stronger within me and I feel the need to listen to God, in contemplative prayer and honest discernment, standing firm on my own reality and the reality of the world.

Hermits in the Society

'Within this common vocation, each one receives her own unique call. We respond to it personally . . .' (1982 Constitutions #25).

During this period there were rscJ around the world who had heard a 'call within a call' to the eremitical life. Each case was unique; some were called for months or years, others could foresee no limit. Joan Scott, rscJ of the English/Welsh Province, has described her experience.

I think my increasing desire to go apart and be in solitude was genuine, although it may well have been connected to my particular situation. I became aware of it in the mid-seventies, at a time when it was virtually impossible to make a retreat in total solitude. This was a time when an obedience had taken me from the headship of the Grammar School at Fenham,[7] to become head of Woldingham,[8] a school with which I was not wholly in sympathy.

After due discernment, I was given permission to look for somewhere to live this solitude. I found a group of hermits living in an Alpine valley, in a remote region of the province of Autal, in France. About ten primitive dwellings were scattered across the hillside, about 3,000 feet above sea level. Every morning I had a fifteen-minute walk down to Mass which was celebrated in 'Le Centre', an old stone barn. This building contained chapel, library, store room, kitchen and one hermitage. There was no electricity; cooking and lighting were by calor gas and heating by wood-burning stoves. Water was piped down the mountain in hosepipes which froze in winter, and except at Le Centre, there were only outside taps. The original buildings were log huts, but the later ones were built of breeze-blocks; each contained a small chapel, furniture made from roughly fastened wooden planks and curtains made from sacking. Food was usually vegetarian; everyone collected supplies as needed from Le Centre for which they paid in kind. Some worked on the buildings, some gardened, others produced craft works for sale. Any other income came from charitable donations in money or goods. Something always seemed to turn up when it was needed.

The hermits made their own order of day and night and were expected to keep to this and to be accountable, but there was great freedom and no common pattern. Decisions were taken communally by those who had been there for more than twelve months and were thinking of permanence. The hermitage was not seen as a place for those who do not get on in community, nor for those wanting to sort themselves out, or to achieve a greater self-understanding. Nor was it for those who were seeking a 'higher or better' form of spiritual life. It was not even for getting to know God. It was seen as the PLACE OF UNKNOWING. If I learnt anything, it was that I do not know anything. After two years I returned to England; I wanted to get back to the province, and at that time I had concerns for my family.

On my return the idea came to me of establishing a place that would give others the opportunity for a period of solitude. By the time this proposal had been acccepted, and we had found both the property and the funds to acquire it, we were receiving many requests for directed retreats which confirmed our decision. Llannerchwen in South Wales, which we bought in 1979, was an isolated stone cottage, standing in eight acres of land, overlooking the Brecon hills. In the grounds there were two cedarwood bungalows and a chapel constructed from a converted shed.

What distinguishes Brecon from other retreat houses is the possibility for solitude and silence, although it took time for this to become known. Now [1999] Llanerchwen has acquired an international reputation and in addition to rscJ from our own Province and farther afield, has welcomed a Benedictine from Stanbrook, assistants from L'Arche and several lay people. There has always been a demand for varying lengths of time for the hermitages, to the point that it became necessary to undertake a modest extension.

Mary Catherine (Mickey) McKay, rscJ of the United States, was a General Councillor, based in Rome from 1970 to 1976. On her return to the States, she was appointed Novice Director of the American Province.

After my time in Rome, I needed to integrate what I had lived, so I went to Israel for six months of prayer and solitude. I found a cave in front of a monastery, but was refused permission to live in it, because it was considered unsafe. Finally I settled in a one-roomed shepherd's hut in the fields of Bethlehem, where I literally went out into the desert to pray. Each night I spent four hours praying by candlelight in what had really become my hermitage. I opened my door around 5 a.m. and prayed facing

the caves in the fields, where families were tending their fires
at the beginning of a new day.

On Christmas Eve I went to Manger Square in Bethlehem to
watch pilgrims arriving from all over the world. It was a scene
of striking contrasts, with thousands of pilgrims submitting to a
military body-search, before being allowed to enter the square.
Above us on top of the buildings were Israeli soldiers with their
sub-machine guns outlined by the setting sun, while below
hymns were being sung in every imaginable language to welcome
the Prince of Peace. With a young South African seminarian, I
went to the cave of the Nativity where we stayed until dawn,
praying for the courage to seek the unity and peace that
continues to elude us . . .

During the final decade of the twentieth century, Anne de
Stacpoole, rscJ of the Australian-New Zealand Province, became
aware of a new and demanding call to a contemplative life.

Our Lord was continuing to say, 'Come apart! I am the living
water. I am sufficient.' From the time I entered, my vocation
had always been strong; it had carried me through my
experience as a member of the founding community of
Uganda, it kept me faithful in illness and during the isolating
experience of serving in the Central Pacific. As this new call
persisted, I did consider transferring to the Trappistines, but
this seemed neither desirable nor practical. I was advised to stay
within the Society as a solitary. This is possible because our
structures are now [1998] flexible and there is no demand to
conform to a uniform pattern of living.

My search and discernment lasted for ten years. Finally,
overcoming my apprehension (based on the knowledge that I
am an extrovert), I arrived in Orewa, which is about an hour's
drive out of Auckland. There in the self-contained flat in the
retreat and holiday house owned by the province, I began a
'new' life in response to the call to solitude. The rhythm of
the hours of Office, meditation and reading provide the
framework of each day. In the two or three free hours that I

have outside formal prayer, I sew and mend for my neighbours. Everything is arranged to enhance prayer and provide the inner space for which God asks. I am aware that to give in to the temptation of seeking security, or to concentrate on becoming self-sufficient would invalidate the reason for living alone.

My life is neither a part-time occupation, nor a seasonal employment. The lifestyle has no community feedback and it imposes the necessity of fidelity to the 'NOW' of the present moment. Each day I try to deepen my prayer, practise interior silence more faithfully and be sufficiently docile to enter new levels of reality. I fail, of course, and constantly have to make the effort to begin again. But until the moment arrives when declining physical energy makes it necessary to accept the love and service of others, I hope that my fidelity to this 'vocation within a vocation' will contribute a beautiful and tuneful note to the orchestration of the Society, whose spirit is based on prayer and the interior life.

All these ministries had the single aim of spreading the knowledge of God's love throughout the world; this has already been said, but it is so fundamental that it can hardly be stated too often. Moreover it was understood as early as 1795 that lay women would play a vital role. 'What good is it to educate men and neglect their wives, when the building of a new social order will increasingly become a woman's work?' Father de Tournély wanted to know, at the time when the Society was no more than an ideal in his head. Much later, in 1852, Madeleine Sophie wrote a letter to all the children of the Sacred Heart in which she told them: 'It is for you, dear children, to continue, I might even say to complete, our own mission by devoting yourselves to the love of Jesus and to the salvation of those who do not know him.'

Recognition of the part that alumnae could play was given more formal recognition during the Generalate of Mother de Lescure (1946–1958) when the alumnae of Sacred Heart schools worldwide were beginning to form themselves into associations.

In 1959 the Association des Anciennes du Sacré Coeur (AMASC) was founded, and when in 1974 a new constitution was passed, it stated that one of the goals of AMASC members 'was to co-operate actively and effectively with the Society of the Sacred Heart in its various undertakings and options'.[9] Josephine Barcelon, who was appointed the first Web Site Editor of AMASC in 1999, generously agreed to describe the work of AMASC. Chapter 11 contains her account.

NOTES

1. Cf. Appendix I below.
2. Published by Collins Dove, Melbourne, Australia.
3. Extract from article in *Religious of the Sacred Heart* by Ilsemarie Weiffen rscJ, edited by Maria Guyonne du Penhoat (Strasbourg: Editions du Signe, 1999).
4. Ibid., Note 1.
5. In 1997 the Bergan Mercy Health System merged with the Immanuel Lutheran Medical Center to form the Alegent Health-Bergan Mercy Health Centre.
6. In 1999 a Secondary, Junior, Primary and Montessori school were educating about 1,400 pupils on the Mount Anville campus. Eight rscJ were directly involved in teaching or management of the schools; two communities were living on the site.
7. The property at Fenham was purchased in 1905 when a teachers' training school was established. At one time there was a primary school and two secondary schools on the campus. The college was closed in 1985; the diocese took over the comprehensive school in 1995 and the primary school in 1999.
8. During World War II Roehampton School was evacuated first to Cornwall and from 1940 to 1946 to Stanford Hall, in Leicestershire; in 1946 the school moved to Woldingham in Surrey. It continued to flourish, but by 1984 there were only ten rscJ on a staff of one hundred, and it was decided to hand the school over to lay management. RscJ continued to serve in the capacity of governors and trustees and it was agreed that the ideals of Sacred Heart education would be enshrined in the future policy of the school.
9. The five 'options' (internationality, education, solidarity with the poor and with the third world, renewal of community life), drawn up by the 1970 General Chapter, were not choices, but were the five areas of mission/endeavour to which members of the Society committed themselves.

❀

A Global Family: AMASC

by Josephine Barcelon

It is only from living soul to living soul that the living tradition can be handed down.

(Janet Stuart rscJ, *The Society of the Sacred Heart* [Roehampton, 1914])

We would like to be God's heartblood outpoured among the women of today's world. All of us together have a world to bring to birth; the whole of society to convert into a home for all; the multitude of human beings to transform into a family, a family of the heart, your Heart.

(Maria Teresa Porcile, Keynote Address to the AMASC General Assembly, San Luis Potosi, Mexico, 1998)

AMASC is the global association which unites Sacred Heart alumnae and alumni in nearly forty countries, in every continent. As stated in the new constitution of the Association (recognised under Belgian law), the aims of the association are:

a) to be at the service of humanity for the construction of a more just and cohesive society, with an increased awareness of its social responsibilities and in the name of a committed faith, lived in its twofold personal and community dimension;

b) to create and maintain friendship and solidarity among all the National Federations and Associations, so as to bring about true collaboration internationally;

c) to co-operate effectively with the Society of the Sacred Heart in its different tasks and options;

d) to be present in other International Organisations with a constant concern for discernment and open-mindedness.

Behind this (necessarily) formal declaration, AMASC is a vibrant organisation numbering many tens of thousands of members coming from an enormous diversity of cultural, social and linguistic backgrounds, and an equally varied range of life experiences. What unites us all is the common experience of having received a true 'education for life'. A hundred years after the foundation of the Society of the Sacred Heart, Janet Stuart, rscJ of Roehampton, summed up the aims of Sacred Heart education in these words: 'All the systems converge on this, to give personal worth to each child, worth of character, strength of principles, anchorage in faith.'

The most heartfelt testimonies to the fact that these aims have been fulfilled come from alumnae who have lived through some of the most tragic personal and social circumstances. Livia Szinna from Hungary, a survivor of the tumultuous postwar years in that country, writes:

It was only because of our education in the spirit of the Sacred Heart that we were able to endure the the difficulties and problems of a grievous life. Among hundreds of examples, I will mention just one: one of our alumnae, who had previously been very wealthy, had lost everything – chateau, land, buildings; her husband, a military officer, was a prisoner of war – [she was living] with three children and her mother and mother-in-law, and had to work as a bus conductor on a long route to support the family. Despite terrible working conditions, she performed this difficult work for nineteen years, always smiling and obliging, never losing her confidence and courage, because of the strength she had acquired from the spirit of the Sacred Heart.

While not all lives call for such heroism, all the regional and national associations of alumnae which constitute AMASC members are actively initiating and participating in work which builds and strengthens communities and promotes social justice. The list of areas of engagement provided by the current German National President, Hieronyma Speyart, is indicative of the commitments of alumnae everywhere: parish work, catechetics, church work, politics, organisations of Catholic women and of Catholic university graduates, social and humanitarian work in many fields. In the case of Germany, alumnae there also have a special commitment to provide support for the re-emerging societies of Eastern Europe.

In the richly diverse but often troubled continent of South America, many alumnae have dedicated themselves to social, humanitarian, educational and political involvement. Across the continent, alumnae work, often on a volunteer basis, to support or provide vital social services such as free or subsidised medical care and pharmaceuticals; visits to the sick or elderly; childcare centres and assistance to mothers; teaching of life and employment skills to underprivileged young people, and work with the mentally handicapped.

In countries such as Spain and Malta, where there is little public provision of care for the aged, alumnae have set up and provide support for retirement homes. In Japan, alumnae associations give practical and financial support to rscJ communities working to provide such necessities as food, education, medical care and social services in some of the most deprived areas of the Asian region.

This list of alumnae activities is far from exhaustive; but it is testimony to the fact that Sacred Heart alumnae live, every day and around the world, the goal of 'building community as a Christian value'. It is also important to stress that challenges which have been met and continue to be encountered by individuals and associations vary widely. This is not only because of the differing circumstances of various countries, but also because, since its inception almost forty years ago, AMASC has obviously not been immune to the social and political changes which have affected the whole worldwide community. One of the most important changes has been in the nature of Sacred eart educational institutions. Most are now under the administration of the laity; changes to government policy and the realities of funding restrictions or other such practical imperatives have necessitated the amalgamation of some schools and, sadly, the closure of many others. For many alumnae communities, the disappearance of their former school, or its re-emergence in a completely unfamiliar form, has represented the loss of a centre around which friendships, commitments and solidarities were based. The fact that the majority of associations have negotiated and overcome these painful transitions and often emerged as stronger and wiser organisations is yet another manifestation of the strength of Sacred Heart bonds!

Indeed, as this millennium draws to a close and a new one begins, there are many signs that AMASC and all its constituent associations are drawing a breath of fresh air and are ready to begin new commitments and embrace new opportunities.

One example of this is the initiative of the European associations to hold a 'grand celebration for the Bicentenary of the foundation of the Society of the Sacred Heart' in Brussels in October 2000. As Kathleen Dor, National President of Belgium and head of the organising committee, says: 'This is a marvellous opportunity to create a link between the past and the future, and like all birthdays, it will be an occasion where important things can be said in a festive and celebratory way.' An important focus of this event is the inspiration and animation of young people; for this reason a special youth forum is being organised for 16–18-year-olds from Sacred Heart schools all over Europe. On every other continent, much thought and effort is also being devoted to the young: the alumni and alumnae of tomorrow. The future of AMASC depends, as it always has done, on the 'succession of generations'.

The spirit of AMASC is also being refreshed by increased communication, helped by new technologies, particularly the Internet. When Trish Burns of Australia was elected World President of AMASC at San Luis Potosi in Mexico in April 1998, she named the fostering of communication as one of the important

objectives of her Presidency. To this end, she initiated the establishment of a Web Site for AMASC which is published in three
languages: English, French and Spanish (Htpp://www.amasc-
sacrecoeur.org). The Web Site was set up in 1998 and by the
following year had received over six thousand 'visits'. As many
individuals and associations are still not connected to the
Internet, this is an extraordinary level of support, and as the contents of the site are also distributed in printed form to the
national associations, there is no doubt that it is reaching
increasing numbers. Because the Internet is designed to be
'interactive', the site has also allowed members to exchange
messages, renew friendships and make new ones, make comments on the contents, submit material and draw attention to
particular areas of interest or concern in various countries and
regions. It has also enabled AMASC to take action on certain
issues on a global basis, such as supporting the 'Jubilee 2000'
initiative to petition governments to cancel the debt of the
world's poorest nations, at the request of the Superior General
of the Society, Patricia García de Quevedo rscJ. The site has also
made it possible for AMASC to propagate information and attract
stronger commitment to the other international associations to
which it is affiliated, such as WUCWO (World Union of Catholic
Women's Organisations) and OMAEC (World Organisation of
Former Pupils of Catholic Schools).

Above all, the site has enabled AMASC to strengthen the ties
which bind all members in a true global family. News from
various asociations banishes any sense of isolation, as people
realise their common aims and concerns. Intimate communication is possible in a way which diminishes difference and
distance. And judging from comments in the guest book of the
site, it is also attracting the very technically conscious young,
which is an extremely healthy development.

The existence of the Web Site has also facilitated the other
objective which Trish Burns has nominated for her Presidency:
reconciliation. Reconciliation had become a tradition even
before AMASC officially existed, and it is to be the theme for a

detailed study process which will culminate in the next AMASC World Congress to be held in Sydney in 2002. Its roots lie in the documents of the 1994 General Chapter of the Society of the Sacred Heart which urge us to 'nurture life by educating to reconciliation'.

A detailed Study Plan has been prepared by Alex Fernon, alumna of Kincoppal-Rose Bay School of the Sacred Heart, in Sydney. In detailed stages covering several years, the plan explores ideas of reconciliation with self, with God, with family, community, country and the world. The final stage includes the preparation and completion of an action-based project which aims to carry the process of reconciliation from each study group into the wider community. The plan has also been carefully formulated to accommodate differences of language, culture, social or national situation. To date, it has been most enthusiastically received by all the participating countries, and serious work and study is now being undertaken by different constituencies around the world.

With strengthening ties between individuals, nations and generations, AMASC realises that its unique international community has much to offer to a 'globalised' world, and is preparing to meet the challenges of the Third Millennium.

One of the primary initiatives is to establish AMASC officially as a Non-Governmental Organisation (NGO). In a new world order where national boundaries and long-held ideas of sovereignty are fast disappearing, NGOs are rapidly becoming the 'third force' to counter transnational economic and political imperatives, most of which have profit or power as objectives rather than human, social or cultural values. In this initiative, AMASC seeks actively to support the goals and endeavours of the Society of the Sacred Heart.

The preliminary document for the Congress of Latin American Alumnae of the Sacred Heart, to be held in Buenos Aires, Argentina, in May 2000, makes this aim explicit. Speaking of a 'post-millennial objective', this document states the importance of:

creating spaces for both action and recognition. The Alumnae associations will have as one of their objectives and within the ambit of permanent formation, the possibility of constructing a critical view of our communities, to be informed analysts of realities, in order to produce documentation of a trustworthy nature which will be of sufficient weight to be taken into account in the decisions of our governments.

This work will not attempt to consist solely of academic contributions or be of a simply fraternal nature, but instead be relevant and instigate new ideas and action. (*Educate for Peace*, Preliminary proceedings of the 5th Latin American Congress of Alumnae)

Because this document, and the forthcoming conference, are specifically oriented towards the progress of AMASC to NGO status, it most impressively addresses ideas of diversity and diverse solutions to problems. This is not the same thing as relativism; it anticipates and aims to address, intelligently and sensitively, the limitations which have hampered many NGOs to date and prevented them from reaching their full potential, particularly a focus on single issues, or narrow points of view. The document continues:

To be an NGO in partnership with the Society of the Sacred Heart, is to assume that we are prepared to confront these problems [of globalisation . . . hunger, loss of rights, etc.] and also to face the fact that the complexity of the world rules out a single solution. It is necessary to search for different solutions for distinct realities. Let us create these, certainly. We are capable of generating different perspectives which will allow us to make valuable contributions in different places.

To work for common goals in a multitude of situations and realities: this is AMASC's challenge for today, and towards tomorrow.

214

A Personal Note and Acknowledgements

Frances Makower rscJ described this book to me as a kind of 'snapshot', of where we are here and now. But the nature of a snapshot depends on who is holding the camera! As I was researching this chapter I became aware that AMASC and I are about as old as each other and so I cannot claim any perspective or experience. I therefore apologise to all of those whose pictures of this organisation must surely be fuller and more mellow than mine, especially Maria Franca Migone, AMASC Archivist, who has given so much assistance. I have been simply privileged to be appointed AMASC's first Web Site Editor, and I thank our world President, Trish Burns, for this extaordinary experience which has changed my life. I am also grateful for what the experience has done for my teenage daughter, Antonia, who is our Site's 'Webmaster', and is currently in her penultimate year at Kincoppal-Rose Bay School of the Sacred Heart in Sydney, and who, against her better instincts, has described what we are doing as 'cool'. From a teenager, there can be no higher praise! My gratitude to so many people who sent material for this chapter, and apologies to so many whose contributions I couldn't accommodate for lack of space. Thanks also to Maryanne Pidcock, Secretary General of AMASC, for redefining the meaning of solidarity; and thanks to Dominique Archambeaud who has taught me more about the AMASC spirit than she will ever know, and whose definition of our spirit (delivered in a speech to the World Congress of Lassalien Alumni in Rome, May 1999) is closest to our hearts:

> We have a spirit of family, of extended families, where there is always a warm welcome, a place at the table for whoever arrives, and help for those who are in need.

CHAPTER 12

Ongoing Renewal

*We must not be blind to the fact that in these times of activity . . .
demands are made on us and obstacles rise so that modifications become
indispensable.*

> (Written by Madeleine Sophie in preparation for the
> 1864 General Council)

*The superior general, with the help of her council, has the responsibility
[among others] to keep the Society alert to the calls of the world and the
Church.* (1982 Constitutions #168)

*Creative collaboration with others is essential in our educational work
as well as in our efforts towards reconciliation.*

> (1994 General Chapter)

Throughout her life Madeleine Sophie was a pioneer; the
education that she received from Louis, her brother, was
many years ahead of the times for girls. She, no less than Philippine, took a leap into the unknown when she agreed to send
her across the Atlantic in 1818, while her insistence that in
foreign lands religious were 'to study the customs of the country
and follow them'[1] foreshadowed the spirit of inculturation which
was to be one of the key issues in the 1988 General Chapter.
Thus she accepted and often promoted change. The Plan of
Studies, the blueprint of Sacred Heart education, was updated
on five occasions in her lifetime, and when travel by rail became
a feasible option, she stepped into a train as readily as she
might have boarded a plane had she been living in the twentieth

century. There is, therefore, every reason to suppose that she would have embraced and encouraged the changes resulting from the renewal that was taking place in the decades preceding the millennium.

At the conclusion of the 1970 General Chapter Concepción Camacho, the Superior General of the time, predicted that 'Our pluriformity will become more marked, [but] . . . far from separating us, our unity in Christ will be strengthened and enriched.' To no small degree this final chapter reflects the pluriformity of the Society at the time of the bicentenary. Unlike the previous chapters it lacks an overall theme; it portrays many diverse apostolates which had developed in response to the current needs and were the means by which rscJ were then making known the love of God.

Changes in Community Lifestyle

At the end of the twentieth century the degree of community openness varied from province to province, but all adhered to the general principle of accessibility so clearly set out in the 1982 Constitutions #34: 'Openness, welcome and sharing with others will make the community a sign of communion.' One example of this style of living was contributed by the community of Taipei.

Yes, [they wrote,] we have, of course been attempting to live up to what we have agreed in our 1982 Constitutions and in so many of our Chapter documents, but we know that we frequently fail. We were therefore pleased and surprised when Mrs Jane O'Shaugnessy ascJ (Associate), from Boston, USA, who had been with us for six weeks, declared that she had been inspired by her experience. She said that the community was 'a place of sharing and open-hearted welcome, where everyone felt at home. The most striking impression I have', she concluded, 'is of a group of women who are truly living in relationship.'
Our living quarters have been likened to a railway station!

217

Retreatants, guests, friends and rscJ meet for our 7 a.m. liturgy and many others come and go throughout the day to share a meal and to keep in touch. The open atmosphere of exchange and affection is tangible. Chinese, English, Spanish and Japanese become a single language of love. At the end of the day a shared reflection on the Word of God brings together all the rscJ. 'This coming together', Jane observed, 'seems to support the bond of relationship which begins and ends in the Heart of Christ.'

While we, as community, are uncomfortably aware how often we fail, nevertheless in the words of the 1994 General Chapter, 'hope impels us to try to make of our world a great banquet, an open table where both bread and word are shared, where Christ wipes away the tears of so much oppression, injustice, violence, division'. In this hope and by continuing to 'give our lives as women of compassion and communion', we desire to live to the end of our days.

There are, of course, various methods of organising open communities; while many, like that of Taipei, have welcomed visitors to stay, others have invited young people, men and women, to join a group of rscJ and form a mixed community. Formed in 1998, Barat House was one such group. There, six students and three rscJ were living in the former convent building on the Digby Stuart College campus, in Roehampton, London. The students had made a commitment to join the community for one year, which could be extended provided there was available space. Bernadette Porter rscJ, the Principal of the College in 1998, had initiated this project as she was aware that several students had expressed a desire to live in a Christian community. The benefit of establishing a visible Christian presence on the campus was understood and welcomed by members of the Province. By 1999 this community was still at an experimental stage, but by then more students wanted to be members than space allowed, and a waiting list had to be drawn up. A glance through the catalogue for 1998–99 revealed that a few lay women and some non-rscJ religious had become members of Society communities. There were also some communities that were intercongregational, as were La Roseraie in Lyons, Centre de la Roseraie in Poitiers, and Weert in the Netherlands; in these communities different groups of religious were sharing facilities and buildings.

Françoise Cassiers, rscJ of Belgium, wrote of an interesting experiment authorised by Miriam Fabri rscJ, a former Provincial of Belgium and Pascal Marie Vandoorne LSU, a former Provincial of La Sainte Union Sisters.

Between 1997 and 1999 our small intercongregational community has made some progress towards furthering European unity, but sadly, although our two provincials have sanctioned this experiment, neither has been able to free more than one religious from each province to carry it forward. Rose-Anne Roussel LSU and I alone made up our community, but we did have the advantage of sharing in similar work: both of us were involved in ministries with refugees and asylum-seekers. As I was also the bishop's delegate for religious, I was in touch with a large number of different congregations. These contacts led to the formation of a group of religious brought together by their common desire to create a more open Europe, where questions of justice would be treated as Gospel imperatives. In this group there were men and women from about twelve different congregations; we met periodically to exchange information, discuss different projects and share our hopes for future developments. Through these meetings we have discovered that many communities are already 'European', either in membership, or in their provincial organisation. The Dominicans have cultural and theological initiatives under way; the Jesuits run both a Catholic European Centre where Rose-Anne and I live and two schools for the children of EEC officials. The sisters of Charity and the Company of Mary have established communities in areas where large numbers of immigrants have settled.

Another advantage of my intercongregational life with Rose-Anne was the similarity of our Constitutions and the historical development of our congregations, both of which were founded at about the same time and for the same type of work. This has facilitated both our life of prayer and our way of living community.

So the benefits of this experiment were never in question; what was more doubtful was the availability of the religious needed to ensure its future. To be uprooted from one's own country is neither easy nor possible for everyone. The question of communication cannot be ignored; we know of one community that has had to abandon its European project for lack of a common language. There are also practical considerations: employment for those below pensionable age can be a problem, while older sisters may lack sufficient stamina. Yet in spite of all the problems, it seems to me that the risk must be taken. Are there any rscJ among us who feel called? Are there any from other congregations? For my part I am grateful for this experience, although I still feel that it has a long way to go.

Living and Working with Organisations outside the Society

Some members of the Society have linked with other organis-ations for a limited period or on a semi-permanent basis. The ministries of Lolín Menéndez rscJ and Denise Calder rscJ with the Jesuit Refugee Service have already been recounted in Chapter 4; Rebecca Loukae rscJ, a Young Professed sister from Uganda, worked in a L'Arche Community in Kampala, Uganda, and described her experience there.

This was a time of giving and receiving, a time of learning a new

way of life. I greatly appreciated the prayer of the community.
We were members of different faiths and churches: Roman
Catholic, Church of Uganda, Seventh Day Adventist and
Muslim; I was clearly aware of the unity in diversity among us.
When a Catholic priest came, we all attended Mass; when the
Protestant pastor came, all without exception attended the
service. Experiencing that Christ is for all, and that he loves us
all as we are, helped me to put aside prejudice. In prayer I have
learned that our God is a God who listens. This was underlined
during prayer in the chapel each evening. The children could
say little more than 'Jesus thank you' or 'Jesus take care of all
who help us'. These disabled youngsters made me look back at
the struggles I had been having with shared prayer in the
community; they helped me to understand that the Lord listens
whether a prayer is short or long. 'I have come that they may
have life and have it to the full' [John 10:10]. For me this text
is revealed in the lives of the people of L'Arche.

I observed that the children were kind and loving. They smiled
so naturally that I would find myself encouraged, however
disheartened I was feeling. They were free in their dealings with
people, whatever their status; this also encouraged me, for
there are times when I become fearful of people. Most had the
ability to tackle such simple tasks as painting, drawing, numbers
and English. At first I was convinced that with me they would
make great progress, but I had to be very patient; writing and
counting, even one to ten, presented genuine problems. When
I left after three months my group had managed to master one
to five!

I chose to live with the children, which helped me to
understand them, both in and out of the class room. I came
to know them as warm and conscientious individuals. They cared
for the community's livestock: rabbits, cows and poultry; they
also made candles and these responsibilities were helping them
to gain self-reliance.

I have learnt so much from the few months that I spent in
L'Arche community, especially the need to change negative

attitudes towards mentally retarded children, who have so much to contribute. The children of L'Arche have led me to question how we, who are also disabled in some way, can learn from them to embrace our disabilities so that we may use them for the glory of God.

Supporting Lay Initiatives

Increasingly as the bicentenary approached, rscJ in different parts of the world were responding to the initiatives of lay people. The Society's first priority has always been to support its members and its ministries worldwide. The 1982 Constitutions also invite rscJ to live in solidarity with those who lack the necessities of life and so in different parts of the world they were increasingly responding to initiatives and requests from lay people, groups and organisations. For this reason in 1978 the Solidarity Fund was created at the central level. The interest from the fund was used to support local projects known to rscJ. In 1996 the fund was renamed the Solidarity-Justice-Peace-Fund, a name which gave a clearer indication of rscJ commitment to solidarity with the marginalised and their work for justice and peace.[2]

Each year the communities were invited to put forward requests for the financial support of projects which responded to the criteria and guidelines laid down by previous General Chapters. In general these would be concerned either with groups who had been marginalised by society, especially projects working with children, young people, women and migrants, or with those that aimed to educate people, thus enabling them to take charge of their own lives and assume greater independence. Support might also be given to projects addressing the causes of injustice and violence and those furthering justice and peace. RscJ and the country concerned were committed to the groups that received assistance, but this was not given to Society works.

These requests were studied by the Mother House community

or by the International Finance Commission together with the General Treasurer; the final decision was made or endorsed by the General Council. Often the requests exceeded the sum that was available in the fund.

In a similar spirit of sharing resources, some provinces find themselves able to support local initiatives. In Canada, for example, in the early nineties, Anne-Marie Conn rscJ was working as a volunteer in a soup kitchen in Ottawa, where she came to know Hélène Dahl. Hélène, a married woman with children, had long nourished a dream to create a centre for carers, where they could meet, find mutual support and be helped to care for themselves. Anne-Marie became convinced both of the need for such a centre and of the viability of Hélène's plan for fulfilling it. In 1994 she asked her Province if there was any way in which this scheme could be supported. It so happened that her request coincided with a time when some property had become re-dundant for the Province; following due reflection Sally Mahar rscJ, the then Provincial, made the decision to invest some of the proceeds from the sale and use the income to provide seed money for Hélène Dahl's project. So the Canadian Province became involved with Tapestry House which by then had gained the support of more than fifty potential clients.

This project opened in 1996 in a spacious four-floored building which was a gift from the congregation of St Anne of Dorval; both the Society and the St Anne Sisters were represented on the Board of Directors. Since the begining, co-operation with the Canadian Province has remained close: Mary Finlayson rscJ worked on the staff as a volunteer from 1996 to 1997. Operating on a 'pay as you can' system social workers, mothers of large families and single parents, as well as women who were sole carers for spouse, parent or child in their own home, have all benefited from Tapestry House. The programmes offered included stress management, massage, health education and a weekend retreat. Anne-Marie Conn, the Provincial in 1999, wel-comed the opportunity to be involved with a creative project enabling women to care for themselves while caring for others.[3]

In Chad the idea of setting up bush schools came from mothers of families who were determined that, unlike themselves, their children should be literate. Their search for educators had led them to Carmen Rosales rscJ, who, as described in Chapter 2, became involved in training teachers for these schools.

The Use of Technology

The Province of the United States was the first to adapt to the advances in Information Technology; resource teams were set up to ensure that every community had both a computer and the skills to make use of it. By the last decade of the twentieth century virtually all rscJ in the States could be reached by e-mail, while in the rest of the Society the number of rscJ that were on-line was steadily increasing.

'We cannot ignore this medium,' commented Catherine (Kit) Collins rscJ, the Director of the Center for Educational Design and Communication (CEDC).[4]

This is a medium which allows us to be international, to participate, to communicate and even to share in the redemption of our world . . . I believe the building of relationships is central to our charism, it is of our very vocation. 'The net' offers a means of strengthening community and bringing new opportunities for relationship. It provides a medium for connecting, relating, interacting and exchanging. Until now, our mode of communication has been from one to many; now as the millennium approaches, technology allows us to communicate many to many.

The Network of Sacred Heart Schools in the United States has played a vital role in the Society's mission; it owed much to the Net, but was set up in 1972, and was already a valued organisation many years before the Net was embraced by the Province. This Schools Network came into being as a response to the many

American rscJ who were seeking their ministries outside the Society's schools and colleges. Between 1968 and 1972 ten schools were closed, the six Sacred Heart Colleges changed dramatically and an increasing number of lay staff were employed. The five provincials[5] agreed to collaborate on all educational matters and in 1972 appointed a Co-ordinator for the Network of Schools.

Three years later, in 1975, the Goals and Criteria were drawn up embodying 'the values, the intentions and the hopes of the Sacred Heart tradition, sharpened to meet the needs of a rapidly changing world . . .' These Goals and Criteria, updated in 1990, commit the nineteen Sacred Heart schools of the United States to educate to a personal and active faith in God, to a deep respect for intellectual values, to a social awareness that impels to action and to personal growth in an atmosphere of wide freedom. This statement was something more than a pious aspiration. The Network Commission on Goals provides for ongoing evaluation of each of the schools according to the stated criteria.

The strength conferred by the Network has been well illustrated by Susan Maxwell rscJ, who in 1974, at the age of thirtyfour, was appointed headmistress of the Academy of the Sacred Heart, Bloomfield Hills. She described how no fewer than eleven rscJ turned down her invitation to join her staff.

It came to me, without resentment and with a sense of grace,
that we would build this school with our wonderful lay colleagues.
I was grateful for the Goals and Criteria. They were the
expression of our charism which I believed would link us, lay
and religious, to a much bigger vision of life and education.

In 1984 Susan gave up the headship of Bloomfield Hills, Massachusetts, to become Executive Director of the Network, a position she held until 1995. Her observations on the working of the Network exemplify the value of this development.

As I saw Board members, administrators, faculty, staff and
students come to life in regional and national gatherings, I saw

the life of our charism being communicated and lived out. Then, as time went on, I became aware of an increasing desire for a deeper and broader spiritual formation. This was clearly indicated in 1990 when we were revising the Goals and Criteria. From across the country came changes in wording expressing an important shift towards the adults in each Sacred Heart school community; the adults were living and modelling the values of the Goals, rather than simply expecting the students to do so. In the light of this call to adult formation, it is clear that Madeleine Sophie's legacy to us is one of a healthy, large view of God, God who is love. As we approach the twenty-first century, I believe that we rscJ are called to play an even stronger role in partnership with our lay colleagues in the area of serious spiritual formation. We need to have more faith in the gifts we have for all those who are searching for meaning at this time.

Communicating by means of 'the net' soon spread to Provinces beyond the United States; it became a valuable tool by which to spread the experience and expertise in Popular Education, a project that was gradually being developed in the Provinces of Latin America, most notably in Mexico. As a result of the inter-action made possible by the net, these provinces have been able to exchange views, conduct a common search, prepare for meetings and finally draw up a document on some of the basic elements of Popular Education in Latin America. The first meeting was held in Colombia in 1984; this was followed by Peru in 1986; three years later delegates involved in Popular Education met in Venezuela, then in Chile and in Mexico in 1996. In 1998 delegates travelled beyond Latin America to Spain. Describing this meeting, Socorro Martínez rscJ said, 'Something new was being born and was beginning to take root. We could feel it, touch it . . .' So the internet provided the means to publish insights and new developments in Popular Education among all the Provinces of Latin America.

However, networking has not been confined to Popular Edu-cation. The net has provided a tool whereby the Society has taken full responsibility for formal education and has been able to share it with the laity. In Mexico, for example, informal networking began in 1991 with students from all the colleges meeting for sports and cultural events. The vision was widened four years later when Mexico played host to a Workshop on Formal Education which was attended by religious and lay staff from the Provinces of South America and the United States. There a decision was taken to work on a new edition of 'The Plan of Studies'. A working document was drawn up in 1998 at a second workshop held at Lima. The aim was to produce a book entitled *The Spirit of Education in the Sacred Heart* which could be presented to the Society as a bicentenary gift.

Many rscJ were inspired by the possibilities that were opening up as a result of technological advance; Catherine (Kit) Collins rscJ was among the first to understand the potential offered by the net as a tool for mission. She has described her ministry at the Center for Educational Design and Communication.

The work of the Center for Design and Communication

CEDC was founded in the recognition that education is not bounded by classrooms, that communication is a matter of relationship and communion, and that the call to work for social justice is integral to our faith.

At CEDC we are in the active ministry of putting communication at the service of social justice – of doing what we do from a profoundly educative perspective. We are in partnership with under-resourced groups that are working for social change – people of passion and commitment, who share something of our vision. They press for educational transformation as integral to systematic change, and they use the media as an agent of liberation that gives voice, visibility and power to those who have been denied the means to communicate. We approach our project partnerships with the

227

belief that 'media' is not about products, but about the thoughtful creation of effective and caring relationships. We try to reflect in all that we do the deepest meaning of our oft-repeated phrase, 'Social Justice: It Happens By Design'. Through our work we have been in contact with countless groups and individuals; we cannot possibly list all that we do, but we can attempt to give the flavour of our ministry.

We are involved in a whole clutch of projects which touch the lives of people who are victims of economic injustice, poor women, homeless people and those working against incredible odds to challenge the prevailing system. We have concrete commitments to those dispossessed, denied their rights, forced to leave their home and country. We are constantly working on projects with groups striving for better information and for educational transformation. They are using electronic communications to build active relationships among communities which have united against the tyranny of local and global control and exploitation.

CEDC has also been involved with grass-root women's groups struggling to overcome the oppression of women. Working in partnership with them, we have produced materials for the women's groups which were attempting to shape the agenda of the United Nations' 'Conference on Women' in Beijing in 1995. We have also provided material to facilitate a six-point Women's Action Agenda to effect and concretise the outcomes of the Beijing Conference.

We have developed electronic communication to support groups seeking to confront and reverse the impact of the Bretton Woods Conference on the poorest countries of the world and those actively working against the Structural Adjustment Programmes of the World Bank and the IMF. In 1999 the effect of these efforts were just beginning to emerge.

We have also become actively involved in such local schemes as a pilot project embracing four community-based organisations in low-income areas of Washington, DC. We also support Networked Learning Centers together with an out-of-school programme for 6–13-year-old children in the neighbourhood; for the most part these are children who have been assigned to the worst city schools. Currently (in 1999) we are collaborating in the development of an inquiry-based project-learning curriculum, and we are also developing a professional staff programme for young teachers who lack training and support.

Another important area of our mission is that of designing and implementing web sites to create on-line communities for those promoting social change through solidarity and joint action. We have, for example, created a web site for the social justice community (www.justicenet.org) and another web site for the Washington DC Housing Network (www.justicenet.org/headinghome). These web sites provide information, discussion forums, and a visible 'Action Alert' on immediate local and world crises such as the 1999 tragic situation in East Timor. The site also provides e-mail links to all members of US Government at state and national levels, to national and local media and to the United Nations.

We also produce videos; *One Child at a Time* depicts an inspirational after-school programme for children in the West Grove, one of South Miami's poorest areas. Its aim was to inform parents of the project and to educate the broader public about the problems of these children; we also hoped that the video might be a means of gaining financial support.

These projects have been undertaken alongside our ongoing commitment to support our own Province and indeed the whole Society. To this end we have produced several publications, many in several languages, and assisted in the production of a video of the 1994 General Chapter. For our own Province we have set up a Web Site (www.rscj.org) and ensured that all communities had Internet access and the use of e-mail.

Although the development of Information Technology (IT) has a potential for serious harm, especially in the matters of globalisation or the transference of huge untaxed sums around the globe, it has become clear that technology is a tool, neutral in itself, which takes on the value and power of the user's hand and intent. We believe that we, as a Society of educators committed to solidarity with the poor, cannot be merely observers and bystanders. We are impelled to make a genuine effort to harness the potential of IT in the service of the world community, of social justice and the marginalised. Unless people of faith and commitment become engaged in this revolutionary means of communication, it will take an unimaginable toll, creating ever greater margins of poverty across the globe. That is why, modest though our efforts are, we work to transform the use of this technology to the service of good. Our greatest privilege and blessing is that we work with and offer hospitality to so many people, who by the vitality of their faith and their compassionate energy, penetrate the darkness, and plant hope squarely in the midst of despair and injustice. To be in partnership with such persons is a precious gift for which we are always grateful.

*Associate Members (Asc*J*) and Volunteers*

At the General Chapter of 1994, the capitulants declared, 'We have the deep conviction that our spirituality does not belong to us alone. It is a gift to be shared, a treasure others help us to discover.' In keeping with this conviction was the recommendation that the movement for Associate Members be encouraged. In 1999 Associate groups had been flourishing in some Provinces for several years; in others they were in the process of forming. Just as there was pluriformity among rscJ, so there was among the community groupings of associates, for a deliberate effort had been made to respond to the desires of the would-be Associates, rather than to impose a central blueprint.

The individuals concerned were united by the common desire to renew and deepen their baptismal vows by living the spirituality of the Society. All made a commitment to this effect by an act of consecration, which followed a period of initiation. The practicalities of how this was to be fulfilled were left to each group under the guidance of an accompanying rscJ.

Thus by 1999, the situation regarding Associates varied from place to place; in Puerto Rico, for example, there were thirty or more Associates in six separate community groupings. In England and Malta, on the other hand, the development was more recent and their formation was still in process. Young and old, married or single, former students, friends and colleagues were drawn to these groups. Their driving force seemed to be a desire to strengthen their active faith and to become formally linked to the Society. For most Associate members their style of life continue unchanged, but there were exceptions. In Austria, for example, Biane Schribl ascJ, a trained nurse, was living in community with two rscJ and worked virtually full-time in the convent infirmary, caring for the elderly sisters. Marianne Keevins, ascJ from Boston, USA, was similarly involved in a ministry with the Society. Marianne, supported by the Boston Associates and the United States Province, was responsible for establishing the Barat Spirituality Centre on Cape Cod.

Several Associates from Austria, Malta, Puerto Rico and Spain have generously contributed information; without exception they expressed appreciation for the support they were receiving from each other and from the Society. Carmen B. Trigo de Villeto ascJ, a Puerto Rican grandmother, wrote of 'a community of faith, of solidarity in joy and sadness, of serene dialogues in all circumstances, even in crisis'. Another said, 'I receive a great deal of spiritual support which has sustained me through the loneliness of being a widow and the trials of living with my youngest son, who is an alcoholic.' Finally Josefina Franca de Quirch, also from Puerto Rico, explained that

being an ascJ has made me realise that we have to walk together as a community; we have to strive for compassion and try to know and love Jesus. It is not really a change in our lives, more

231

like a step forward, like continually walking towards an intimacy with Jesus and towards discovering day by day his will in our life.

Marie Miller, an Englishwoman who has a strong link with the Society, having spent several years in initial formation, is one of the group who are in the process of becoming Associates. She has kindly described what the spirituality of the Society has meant to her life.

Knowing 'how' but not 'where' I should be led, I left school in 1958, full of hope and expectation, clasping a bag of 'jewels': Gerard Manley Hopkins, Teilhard de Chardin and Thomas Merton.

The Sacred Heart College of Fenham, in the North of England, provided a revisioning of my earlier Marian view into the more acceptable image of a simple girl 'waiting', in preparation, to reveal her great inner secret. At last I felt more comfortable with such a model: Mater Admirabilis. More significantly I sensed an enlightenment on my arrival at a place where I felt I could share my treasures. Firstly I was aware of Christ's welcome, in his 'Come to me ... all who labour ...' I found an inclusiveness which opened up possibilities of a space for everyone in the heart of God. Secondly I found myself on the threshold of a charism which was both 'hic et nunc' as well as something for which I would have to wait. Gradually I built into my life the reality of that hopeful phrase, 'It will come', and in the waiting began to learn what paradox can offer. However, it was not until 1967 that I took my next steps on the way, thanks to the generosity and understanding of a loyal friend.

The desire to serve through a community of like-minded people (rscJ), was eventually embraced in 1971 when I had become a mature teacher. I was encouraged particularly by the sacrifice of Janet Stuart rscJ and her spirit of adventure. Four wonderful years within the charism of the Society gave me a unique opportunity to experience further spiritual formation. I witnessed how this 'little Society' was in the van when it came to embracing Vatican II, and I also observed the courage and pain that accompanied those years of transition. The letting go in love is what I keep with me, as well as the discernment of seeking what is valuable enough to treasure. Then I was presented with another paradox while I was on my way to Joigny and was preparing to start a new job as warden at Digby Stuart College.

The amazing years in a vibrant college followed and led to my awareness of the riches of Taizé, the need for reconciliation and healing in the world. I discovered L'Arche and was caught up in the desire to push back more boundaries and cross further bridges. So, taking the charism of the Sacred Heart with me, my heart found its new home in Little Ewell, in Kent, the first of the L'Arche communities in England. Finding the image of God's open heart is rarely a problem for vulnerable people, but for the powerful it is often more difficult. Witnessing closed minds leads me to ponder Christ's challenge to 'Love your enemies', and here lies another paradox.

Now, in 1999, I am driven by the ecumenical and inter-faith demands of Vatican II, which I believe presents us with an imperative to overcome the divisiveness of this violent world. Rather than striving for human unity, perhaps we will only be led to peace through the global harmony of thought and action. I have never found academia a comfortable bed on which to lie. Personal experience, however, always displays within the centre of all faith, all spirituality, all wisdom, a small space of peace reflected in the universal love of an Ultimate Being.

Thus the charism which touched me at Fenham has remained throughout life's pilgrimage; at no time has it been incompatible with the watering places on my journey. Often I have opened up my bag of jewels to add others; recently Bede Griffiths, Capra, O'Murchu, O'Donohue. I see more clearly the link between 'hic et nunc', the Sacrament of the Present Moment, the Mindfulness of Buddhism, the OM of Hinduism in the deep unconditional love of the Heart of God. All of these treasures are found both within the 'cave' of each human heart, and in the universe. For me now, all paradox has become challenge, as with two sides of one coin, interconnected in the non-duality of the wholeness of existence. Furthermore, I acknowledge the setting of those jewels as the link, the circle, the ring of the all-embracing love of God manifested for us, who are his disciples, in the heart of Christ. Thus I am led each day to listen to the signs of the times, where I try to find a blessing within any curse I encounter, perhaps my final paradox. Having just attended the Provincial Chapter of England/Wales, I realise that there will always be a space within this rich and free charism which offers a model of unity in diversity. Here I have found the gift of friendship, a harmony in which to live out the Kingdom.

In 1995 the *Act of Hope* document, drawn up by the United States Province, was another initiative that reached out to the laity, and aimed at providing an opportunity for young women to share in the life and mission of the Society. Participants were offered an experience which would integrate spirituality, service to the poor and a simple community lifestyle. Committing themselves for a year, the volunteers lived in community with rscJ and each other, where they shared prayer and reflection in a milieu which encouraged co-operation rather than competition, and fostered community rather than individualism. The integration of ministry and spirituality was designed to enable the participants to become more committed to their own spiritual transformation as well as to the struggle of the poor for the resources and conditions essential for human well-being.

One volunteer served as an outreach worker in a children's home in East Harlem and another as a pre-kindergarten teacher in Central Harlem. A third volunteer who later wrote a thesis on 'The Kingdom of God and the Food System: God's Table Order', commented: 'The poor have forced me to reconsider the meaning of food ...' By 1999 the programme had spread to Venezuela and news of it had reached Europe; a former pupil of the Sophie Barat School in Hamburg, Germany, travelled to the States especially to take part in the programme.

NOTES
1. Letter written by Madeleine Sophie in 1843.
2. Information on the Solidarity fund was kindly provided by Monique Fabre rscJ, General Treasurer.
3. Information on Tapestry House was kindly provided by Hélène Dahl and members of the Canadian Province.
4. CEDC was founded by Kit Collins in 1987 for the mission of developing social justice projects which integrate education, communications and leadership; the Center offers consultation, graphic design, video production, web-site design and conference facilities.
5. In 1981, after due consultation and discernment, the five Provincials of the United States drew up a new Government Plan by which the five Provinces were united in a single Province governed by one Provincial assisted by a council.

✻❀✻

End Piece

In 1997 Patricia García de Quevedo, then Superior General, and Mary Hinde, one of her Councillors, made an official visit to the English/Welsh Province. Various events were arranged, including 'the Market Place', a display which depicted all the ministries undertaken by members of the Province. This had been mounted to provide an introductory orientation; in the event it proved almost as enlightening to the English hosts as it was to their Roman visitors.

At that time *Towards Tomorrow* was beginning to take shape and the ambition that the completed book would set out 'a market place' for the whole Society, took root. The whole project became the most exhilarating, frustrating and humbling task I have yet undertaken. Overwhelmed by papers which escaped every filing system I contrived, I nevertheless feared that there was insufficient material; yet by the end some excellent pieces had to be excluded to accommodate the length agreed by contract. Furthermore few days passed when I did not doubt the whole endeavour, shamed by the knowledge that while I was fiddling about with words, colleagues were confronting the pierced heart of Christ in the reality of the world.

'So what made you go on?' a good friend asked.

'The support, encouragement and inspiration that accompanied every piece; I had to try to do justice to all the contributors. They were living and extending Madeleine Sophie's vision, a vision grounded in God's unfailing love. If I doubted myself, never did I doubt God's love or the compelling commitment to make that love known.'

❊❊❊

Changes in the Society of the
Sacred Heart 1964–94

by Rosemary Bearss rscJ

Human relationship is an apt analogy for the charism of the Society of the Sacred Heart; some have even called it the core metaphor for its spirituality. To be in relationship requires commitment to attentiveness, listening, insight, intimacy and connection. Each decade brought further growth concerning how to be in relationship. With outward changes came not only new understandings about the call to be related to one another, as well as to those with and to whom we minister, but also about a new openness to the world – we were called to be in relationship to that world. The charism has often been described as 'the love of God made human'. It became our task to make this concrete in our daily lives first, and then to push our boundaries to include the entire world.

As the Society matured, the task of understanding, clarifying and articulating the charism for new times and places became the work of the General Chapters. These General Chapters evolved over time to include not only those holding the authority delegated directly by the Superior General, but also elected delegates, given the task of reflecting upon the living out of the charism since the last General Chapter and looking forward to the future as best as this can be foreseen.

The General Chapter of 1964

This was the last Chapter made up of the Superior General, her Council and the Superior Vicars; chapters to follow would include elected delegates. It was an important turning point for the Society in the sense that all subsequent changes had their roots in the opening toward the world that this Chapter embraced. The Society was paying attention to the changes in the Catholic Church as articulated by the Second Vatican Council.

An important influence on the Chapter was the fact that our Superior General, Sabine de Valon rscJ, was invited as an 'auditrice' to the Vatican Council; she then adopted the method of the conciliar sessions for the Society's General Chapter. This included working documents prepared ahead of time by commissions, discussions of these 'schemata' in small groups, presentation of the results of the discussions to the assembly of the whole with opportunity for comments, reworking the document several times, and finally a vote.

Mother de Valon called upon the Vicars to follow this procedure for the following topics: cloister, coadjutrix sisters, doctrinal formation and secular education of the religious, poverty, the missions, and insertion among the working classes. The Vicars were asked to keep their work completely confidential; the membership-at-large was not told of this new format of preparation for the Chapter.

As a result of their deliberations and decisions, this Chapter lifted the rule of cloister and began the work of shifting the membership from a cloistered mentality toward one open to the world; a new understanding of our apostolic purpose was developing. It eliminated the division of the religious into two classes, the choir religious and the coadjutrix sisters. It recognised that our membership needed a better theological education. A new programme of theological studies was inaugurated for our young religious following the noviceship.

The work of this Chapter provided the context for living out the charism in the early sixties. Just as the Second Vatican Council influenced the methodology of the 1964 General Chapter, so too did it influence the lives of the religious. The desire for change that was prevalent at this time was pronounced. The 1964 Chapter validated the need already felt by so many in the Society to be better educated and prepared to probe our own questions, to educate our students with greater depth and to be of service in whatever way we were called.

Monasticism had impacted deeply on our lives; the choice to be apostolic while remaining deeply contemplative required the change of many of our customs. The outward manifestations were easier to change; some of the inner choices are still with us nearly forty years later. The more deeply each rscJ accepted these customs as integral to our charism, the more difficult it was to accept their demise.

These were poignant times. The desire for change crossed boundaries of age and generation; it was not just the young who wanted change.

The actual experience of change, however, marked our lives with both joy and pain. Those eager for the changes experienced life in the very same realities that were a death for others. Everyone, whether experiencing a death or a new life, was engaged in the task of integrating new choices and thus differences into our common life. Many experimented in the realm of ideas, prayer, and the use of 'free time' at the very same time that the usual demands of work continued. 'Turmoil' disrupted the structures and the rule of our former lives as a new paradigm became more and more a part of our evolving lives. Fresh air and fresh insights brought tremendous challenge; we understood both the struggle and the gift contained in the diversity we experienced among ourselves.

The Chapter of 1967

This was termed a 'Special Chapter' because it was called by the Church for all religious congregations, following the period of renewal after Vatican II. The preparation for the Chapter was characterised by the call for a 'desiderata', that is, the hopes and desires of the membership. This was the first time that the membership had been asked to submit input to the General Chapter. It was also the first time that elected delegates were admitted as participants along with the Vicars as capitulants to the Chapter.

The reading of the 'desiderata' at the Vicariate Chapters in preparation for submitting the agenda to the General Chapter was a time of anguish, soul-searching and great concern as the delegates heard the pent-up pain of decades. The task that was put upon this General Chapter was to provide a passage from the past forms of religious life into a future marked by collaboration and participation.

In order to help guide the membership's responses to the challenges of the times, the General Chapter introduced several concepts including subsidiarity, decentralisation and participation. Practically it endorsed freedom with regard to the time and form of individual prayer, as well as to liturgical and sacramental practice. Stress was placed on personal responsibility in the organisation of community life; there was encouragement to form smaller groups within the larger communities. New perspectives were promulgated on an apostolate within the local Church in collaboration with lay people.

The change from Vicariates to Provinces marked a change to

decentralisation which became real to the membership only many years later when we understood the significance of this development.

During this Chapter the Superior General, Sabine de Valon rscJ, resigned and Maria Josefa Bultó rscJ was elected to replace her. This was the first time that a Superior General did not remain in office until her death.

It has been said that the 1967 Chapter was a 'small revolution'. The invitation to the membership to participate through the 'desiderata' was accepted and responded to in great detail. The delegates to the General Chapter, in turn, responded by listening deeply to hear the pain and the hope of the membership.

The interiorisation of our spirituality was the work of these times. The tumultuous world around us touched us as well, as we entered a time of experimentation, of trial and error, of casting off old ways, only to reclaim some anew. It was a time for gaining new understanding of the deeply relational dimension of our charism. It meant being personally responsible for the depth of our individual and communal lives. For some, it was a time for beginning to share with one another about our spiritual life, of choosing to make our first directed retreat and to have a personal spiritual director. By the same token, some chose to lead an even more independent and privatised life than before. The possibilities were innumerable; the choice was ours to make.

There was excitement, hope and energy as we worked out the deeper meaning of our apostolic vocation. Change was coming rapidly, too rapidly for some to integrate, and many of our former students suffered as they watched what they held dear being called into question. These were not easy times.

The General Chapter of 1970

The General Chapter of 1970 came only three years later. These were years marked by turmoil, as external structures lagged behind the organic shift already occurring. Those who yearned to implement new structures in order to facilitate this movement found themselves confronted by those who grieved for the past and feared the unknown face of these new structures. Prior to this Chapter the Superior General engaged a socio-religious research institute to conduct a worldwide survey of the Society by Province. There was an 85 per cent response to this survey, which gave each Province concrete data to reflect upon, that came directly from the lived experience of the membership.

The 1970 Chapter has been termed the 'Prophetic Chapter'. The capitulants recognised 'change' to be the dynamism of this Chapter. They understood the charism of St Madeleine Sophie to be precisely adaptation to the needs of the times in order better to manifest to humanity the love of God.

The following synthesis of the responses of the ten working groups of the Chapter reflect what was on the minds and in the hearts of the rscJ regarding the living out of our charism in the early 1970s:

> To become aware of what the Spirit requires of us,
> for a life that is radically evangelical,
> open to God's moment by prayer,
> committed to a community of sisters,
> inserted in the world as a liberating witness,
> and integrated in international communion in the love of Christ,
> which presupposes today unity in plurality.
> The Chapter must make a fundamental option in this direction.
> And in a world where change will henceforward require
> a flexible dynamic, the Chapter must create liberating
> structures which allow for response to the demands of the Spirit.
> (Taken from 'A Re-reading of the Life and Evolution
> of the Society 1964–1994' by Agota Baternay rscJ)

Put in simpler language this Chapter committed the Society to five essentials: to internationality, to the mission of education in the service of the Church, to solidarity both with the poor, and the countries of the 'third world', and to the renewal of community life. Concepción Camacho rscJ was elected Superior General and with her newly selected team set out to travel to each Province, to create personal bonds with the membership. Her purpose was to show the Society that renewal is what St Madeleine Sophie would have wanted.

Renewal, however, was not to be confused with complete abandonment of the past. During the years after the 1970 Chapter the membership reflected on how to remain authentic to our religious life while at the same time heeding the call to discern new ways to live and pray together.

Efforts were made to ensure that the membership learned the dynamics of discernment: therefore workshops, courses and faith experiences of various kinds were organised. Many pursued spiritual direction and directed retreats as avenues for monitoring their own journey in these changing times. Clearly each was being invited to take responsibility for the depth and authenticity of her own vocation, an invitation that necessitated a reply, or our lives would cease to have meaning altogether.

The General Chapter of 1976

The General Chapter of 1976 focused on mission and it was a profound experience of communication, listening and discernment for those who participated. The time following this Chapter was greatly influenced by preparation for the revision of our Constitutions called for by the Church.

Study of our charism was an integral part of these years of reflection on our Constitutions. We returned to the writings of those who articulated our charism in times past, in order not to lose essential elements which were so important to our reflection. Janet Stuart wrote many years ago about the union of contemplation and action; she used the image of breathing in and breathing out to signify the intimacy and the complementarity of the two aspects so central to our life. These are her words about our call to what she terms 'the mixed life':

> It must consist, not of two separate parts, but of an inward spirit of consecration which has two movements, like the vital act of breathing, the outward and inward movement are each incomplete without the other. The deep intaken breath of prayer is given back again as the sound of a voice, carrying its gift from God. (Janet Erskine Stuart, *The Society of the Sacred Heart*, p. 55)

Jeanne de Charry articulated this in the early 1970s, using the term 'the single movement' to describe the unity of contemplation and action. Many of us were beginning to develop a sense of the depth of contemplation in the midst of action.

In 1979 there was a significant meeting of Provincials in Mexico when the concept of international planning took on an importance never before so deeply understood. It was following this meeting that the five Provinces in the United States seriously began the merger to one national Province.

The General Chapter of 1982

The Chapter of 1982 built upon the experience of the Mexican Assembly of Provincials; its essential work was the revision of the Constitutions. The capitulants worked intensely in order to find the best expression of the charism of the Society and the essential elements of its spirituality. They had at their disposal a wealth of material that had been contributed from all the Provinces. Thus the revision was based both on the experience and evaluation of changes that had been introduced as a result of Vatican II, and on the historical and traditional documents of the Society. The capitulants wrote the text of the 1982 Constitutions, but it is also true to say that the whole membership played a part in this revision. At the end of the Chapter Helen McLaughlin rscJ was elected Superior General.

The Constitutions were well received; the whole Society set to work to study them, to make them their own and to continue to live them. Many workshops and retreats centred around the themes of these new Constitutions: solidarity with the poor, contemplation in the midst of action and the promotion of justice and peace, to name a few.

The long and difficult dialogue with the Church began; the process of securing approval took five years. During this time many religious orders were experiencing anguish in relation to the Church and issues of women in the Church. The renewal begun by Vatican II called women out of the cloister and into the world. This same renewal encouraged women to participate in theological formation which helped them to understand the theological underpinnings of a variety of issues. With understanding came the capacity to become articulate on these same issues in public forums. The Church authorities were not prepared for the latter, for the very dialogue to which they had invited participation. This dialogue and struggle which continue to the present are important to the future of both religious life and the Church.

Following the Chapter of 1982 an International Education Commission was formed to lead the entire Society in a process for reflecting upon our educational mission. A process of social analysis was applied to all of our ministries in an effort to reflect upon our apostolic response to our world.

The General Chapter of 1988

The General Chapter of 1988 has been termed the 'political' Chapter because the capitulants dealt with the political dimensions of our life in mission. The general theme was international apostolic community. It was the topic of 'inculturation' that was the source of both the greatest anguish and the greatest growth of this Chapter. Some understood the term to be theological, while others understood only its sociological meaning. In the end we came to recognise the theological dimensions of our respective cultures as these cultures are the birthplaces of our spiritual understandings.

One of the catchphrases from this Chapter, often repeated, has been 'Let the world set our agenda'. Our relationship with the world that began in a new way in 1964 deepened, and we experienced a further development. Equipped with age-old values and timeless truths such as the creating and transforming power of the Spirit, the Gospel as the starting point, with all that it demands from us of love, forgiveness and justice, the belief that God's mercy and faithfulness shine forth in a world wounded by sin – these were the tools with which we sought to penetrate and heal the pain of our world. We plumbed the depth of struggle in order to move beyond it. We came to know experientially that being contemplatives in the midst of action necessarily engages us with the pain of our world.

Now, more than ever before, comes the desperate cry of a world in flux. Now, more than ever before, we are called to be prophetic, to be courageous, to be contemplatives in action. Our world is in dire need of contemplation. It is a world full of activity in the name of progress, yet lacking in reflection for the sake of humanity. The pierced heart of Jesus leads us to the pierced heart of humanity, and in so doing we live the union of our contemplation and action.

The General Chapter of 1994

In preparation for the Chapter of 1994 the entire Society was invited to be in dialogue with the Gospel story of the disciples of Emmaus by retelling our own salvation history in small groups of faith-sharing. This Chapter centred on the topics of internationality, education for reconciliation, community life and the eucharistic dimension of our life. Patricia García de Quevedo, rscJ from Mexico, was elected Superior General and was the first non-European to hold this office.

It is clear that we continue to probe the grace of our charism in each new decade. The call to live out the single movement of contemplation as it embraces our action requires of us new understandings of the depth of relationship as central to our charism, for we are, in fact, called to live lives of attentiveness, listening, insight, intimacy and connection. Because of this call to be in relationship with others no matter where we are living or what we are doing, the height, depth and breadth of our vocation is awesome; to live it requires of us a response in mutuality with the God who called us to it, to live it fully demands of us a wholeness to which we can only aspire.

I have found the paper entitled 'A Re-reading of the Life and Evolution of the Society 1964–1994', which was presented by Agota Baternay rscJ to the 1994 General Chapter, helpful in regard to the content and process of the Chapters.

Brief Descriptions of Some Contributors

Elaine Abels   1943   Finally Professed 1975   USA
Elaine taught in Society schools. In 1981 she was appointed Chaplain to the medical staff in the Omaha area. In 1996 she combined her ministry of spiritual direction with that of chaplaincy work.

Elizabeth Amarante   1933   Finally Professed 1963   Brazilian
Since the 1970 General Chapter, Elizabeth has served poor people and been committed to defending the rights of Brazilian ethnic minorities; in 1999 she was continuing to live with the Myky people, to work for indigenous education and for the CIMI.

Maria Teresa Arbeloa   1925   Finally Professed 1952   Spanish
Maria Teresa taught young children until she went to Egypt in 1955. She taught in Society schools, first in Cairo and then in Upper Egypt. In 1995 she was appointed to the Provincial Council, returning to Upper Egypt in 1999.

Dominique Archambeaud   (AMASC Advisor)
Dominique was born in Dordogne, France in 1945; she is married and has two sons. Always active in AMASC, she previously served as an AMASC Advisor for Europe; she also translates into French for the AMASC Web Site. She was the French President in 1999.

Maria Eugenia de la Arena   1937   Finally Professed 1968
Spanish
Maria Eugenia taught; in 1987 she was missioned for Brazil and worked on the Pastoral of the Child, in Brazil. She continued this work in Paraguay and Venezuela.

Arita Yuka   1961   Finally Professed 1998   Japanese
Yuka entered the Society in the Philippines where she had studied and

worked as a volunteer. She has worked as a catechist, pastoral worker, campus minister and teacher.

Josephine Barcelon　　(AMASC Web Site Editor)　　1959
Born in the Philippines, Josephine was educated at Kincoppal-Rose Bay in Australia and at Somerville College, University of Oxford, UK. She has worked as a writer, editor and publisher and in 1999 was responsible for all external publications at Kincoppal-Rose Bay.

Charlotte Bardenhewer　　(AMASC Germany)
Charlotte was born in Goslar, Germany, in 1936 and attended the Society school in Putzchen. Married with three children, she has been President of the Sacred Heart Association in Germany. In 1999 she was on the AMASC board with a special portfolio for the younger alumnae in Europe.

Rosemary Bearss　　1931　　Finally Professed 1960　　USA
Rosemary taught and administered in schools; she was involved in provincial administration, and named Provincial of the recently formed United States Province in 1988. Since 1994 she has worked with disadvantaged children and adults.

Doreen Boland　　1930　　Finally Professed 1960　　Irish
Doreen went to Uganda in 1963, where she was still serving in 1999. From 1968 to 1976 she served in the General Treasurer's office, and as a General Councillor in Rome. She has served in administration in Kenya/Uganda. In 1999 she was doing pastoral work and assisting in the formation of women.

Bernadette Bovagnet　　1926　　Finally Professed 1956　　French
Bernadette taught in schools until retirement in 1994 when she worked with under-privileged people. In 1999 she was serving as a public scribe and assisting with the formation of women.

Mary Karuna Braganza　　1923　　Finally Professed 1950　　Indian
Karuna has held administrative posts both within and outside the Society; she has been Provincial and a General Councillor, and has held positions on national educational bodies. In 1999 she was working with 'grass-root' women.

Mary Brennan   1932   Finally Professed 1951   Australian
Mary taught for many years, studied social work and in 1999 was Director of Social Services in a rural area of Queensland. She is a member of the AMASC 2002 Committee and advises on rscJ ongoing projects.

Patricia (Trish) Burns   (AMASC Elected World President in 1998)
Born in Sydney, Australia, in 1942, Trish was educated at Society schools in Australia; she is widowed with two adult sons. She has served on several AMASC boards as an Advisor and in 1998 was elected World President.

Denise Calder   1940   Finally Professed 1972   British
Denise taught in Society and state schools. Later she helped to develop a new approach to teaching biology. She was involved in the training of teachers in Uganda and was also responsible for health education. After working with JRS in Zambia, she worked on environmental matters for the Bishops' Conference.

Minda Caoile   1941   Finally Professed 1975   Filipino
Minda has been involved in formation work for many years. She was Director of Novices of the Philippine District before becoming District Superior in 1995.

Françoise Cassiers   1933   Finally Professed 1961   Belgian
Françoise taught and was an administrator in Society schools. From 1970 to 1974 she was a member of the General Council; from 1974 to 1978 she was Mistress of Novices in Egypt and then worked in the international Formation Team. In 1999 she was working for JRS in Europe and was the episcopal delegate for religious life.

Elisa Castillo   1950   Finally Professed 1994   Peruvian
Elisa has been involved in pastoral work in Lima; she has worked in secondary and tertiary education. In 1997 she was appointed Director of an adult training college while continuing her work for women in the province of Bambamarca.

Chow Ching-ming   1924   Finally Professed 1967   Chinese
Ching-ming entered in Japan, in 1961; as a YP she was sent to the newly established Taiwan Area where she worked in the school. After social

work training in Hong Kong she was asked to set up the Young Friends' Centre, where she was working in 1999.

Lydia Collado   1959   Finally Professed 1993   Filipino
In 1993 Lydia was Vocation Director; later she was appointed Director of Candidates. In 1997 she became programme co-ordinator of the Ministry of Youth Affairs for the Archdiocese of Manila.

Catherine (Kit) Collins   1937   Finally Professed 1961   USA
Kit taught and administered in school; the Network of Sacred Heart Schools was founded under her direction. In 1987 she was the founder and Director of CEDC.

Mary d'Apice   1922   Finally Professed 1949   Australian
Mary, a medical doctor, taught and was then involved in provincial administration, and that of two university colleges. In 1980, having studied, she ministered in psychotherapy and spiritual direction, giving seminars and retreats in several countries.

Mary D'Arcy   1942   Finally Professed 1964   Australian
Mary taught and undertook youth work. Since the mid-1970s she has been involved with justice and environmental groups. In 1999 she was supporting migrant Filipino women and was teaching permaculture (a system of natural agriculture).

Carmela Deguara   1930   Finally Professed 1962   Maltese
Carmela taught and administered in Society schools in UK, Malta and Congo. From 1981 to 1987 she served in District Administration. In 1999 she was involved in parish work and was collaborating with the Jesuits' Literacy Programme.

Anne de Stacpoole   1927   Finally Professed 1957   New Zealander
Anne was involved in practical employments. In 1962 she was in Uganda, but left in 1967 on account of her health. From 1983 to 1994 she acted as administrator for the first local bishop of Kiribati in the Central Pacific. In 1999 she was living as a solitary.

Luz Dolalas   1950   Finally Professed 1989   Filipino
Luz first worked as a campus minister; since 1998 she has been involved

in advocacy for the protection of the environment and secretary to the NGO attempting to safeguard the mountains of Montalban.

Marie Rose Droulers   1922   Finally Professed 1954   Australian
Marie Rose, a trained nurse, worked in school and community infirmaries, and in community administration. From 1973 to 1975 she nursed in Papua New Guinea; later she worked with marginalised people and refugees. Since 1998 she has had a ministry of prayer and presence in outback Queensland.

Ada Duarte   1925   Finally Professed 1956   Cuban
Ada taught in the Society's schools. In 1999 she was visiting young children in a pediatric hospital and making cards to raise money for St Helen's orphanage, in Haiti.

Marijke van Eechoud   1938   Finally Professed 1968   Dutch
Marijke taught first in Holland and from 1973 to 1987 in Congo. She then worked with an organisation financing projects in developing countries. In 1992 she was appointed superior of the elderly community at Venlo.

Rita Egan   1917–1998   Finally Professed 1946   Canadian
Rita taught in Society schools until 1952 when rheumatoid arthritis was diagnosed. She continued to teach in a school for deprived youngsters. From 1993 to 1998 she worked for refugees, determined, despite intermittent surgery, to serve those in need.

Joan Faber   1925   Finally Professed 1954   English
Joan taught and administered in Society schools. From 1970 to 1975 she was responsible for international formation; she then served in provincial administration while training as a psychotherapist. In 1999 she was working with AIDS sufferers and with local projects.

Alexandra Fernon   (Head of AMASC Study Committee)
Alexandra was born in Sydney in 1958, educated at Kincoppal-Rose Bay and the University of New South Wales. She has worked in the fields of drug and alcohol abuse and grief counselling with cancer patients. Married with three sons, she is an active member of the community and parish and the co-ordinator of the study plan for AMASC World Conference in 2002.

Marie-Louise Fey   1932   Finally Professed 1961   French
Marie-Louise was a school caterer, and secretary in provincial administration; she also worked in a community for elderly rscJ. In 1999 she
was involved with a project for homeless people.

Angela Galletto   1943   Finally Professed 1972   Italian
Angela, a trained nurse, served in community infirmaries. In 1981 she
trained as a teacher and later became headmistress of an elementary
school. In 1999 she was head of a nursery school and was ministering
in her local parish.

Mary Germani ascJ   Italian
Mary, an alumna, is a lay celibate, who has shared the life and apostolate
of Sacred Heart communities in Bordeaux, Alsace, Paris and Poitiers.
In 1981 she became a member of KAIRE and in 1996 founded the
Association Aghia Sophia for the promotion of ecumenism.

Virginia (Vickie) Grieg   (AMASC Vice-President)
Vickie was born in Sydney in 1946. Educated at Rose Bay, she trained
as a librarian, and is married with three adult children. She has been
President of the Sacred Heart Association of NSW and played a pivotal
role in the organisation of the AMASC World Conference in 2002.

Maria del Carmen Guerrero   1922   Finally Professed 1954
Colombian
Between 1949 and 1990 Maria was involved with college administration
and catechetics. She has worked in Puerto Rico, Cuba, Argentina and
Uruguay; in Colombia she has led many workshops, worked with CEBs
and rag-pickers and has accompanied displaced peasants, especially the
Choco in Turbo.

Hayami Yayoi   1922   Finally Professed 1965   Japanese
Yayoi taught until she was appointed Mistress of Novices 1978–1983,
followed by a term as Provincial 1983–1989. Since 1989 she has undertaken retreat work and spiritual direction.

Tricia Ho   (AMASC Treasurer General)
Tricia was born in Melbourne in 1972 and educated at the Sacred Heart
College in Melbourne; she has degrees in Economics, Law and taxation
law. She was Co-President of the Sacred Heart Alumnae Association of

Melbourne – the youngest person to hold the post – and was responsible for attracting younger alumnae.

Lucy Hu   1918   Finally Professed 1951   Chinese
Lucy entered the Society in Shanghai, and later was sent to Tokyo to work for the school and community. In 1960 she was missioned for Taiwan. She has been involved in parish work and in 1998 she was helping in the spirituality centre.

Margarita Hurtado   1934   Finally Professed 1955   Chilean
Margarita taught and was principal of Apoquinda College, in Santiago. Later she worked with the poor until appointed Provincial in 1979. She has been involved with international formation, superior of a house for elderly sisters and in 1999 was again working with the poor.

Mary Louise Jenkins   1924   Finally Professed 1951   USA
Mary Louise was a teacher and administrator in Society schools. She retrained as a music therapist and then ministered to Alzheimer sufferers and physically handicapped youngsters. In 1999 she was working in school and continuing her therapeutic ministry. She is a Charter member of the national Black Sisters' Conference and Vice-President of the Sister Senate in Washington.

Margaret Mary (Marnie) Kennedy   1927   Finally Professed 1955   Australian
Marnie was a teacher and administrator and has assisted in provincial administration. After further study she became a spiritual director; since 1984 she has attempted to develop a spirituality bringing together contemplation and justice.

Brigid Keogh   1909   Finally Professed 1938   Irish/American
Brigid taught in Society schools in USA before going to Japan in 1947. She served in provincial administration; she has taught in the universities of Taiwan, Nicaragua, Indonesia and China. In 1999 she was living in community in Tokyo.

Maryvonne Keraly   1931   Finally Professed 1961   French
Maryvonne taught in Society schools before becoming Provincial of France. She was responsible for formation in several congregations,

both in Europe and in developing countries. Since 1994 she has been a General Councillor in Rome.

Phil Kilroy   1943   Finally Professed 1970   Irish
Phil taught in Society schools, was involved in initial and international formation and served as the Irish/Scottish Provincial. Among her published works is a new biography of Madeleine Sophie Barat.

Aideen Kinlen   1937   Finally Professed 1971   Irish
Aideen was a practising barrister. In religious life she taught in schools, assisted in provincial administration, gave retreats and served on a church marriage tribunal. In 1999 she was a member of the provincial council and a co-ordinator of the Irish Scottish Network of Sacred Heart Schools.

Joan Kirby   1926   Finally Professed 1956   USA
Joan taught and administrated in Society schools; in 1980 she worked with homeless families. In 1998 she was working for the Temple of Understanding, an inter-faith organisation, and was a member of the rscJ International Commission for Justice and Peace.

June Kirk-Smith   1929   Finally Professed 1959   New Zealander
June taught and administered in schools; she was involved in national and international formation. In 1987 she was involved in provincial administration. In 1999 she was working with the NGO Tenants' Protection, and with various justice groups.

Eileen Lawless   1949   Finally Professed 1989   Irish
Eileen worked at all levels in school and had extensive experience in youth ministry; she has undertaken retreat work amd pastoral counselling with young adults.

Anna Lazár   1928   Finally Professed 1958   Hungarian
Anna entered as a coadjutrix sister, shortly before the Communist regime was established. Unable to leave Hungary, she was imprisoned, but reached Austria in 1956 where she undertook domestic responsibilities. In 1996 she returned to Budapest.

Norah Lester   1935   Finally Professed 1960   British
Norah taught and administered in schools, colleges of education, and

as a member of an educational team in a men's prison; she has served in provincial administration. In 1999 she was teaching in her parish primary school.

Lee Mi Kyung   1965   First Vows 1995   Korean
Mi Kyung worked in the Maumto study room until 1998 when she started work in the campus ministry of the Catholic University of Korea; she was also in charge of the Blick Light study room for neighbourhood students.

Edmée Lesne   1910   Finally Professed 1940   French
Edmee has taught and administered in Society schools. In 1994 she joined the community of La Roseraie for elderly and frail sisters; in 1999 she was acting as a guide for visitors to the Basilica of Fourviere.

Caroline Joy Luz   1964   Finally Professed 1997   Filipino
Since her profession Joy has worked with young people, she has been a pastoral worker in Samar and in 1998 became a member of the District Council.

Frances Lynch   1930   Finally Professed 1961   British
After a period of general work, Frances trained as a nurse and served in the infirmaries in England and Malta. In 1981 she was missioned for Uganda where she ran a mobile clinic and a dispensary. In 1999 she was working with handicapped youngsters in Western Kenya.

Maria Casabonne de Machiavello   (AMASC Peru)
Maria was born in Tacna, Peru, in 1936 and educated at Society schools. She has been President of the Peruvian Alumnae Association and in 1999 was delegate to OMAEC (World Association of Former Pupils of Catholic Schools), representing the Americas.

Frances Makower   1930   Finally Professed 1976   British
Frances converted from Judaism in 1952; she worked with drug-users and homeless youngsters. She had been disabled in a fencing accident which led to thirteen years in the provincial infirmary; there her ministry of writing developed.

Socorro Martínez   1944   Finally Professed 1981   Mexican
Since 1974 Socorro has collaborated with BECs at parish, regional and national level; in 1999 she was serving as the National Executive

Secretary; she has contributed much to the Network of Popular Education. In 1999 she was the Provincial of Mexico/Nicaragua.

Susan Maxwell 1941 Finally Professed 1973 USA
Susan taught and administered in Society schools. From 1984 to 1995 she was the Director of the USA Network of Sacred Heart Schools. In 1997, she was appointed Director of Sacred Heart Schools in Chicago.

Laurent Mayasari 1971 Indonesian
Laurent was born in Bogor, on the island of Java; she trained as a teacher and worked at the Jakarta Social Institute where she met the Society. In 1999 she was a postulant and entered the noviceship in November.

Mary Catherine (Mickey) McKay 1929 Finally Professed 1960 USA
Mickey taught and administered in Society schools. In 1970 she was appointed to the General Council in Rome. She spent six months in the Holy Land before becoming Director of Novices in US, after which she worked in Nicaragua, 1985–1996. In 1999 she was working with Hispanics in East Harlem.

Mary Ethna McLoughlin 1919 Finally Professed 1950 Irish
Mary Ethna taught and administered in school and community; later she studied theology at the University of San Diego. In 1999 she was tutoring and animating several prayer groups.

Dorothy McMichael 1926 Finally Professed 1957 USA
From 1952 to 1985 Dorothy taught in Society schools. Since 1986 she has worked as a graphic designer with an inner-city screen-printing training programme in Detroit.

Virginia McMonagle 1921 Finally Professed 1959 USA
Virginia taught in Society schools; in 1978 she was appointed Assistant to the Vice-President of San Diego University. In 1987 she assisted in the foundation of an orphanage and infant hospital in Haiti. In 1999 she was working in San Diego and in Haiti.

Fuensanta Meléndez 1934 Finally Professed 1957 Spanish
Fuensanta taught in secondary and tertiary institutions. In 1975 she

collaborated in the foundation of ASTOR, a parents' association for mentally retarded people. In 1999 she was working for ASTOR and was a diocesan representative for RE in Schools.

Rosario Méndez   1936   Finally Professed 1962   Spanish
Rosario taught teenagers and assisted in formation. In 1962 she arrived in Egypt where she taught in Heliopolis and in Upper Egypt. After a motor accident in 1975 she became paraplegic, confined to a wheel-chair. In 1999 she was the Director of the Sacred Heart College at Heliopolis.

Dolores Maria (Lolín) Menéndez   1943   Finally Professed 1968
Puerto Rico
Lolín was educated in Puerto Rico, Spain and the US. She taught in the States and Uganda, where she trained teachers and parish leaders. She worked for JRS and was appointed JRS Resource Person for Africa in 1996.

Catherine Mifsud   1941   Finally Professed 1978   Maltese
Catherine taught and administered in schools. From 1978 to 1987 she served as District Treasurer of Malta. In 1999 she was teaching English to refugees and was involved in vocation promotion.

Maria Franca Migone   (AMASC Archivist and Emeritus Member)
Maria was born in Genoa in 1927. Educated at the Sacred Heart College and Genoa University, she has taught in secondary schools. She is married, has three sons and several grandchildren. She has been an Advisor to AMASC, and World President 1990–1994. She was appointed AMASC Archivist in 1994.

Marie Miller ascJ   1940   English
Marie trained in the Society College at Newcastle upon Tyne. She taught before entering the noviceship in 1972. She left the Society without making first vows and returned to special teaching. She was invited to attend the General Chapter at Amiens in 2000.

Nagano Koko   1940   Finally Professed 1978   Japanese
Koko taught and administered in schools; later she trained for the

ministry of spiritual direction. From 1993 to 1999 she served as principal. In 1999 she taught children, students and adults in school.

Margaret Nourse   1924   Finally Professed 1973   English
Margaret was appointed Principal of the Sacred Heart College at Newcastle upon Tyne. After retirement she spent time in India and Bangladesh. In 1999 she was living in a small community in multi-ethnic Southall.

Herminia (Hermie) Noval   1944   Finally Professed 1995
Filipino
Hermie has helped to establish CEBs in the diocese of Catarman, Northern Samar. In 1999 she was working with the community-based programme of the SMSF.

Maria Carmen Núñez-Lagos   1926   Finally Professed 1954   Spanish
Maria Carmen taught in school. In 1971 she joined the Archbishop Claret Institution to train students by correspondence. In 1973 she joined the Institute of Theology at a Distance, later serving on the Governing Body; in 1999 she was Secretary General of the Institute.

Deirdre O'Brien   1931   Finally Professed 1959   Irish
Deirdre taught and administered in Society schools and colleges. After re-training she was appointed Diocesan RE advisor to Secondary Schools. After retirement she taught in China with the Voluntary Service Overseas, and was in that ministry in 1999.

Marcia O'Dea   1938   Finally Professed 1966   USA
Marcia taught English in the Network of Sacred Heart Schools. Since 1974 she has been at Forest Ridge School where for many years she has been the English Department Chair.

Anne O'Keeffe   1958   Finally Professed 1991   Irish
Anne worked in Society schools in both Scotland and Ireland; she went to Colombia to work with rural Christian communities. In 1999 she was studying and working in a community-based educational project in a disadvantaged area of Dublin.

Erminia Oliva   1946   Finally Professed 1982   Italian
Erminia taught in Society schools from 1971 to 1997. Since 1998 she has been a member of the National Missionary Network.

Helen O'Regan   1941   Finally Professed 1975   USA
Helen taught before training as a nurse. In 1975 she went to Uganda/ Kenya where she served in Kenya as a rural nurse. In 1999 she was an AIDS educator for the Diocese of Eldoret.

Dorothy Ormesher   1922   Finally Professed 1950   English
Dorothy taught and administered in Society schools. After training as a remedial teacher she taught special needs children until appointed Provincial Secretary in 1993. Since 1995, she has been living among Aboriginal people in inner-city Sydney.

Patricia Ormesher   1928   Finally Professed 1957   Australian
Patricia taught in Society and parish schools. A renewal/retreat led to a 'call' to live and work with poor people; in 1999 she was working among Aboriginals in Sydney, with Dorothy, her sister.

Micheline Ortegat   1928   Finally Professed 1959   Belgian
Micheline taught and administered; later she worked at a Christian-Islamic Centre, making contact wth immigrants, delinquents and prisoners. She collaborated in setting up a centre for children and mothers. In 1999 she was continuing to visit prisoners.

Oshima Kumiko   (AMASC Japan)
Kumiko was born in Kamakura in 1934, and was educated in the Society's school and university. She is married with one daughter. She was the elected AMASC advisor for Asia and active in all Alumnae Associations in Asia.

Raquel Pérez   1912   Finally Professed 1944   Cuban
Raquel taught and administered in Society institutions in Cuba and Puerto Rico. In 1970 she worked with poor people in Venezuela; returning to Cuba in 1972, she worked in the parish. In 1999 she was provincial archivist and was writing books on the Society.

Maryanne Pidcock   (AMASC Secretary General)
Maryanne was born in Sydney in 1967 and educated at the Society's Kincoppal-Rose Bay School and Sydney University. She was Director of Development at her former school and was actively engaged in alumnae associations at local, national and international level.

258

Bernadette (Bernie) Porter   1952   Finally Professed 1983
English
Bernie taught in the UK and Uganda. In 1983 she moved to higher education and became Principal of Digby Stuart College in 1989. In 1999 she was appointed Rector and Chief Executive of the University of Surrey, Roehampton.

Françoise de Pous   1942   Finally Professed 1970   French
Françoise was missioned for Chad in 1970, where she taught in the Society school in N'Djamena. In 1991 she was appointed to parish work in Bongor. In 1998 she was living in Guelendeng.

Margarita Recavarren   1930   Finally Professed 1957   Peruvian
Margarita taught, was involved in formation, became a member of the Conference of Latin American Religious and held national responsibility for religious renewal. In 1989 she worked for human rights and trained rural teachers in a deprived zone. She is based in Cusco, a poor area with a high level of illiteracy.

Ana Elena Ogario de Reyes Retano (AMASC Mexico)
Ana Elena was born in Mexico City in 1924. She attended the Society school in New York and Manhattanville College. She is married and has several children and grandchildren. She was Vice-President of AMASC 1994–98.

Livi Rodrigues   1933   Finally Professed 1969   India
Much of Livi's ministry has been at Sophia College, Mumbai, as lecturer and Principal. In 1999 she was the Executive Director of the Training for Development Scholarship Society, an NGO working in several states of India.

Philomena Prabha Rodrigues   1937   Finally Professed 1969
Indian
Prabha taught; after nursing training, she became involved in health education and was principal of the nursing college. In 1999 she was a member of an organisation working for world health for the Food and Agriculture Organisation (of the UN).

Olga Rome (AMASC USA)
Olga was born in Louisiana, USA, in 1935 and went to a Sacred Heart

school, before graduating in music therapy at New Orleans. She is married with five children and several grandchildren. She has been president of AASH (American Association of the Sacred Heart), and served on its Hospitality Committee on which she has given long service.

Carmen Rosales　　1928　　Finally Professed 1955　　Spanish
For fourteen years Carmen taught and administered in Sacred Heart schools in Spain. In 1974 she was missioned for Chad and taught in the Society's N'Djamena school. In 1994 she was training teachers for bush schools; in 1998 she helped to establish the first agricultural college in Chad.

Odile de Rousiers　　1927　　Finally Professed 1957　　French
Odile taught in Society schools until 1975 when she worked as an almoner in a state hospital. In 1999 she was a member of an organisation providing a social facility for people suffering from mental illness.

Joan Scott　　1920　　Finally Professed 1956　　Welsh
Joan taught and administered in secondary and tertiary Society institutions; after two years as a hermit in France, she helped to establish a retreat house in the Welsh hills with an emphasis on solitude. In 1999 she was attached to a community in Middlesex.

Jadwiga Skudro　　1914　　Finally Professed 1947　　Polish
Jadwiga taught and in 1974 collaborated with Professor Francis Blachnicki, founder of the Authentic Christian Families Movement. She carried on his work after his death and was working full-time for the movement in 1999.

Inmaculada Subirá　　1941　　Finally Professed 1968　　Spanish
Inmaculada taught as a professor in Society institutions. Later she joined the Engrunes Co-operative which attempted to rehabilitate marginalised people. In 1999 she was working in a centre for the promotion of women in a suburb of Barcelona.

Eusebia (Eby) Talastas　　1944　　Finally Professed 1970　　Filipino
Eby entered the Society in Japan before the establishment of the Filippino foundation in 1969. In 1999 she was a formation consultant to religious communities and institutes.

Mary Totton   1929   Finally Professed 1963   British
Mary taught in Society schools until she became Director of Novices. She taught and worked in the chaplaincy of the Roehampton Institute. In 1993 she joined the Moscow community for five years. After her return she joined the Oxford community, maintaining her links with Moscow.

Tsai Su-fang   1942   Finally Professed 1974   Chinese
Su-fang nursed in schools; later she served as principal of primary and secondary schools; she assisted in Area administration and in 1986 became Area Treasurer. She has made many brief visits to mainland China.

Irène-Marie Uyttenhove   1905   Finally Professed 1935   Belgian
Irene taught for most of her active life. Later she lived and worked in a parish in a deprived area of Brussels. Since 1979 she has been a member of the Tele-Accueil service. In 1999 she was active in the parish.

Vandana   1924   Finally Professed 1948   Indian
Vandana spent years studying Indian culture, searching for ways of meeting 'the Christ of the Indian Road'. Convinced that the traditional ashram lifestyle would suit religious life, she founded several ashrams and studied under a Hindu guru. She is the author of several books.

Margaret Wilson   1948   Finally Professed 1981   Irish
Margaret worked in school until 1990 when she was appointed Novice Director. In 1999 she was living in a student/rscJ community on the Digby Stuart campus of Roehampton.

Hannelore Woitsch   1941   Finally Professed 1972   Austrian
Hanni taught and held pastoral responsibilities in school. Since 1977 she has served in provincial administration, as Provincial, and as a General Councillor in Rome. In 1998 she assumed responsibility for the novices who had temporarily been transferred from Budapest to Vienna.

Yabuki Keiko   1931   Finally Professed 1962   Japanese
Keiko served in school and in community; after probation she worked
in the school office. Later she worked in the parish, teaching in the
Sunday School. She worked in a rehabilitation centre for recovering
alcoholics and also worked for the homeless. In 1999 she was serving
as a sacristan.

FURTHER READING*

Margaret Williams, *The Society of the Sacred Heart: History of a Spirit 1800–1975* (Darton, Longman & Todd, 1978).

Religious of the Sacred Heart (Strasbourg: Editions du Signe, 1999).

Phil Kilroy, *Madeleine Sophie Barat: A Life* (Cork University Press, 2000).

Prue Wilson, *My Father Took Me to the Circus: Religious Life From Within* (Darton, Longman & Todd, 1984).

Connections: An International Journal Published by the Society of the Sacred Heart

Vol. 1 No. 1 (1991), *The World of Migrant Peoples.*

Vol. 2 No. 1 (1992), *Politics Behind the Utopia.*

Vol. 3 No. 1 (1993), *Inculturation.*

*There are few published works on the whole Society in the late twentieth century. However the Central Archivist in Rome and the local archivists do have unpublished material which may satisfy further queries.

Index